Cinema, democracy and perfectionism

MANCHESTER 1824

Manchester University Press

CRITICAL POWERS

Series Editors:
Bert van den Brink (University of Utrecht),
Antony Simon Laden (University of Illinois, Chicago),
Peter Niesen (University of Hamburg) and
David Owen (University of Southampton).

Critical Powers is dedicated to constructing dialogues around innovative and original work in social and political theory. The ambition of the series is to be pluralist in welcoming work from different philosophical traditions and theoretical orientations, ranging from abstract conceptual argument to concrete policy-relevant engagements, and encouraging dialogue across the diverse approaches that populate the field of social and political theory. All the volumes in the series are structured as dialogues in which a lead essay is greeted with a series of responses before a reply by the lead essayist. Such dialogues spark debate, foster understanding, encourage innovation and perform the drama of thought in a way that engages a wide audience of scholars and students.

Published by Bloomsbury

On Global Citizenship, James Tully
Justice, Democracy and the Right to Justification, Rainer Forst

Forthcoming from Manchester University Press

Rogue Theodicy – Politics and power in the shadow of justice, Glen Newey
Democratic Inclusion, Rainer Baubock
Law and Violence, Christoph Menke
Autonomy Gaps, Joel Anderson
Toleration, Liberty and the Right to Justification, Rainer Forst

Cinema, democracy and perfectionism

Joshua Foa Dienstag in dialogue

Edited by Joshua Foa Dienstag

Manchester University Press

Published by Manchester University Press
Altrincham Street, Manchester M1 7JA
www.manchesteruniversitypress.co.uk

British Library Cataloguing-in-Publication Data
A catalogue record for this book is available from the British Library

Library of Congress Cataloging-in-Publication Data applied for

ISBN 978 1 784 99401 3 hardback
ISBN 978 1 784 99402 0 paperback
ISBN 978 1 784 99735 9 open access

First published 2016

Typeseby Out of House Publishing
PrintedinGreatBritain
by Bell & Bain Ltd, Glasgow

Contents

List of contributors *page* vii
Series editors' foreword x
Acknowledgments xiii

Part I Lead essay 1

1 The tragedy of remarriage: letter to M. Cavell about cinema (a remake) 3
Joshua Foa Dienstag

Part II Responses 83

2 Emancipated perfectionism – or, In praise of dreaming 85
Clare Woodford

3 The phenomenology of the political: a reply from Saturday Night to Mr. Dienstag 110
Tracy B. Strong

4 The tragedy of remarriage in the Golden Age of television 131
Margaret Kohn

5 "That dangerous contention": a cinematic response to pessimism 147
Davide Panagia

6 Letter to Mr. Dienstag 167
Thomas Dumm

Part III Reply 179

7 A reply to my critics 181
Joshua Foa Dienstag

Bibliography 206
Index 212

Contributors

Joshua Foa Dienstag is Professor of Political Science and Law at UCLA. His writing is broadly concerned with the roles of time and narrative in political theory and he has published essays on Nietzsche, Gadamer, Wittgenstein, Cervantes and the American Founders, among others. He is the author of two books: *Dancing in Chains: Narrative and Memory in Political Theory* (Stanford University Press, 1997) and *Pessimism: Philosophy, Ethic, Spirit* (Princeton University Press, 2006), which won the Best Book award in Philosophy from the American Association of Publishers. His current projects include a collection of essays on film and political representation, and a book on the boundary of the human.

Thomas Dumm is the William H. Hastie '25 Professor of Political Ethics at Amherst College. He served as a founding editor of the journal *Theory & Event*, and is the author of six books, including most recently *Loneliness as a Way of Life* (Harvard University Press, 2008) and *My Father's House: On Will Barnet's Paintings* (Duke University Press, 2014). He is currently completing a book-length study on the fate of home in the twenty-first century.

Margaret (Peggy) Kohn is Professor of Politics at the University of Toronto. Her main research interests are urbanism, critical theory, the history of political thought, and colonialism. She is the author of three books and over a dozen scholarly articles in journals such as *Political Theory*, *Journal of Politics*, *Theory & Event*, *Polity*, *Constellations* and *Dissent*. Her current book project is entitled *The Death and Life of the Urban Commonwealth* (forthcoming, Oxford University Press). It advances a novel theory of social rights and examines displacement in cities (including gentrification, slum clearance, privatization of public space) from a critical and normative perspective.

Davide Panagia is Associate Professor of Political Science at UCLA. He is a political theorist with multidisciplinary interests across the humanities and social sciences including democratic theory, the history of political thought, interpretive methodologies, cultural theory, media studies, aesthetics, literary studies and visual culture. His work specializes in the relationship between aesthetics and politics, with an ongoing curiosity about the diverse ways in which the sensation of value is generated and assembled in political societies. He has published three books: *The Poetics of Political Thinking* (Duke University Press, 2006), *The Political Life of Sensation* (Duke University Press, 2009) and *Impressions of Hume: Cinematic Thinking and the Politics of Discontinuity* (Rowman and Littlefield, 2013).

Tracy B. Strong is Professor of Political Theory and Philosophy at the University of Southampton and UCSD Distinguished Professor Emeritus. He has broad interests in political theory and in related fields in political science, aesthetics, literature and other areas. He is the author of several books including, most recently, *Politics Without Vision: Thinking Without a Banister in the Twentieth Century* (Chicago University Press, 2012), Winner of the David Easton Prize, 2013. He is currently working on a book on music, language and politics in the period that extends from Rousseau to Nietzsche. He has been the recipient of fellowships from the National Endowment for the Humanities and the Rockefeller Foundation, has been Visiting Professor at the Juan March Instituto in Spain and Warwick University in England, and was a Fellow at the Center for Human Values, Princeton University (2002–3). From 1990 until 2000 he was the editor of *Political Theory*.

Clare Woodford is Senior Lecturer in Political Philosophy at the School of Humanities, University of Brighton. Her research interests include poststructuralism, theories of democracy, ethics, queer theory, psychoanalysis, democratic activism and aesthetics. She is the author of articles and chapters on the work of Cavell, Rancière, Honig, Rawls, Butler, Laclau and Foucault with respect to topics including political extremism, cosmopolitanism, democratic activism and the ethics of friendship. Her book *Dis-orienting Democracy* (Routledge, 2016) puts Rancière's work in conversation with Menke, Cavell, Derrida and Butler to expand the impact of his thought on democratic theory and practice today.

Series editors' foreword

Joshua Foa Dienstag's engagement with Stanley Cavell's work on cinema is both homage and critique. Deliberately echoing the form of Rousseau's 1758 essay *Lettre à M. d'Alembert sur les spectacles* (*Letter to M. d'Alembert on the Theatre*), it revisits and updates the question of the relation of aesthetic culture to morality raised by the Rousseau–d'Alembert exchange in terms of a meditation on the relation of cinema and democracy.

Rousseau's essay addresses his friend Jean d'Alembert's article "Genève" (Geneva) in the *Encyclopédie* proposing the establishment of a theater in Rousseau's home city. After making clear his respect for d'Alembert, Rousseau proceeds to express skepticism concerning the moral and political effects of the content of theatrical productions, especially comedies such as those of Molière; to express concern about the likely effects of the establishment of a theater (and the presence of actors) on the existing culture of Geneva; and to propose that open-air festivals offer an alternative that is more attuned to sustaining the patriotic unity of Geneva's political culture. *Lettre à M. d'Alembert sur les spectacles* is an acute and highly influential expression of the philosophical pessimism that Rousseau opposes to the philosophical optimism of the Enlightenment – and it is no coincidence that Dienstag's prior work, especially his award-winning 2006 book *Pessimism: Philosophy, Ethic, Spirit*, offers both a cogent reconstruction of the tradition of philosophical pessimism and a forceful advocacy of this orientation. Notably, philosophers who exemplify the pessimist tradition, on Dienstag's account, such as Rousseau, Schopenhauer, Nietzsche, Freud and Camus are without exception philosophers of culture, centrally concerned with the relations of culture to ethics, society and politics or, put more abstractly, the government of self and of others.

The constitutive features of the pessimistic tradition as Dienstag reconstructs it are fourfold: that time is a burden; that the course of history is, in some sense, ironic; that freedom and happiness are incompatible; and that human existence is absurd. This pessimism is opposed to an outlook ("optimism") according to which the world is, in principle, fully knowable by us and receptive to our ethical interests; that is, a condition in which we and the world are, in some happy sense, made for each other and in which, rightly understood, the world makes epistemic and moral sense to us *as if* it were designed to satisfy our rational desires and to reconcile moral freedom and personal happiness.

It is the pivotal concern of the pessimistic tradition with culture (as central to freedom, happiness and the tension between them) that motivates Dienstag's engagement with Cavell and cinema. The work of Stanley Cavell has a strong claim to be the most significant philosophical engagement with culture in contemporary thought, while cinema is one of the most vital media of contemporary culture (arguably akin to that of theater for the Enlightenment period) and Cavell's philosophical engagement with cinema, perhaps especially in his work on comedies of remarriage, offers the best argument for the ethical and political value of cinema in contemporary democratic cultures. In this respect, Cavell's work on cinema represents the most important contemporary challenge to the pessimistic orientation that Dienstag reconstructs and advocates. Dienstag's essay is thus a testing of his own philosophical stance against its most worthy opponent. This is not to say that Cavell's work represents a full-blown "optimism" in the sense that pessimism opposes, but, rather more modestly, it is to say that, for Dienstag, Cavell's engagement with cinema has not fully freed itself from the grip of the philosophical optimism that has been the dominant feature of the philosophical tradition, especially with respect to the reconciliation of freedom and happiness.

At the heart of this agonistic encounter is Dienstag's skepticism that cinema can perform the work of ethical exemplification that Cavell finds in such films as *The Philadelphia Story*. This skepticism is developed in three stages. In the first, Dienstag offers an alternative reading of *The Philadelphia Story*, one that foregrounds more explicitly its relation to the political refounding of the USA in this city and, through this foregrounding, draws out the relations between the publicity and secrecy, institution and eros, and participation and spectacle that link the political and the personal in this film. In the second, Dienstag contrasts *The Philadelphia Story* with Renoir's contemporary film *The Rules of the Game* (*La Règle du jeu*), a film that bears many parallels to *The Philadelphia Story* in terms of its treatment of the themes of union, of erotic desire and of the household as symbolic of the nation, but which presents a stark counterpoint to the optimism of the former that eros can be stably channeled into bonds of (civic) friendship, namely, that freedom and happiness can be fully reconciled. On the contrary, *The Rules of the Game* offers a working out of the costs to individuality and spontaneity of establishing a stable union. In the final stage, Dienstag addresses the nature of viewing cinematic film as a mode of experience, arguing against Cavell that it is akin to dreaming rather than lived consciousness and, crucially, cannot be shared. Democracy is a relation of seeing and being seen; cinema is a relation of seeing and not being seen. For this reason, film may be a source of pleasure but it cannot engender or sustain relations of freedom.

These remarks only sketch the barest outlines of Dienstag's challenge to Cavell's work on cinema and, as such, cannot communicate the depth or richness of his engagement with that work nor of the clarity with which his essay articulates the implications of philosophical pessimism for addressing contemporary culture in its relationship to political life. But it is hoped that they indicate the philosophical and political stakes of this encounter and of the dialogue that Dienstag's essay engenders. Recent years have seen a welcome burgeoning of the engagement of political theory with cinema and this volume provides a dialogue in which what is in play is the question of the precise significance of this engagement.

Acknowledgments

The contributors would like to offer their collective thanks to David Owen for conceiving of this volume, soliciting the authors' contributions, and encouraging a robust dialogue. Without his interest, editorial judgment and perpetual good cheer, this exchange would never have come about. We also thank Caroline Wintersgill for shepherding the result through some unexpected editorial obstacles, and Isla Rosser-Owen for excellent copy-editing. And we thank Stanley Cavell, above all, for inspiring the conversation.

Joshua Foa Dienstag: I am grateful to UCLA Division of Social Sciences and the School of Law as well as the Center for Advanced Study in the Behavioral Sciences (Andrew W. Mellon Fellowship) for sabbatical time and research support which enabled the writing of this Letter and supplemental response. I would like to particularly thank Elisabeth Anker, Lori Marso, David Owen, Davide Panagia and Tracy Strong for their encouragement of this project through a long period of development. I would like to also thank my colleagues and students at UCLA for their feedback during presentations and classes on political theory and film. Finally, as always, Jennifer Mnookin, Sophia Dienstag and Isaac Dienstag are a source of unmediated joy and support and have my endless love and gratitude.

Part I

Lead essay

J.-F. DIENSTAG

CITOYEN DE LOS ANGELES

To M. CAVELL

Walter M. Cabot Professor of Aesthetics and the General Theory of Value Emeritus, MacArthur Fellow, Past President of the American Philosophical Association (Eastern Division), Winner of the Zabel Award in Criticism, the Bucknell Award of Merit, etc.

Sur Le Cinéma

ET PARTICULIÈREMENT,

Sur son Article LE BON DE FILM

Tout nous force d'abandonner cette vaine idée de perfection qu'on nous veut donner de la forme des spectacles, dirigés vers l'utilité publique.

1

The tragedy of remarriage: letter to M. Cavell about cinema (a remake)

Joshua Foa Dienstag

Introduction

In 1757, Jean d'Alembert wrote an entry on "Genève" (Geneva) in the seventh volume of the *Encyclopédie*, the great encapsulation of the Enlightenment, of which he was also one of the general editors. Among other things, the article proposed that Geneva should relax its sumptuary laws so as to permit the establishment of a theater. It was generally suspected that this part of the article was either written or suggested by Voltaire, who was living in exile there at the time and complaining bitterly to his friends about the lack of a theater.

Jean-Jacques Rousseau, born in Geneva, had contributed many entries to the *Encyclopédie* on music and political economy and was well known as a composer and patron of the theater. He had recently reconverted to Calvinism, however, and reclaimed his Genevan citizenship. Determined to oppose Voltaire's suggestion that theater represented cultural and political progress, he wrote a public letter to his editor and friend. It was published in 1758 as *Lettre à M. d'Alembert sur les spectacles* (*Letter to M. d'Alembert on the Theatre*). It provoked an extended public exchange and represented Rousseau's permanent break from d'Alembert, Diderot and all his former Enlightenment allies.

In our day, the optimistic view that a nation's political culture may be improved by the exposure of its people to spectacles of a particular kind has again become popular. It has been endorsed by many but celebrated by one distinguished voice in particular, especially with reference to film, that of Stanley Cavell. It is therefore necessary, once again, to rehearse the opposing view, not out of any dislike for that medium, but out of a greater concern for its corrosive effects on our democracy. Not having found any way to improve on Rousseau's style of presentation, I have adapted it to my own ends. As for the arguments, no doubt I have debased them.

Cavell's contributions to aesthetics, philosophy and film theory are immense and anyone who reads what follows will see how much I have benefited from them. I regret that his current poor health makes it impossible for me to address these remarks to him directly or to expect any reply from him, but I trust that the other respondents will hold me to account on his behalf as well as their own. I thank them for this, as well as for tolerating a form of presentation that is out of fashion.

Preface

I am wrong, if I lay my hands on my keyboard on this occasion without good cause. It can be neither advantageous nor agreeable to me to attack M. Cavell. I respect his person; I admire his talents; I love his works; I am moved by the good things he has said of my country. A just response to his decency obliges me to every sort of consideration toward him; but consideration outweighs conviction only with those for whom all morality consists in gratitude. Humanity and truthfulness are our first duties; every time that particular discretion causes us to change this order, we are culpable.

Since not everyone will have M. Cavell's encyclopedic works on film before their eyes, I shall here transcribe some of the passages, from an essay entitled "The Good of Film," that set me, on this occasion, before my private screen.

> [M]y attention has over the years rather been attracted to cases that show film, good films, to have an affinity with a particular conception of the good ... It is the conception found in what I have called Emersonian perfectionism.
>
> As a perfectionism it is going to have something to do with being true to oneself, or, in Foucault's title, the caring of the self, hence with a dissatisfaction, sometimes despair, with the self as it stands; so something to do with a progress of self-cultivation ... The decisive difference of Emerson's outlook from that in Plato's *Republic* is that the soul's journey to itself is not pictured as a continuous path directed upward to a known point of completion but rather as a zigzag of discontinuous steps following the lead of what Emerson calls my "unattained but attainable self" (as if there is a sage in each of us), an idea that projects no unique point of arrival but only a willingness for change, directed by specific aspirations that, while rejected, may at unpredictable times return with new power ... The sage in us is what remains after all our social positionings.
>
> [T]he genre of Hollywood comedy ... [that] I name ... comedies of remarriage were working out ideas in Emersonian perfectionism ... The

> lives of the remarriage couples … arrive at a moment in which they have to reaffirm their marriages by taking them intact back into participation in the ordinary world, and attest their faith, or perception, that they consent to their society as one in which a moral life of mutual care is pursuable, and worth the show of happiness sufficient to encourage others to take their lives further, as if happiness in a democracy is a political emotion.[1]

This is certainly the most agreeable and seductive scene that could be offered us, but it is, at the same time, the most dangerous advice that could be given. At least, such is my sentiment and my reasons are in this writing. With what avidity will the young of philosophy, swept away by such a sage of our sageness, give themselves to ideas for which they already have too great a penchant? How many young Americans, otherwise good citizens, are waiting for the moment to dash off to the multiplex, believing that they are rendering a service to their country and nearly to humankind? This is the subject of my alarm; this is the danger that remains unacknowledged. I have no more desire to displease M. Cavell than he to do us injury, but, even if mistaken, must I not act and speak according to the world as I have viewed it? Would it not be a treason to that world and my place in it to do otherwise?

Widespread printing and reading destroyed the art of memory; recording and broadcasting destroyed the household practice of music; motorized transportation destroyed the art of horsemanship; the great singing and dancing movies of the twentieth century coincided with the demise of routine instruction in singing and dancing for the middle class. How is it that I, a supposedly well-educated individual of the twenty-first century, can neither recite poetry nor play an instrument, nor ride a horse, nor dance with even the slightest competence? All I am good for is reading and karaoke. Shall we really, then, hope to become better democrats by putting our hopes and dreams for democracy on film and expecting them to inspire us? For what other practice has this method proven successful? For every popular representation that is created, a human activity is destroyed; let anyone who can show me where this is not the law.

[1] Stanley Cavell, "The Good of Film," in *Cavell on Film*, edited by William Rothman (Albany, NY: State University of New York Press, 2005), pp. 334–7, 348.

What reception can such a writer expect to receive who defends democracy *against* happiness and perhaps also the reverse, against the greatest aesthetic achievements of the twentieth century. Against happiness! Against art! What delightful recommendations for a book! How slight is the audience with a disposition to tolerate this! Yet, if this letter fails to reach its destination with the public – the small, remnant reading public – there is no place to put the blame but on the hands that type these words. Blessed with every kind of fortune – good health, good friends, a fine family and position – I am nonetheless in the grip of trepidation that I cannot exorcise and I tremble when I consider the duty set before me. I have seen what must be done but lack the courage and wit to do it. Isolation may temper the passions that sociability excites, but it cannot extirpate them nor produce new resources of audacity by itself when the material is lacking. Reader, if you receive this work with indulgence, you will see the moment of substance that casts the shadow; for, as for me, I am less, and more, but not equal to the task.

I

How many questions I find to discuss in what you appear to have unsettled! Whether the cinema, or even just the genre you specify, is good or bad in itself? What it is that attracts us to it? What sort of experience the cinema is? What the time of cinema signifies or whether it signifies anything at all? Not to be of your opinion on some of these points is to make myself clear enough about the others.

Of no less importance: what are the ties – economic, moral, erotic – which make possible the constitution and continuous reconstitution of a people as such from an assortment or multitude of humans? And at what cost to their souls or their individuality? How can the bonds of union be those of liberty?

I believe it was a previous letter writer who first grasped (or perhaps first translated from Greek tragedy into modern terms) the fundamental political problem that the mobility of eros is incompatible with the political need for institutional stasis.[2] We must speak precisely here: it is not the irrationality or strength of eros, per se, that is the problem. Avarice, in the sense of desire for money, is a passion both irrational and powerful, but our political and economic theorists have found many ways of channeling it into stable institutions because, for all its irrationality, avarice is predictable. Its object is unchanging and the paths to that object are relatively well known. Eros, however, is not predictable in that way. Its objects are *not* fixed and the paths to them are so various as to be incomputable. Therefore, the institutionalization of eros must, initially at least, be a more vexing task.

Marriage, we might say, is a stable (or unstable) institution of eros in the same sense that the market is a stable (or unstable) institution of avarice. Indeed, the forms and systems of marriage have been various enough that one might define marriage simply as any institution that succeeds in ordering some particular set of erotic desires. But, eros being different from avarice, the mechanism of stability in the two institutions cannot be the same. Nothing is "maximized" in a marriage and certainly not erotic pleasure. How, then, does the institution work, when does it fail, and what is the price of it "working"? And can these mechanisms, however they function in marriage, inform us in turn about the bonds of a democratic political union which faces its own erotic challenge? Is our polity at stake in our system of marriage, as many today for very different reasons suppose? I think perhaps you and I agree that it is, but, again, for reasons very much other than the ordinary.

The democratic state, that is the state that is freely founded and persists in freedom, is some kind of union: on this much many can easily agree. But which kind? To say it is founded by "contract" is no answer, for we use this term in a way that is irreducibly plural. On the one hand, a contract could be a meeting of interests that are selfish and perhaps

[2] A point well made in Elizabeth Rose Wingrove, *Rousseau's Republican Romance* (Princeton, NJ: Princeton University Press, 2000), and Tracy B. Strong, *Jean-Jacques Rousseau: The Politics of the Ordinary* (Thousand Oaks, CA: SAGE Publications, 1994), wise books from which I have learned much.

economic in nature. But, if we use the word this way when we speak of a wedding contract, we either debase marriage beyond all recognition (though some would do this) or we mean something else. Indeed, we could just as easily turn around the problem (and the metaphor) by referring to economic agreements as a "marriage of interests," and it is just as plain that we clarify nothing in doing so.

To know whether the cinema of remarriage – the "comedies of remarriage," as you have called them[3] – is good or bad for the union of the state, we must know the second as well, if not better, than the first. Can we really, then, reach a conclusion on this relation by removing ourselves from active participation in politics in order to reflect in a movie theater? But, I suspend this objection, for it applies to so many others, and with such greater force, that it would be unfair to apply it to those who are most conscious of it. Still, we must bear in mind the difficulty and ambiguity of investigating both sides of the equation simultaneously or we will end by adding to the confusion rather than reducing it.

* * *

Postponing some of these questions for later, however, I propose to begin where these questions meet, in Philadelphia, a name with such delicious ambiguity of state, sex, love and marriage that it perfectly encapsulates our problem, and, further, to begin where we find ourselves in perfect agreement, namely, in the judgment that *The Philadelphia Story* is one of the most nearly perfect films ever made. Perhaps in exploring our disagreement in the reflected glow of this particular concord we will reach our destination, the disputed contribution of film to our democracy, that much more quickly.

You have written of this film that it asks the questions of "what is it that constitutes the legitimacy of marriage?" and "whether America has achieved its new human being, its more perfect union and its domestic tranquility, its new birth of freedom, whether it has been successful in

[3] Stanley Cavell, *Pursuits of Happiness: The Hollywood Comedy of Remarriage* (Cambridge, MA: Harvard University Press, 1981).

securing the pursuit of happiness."[4] While you offer no firm answers to these questions, you have repeatedly emphasized how the comedies of remarriage embody the Emersonian perfectionism you champion. Indeed, *The Philadelphia Story* is the film you pair with Emerson himself in your own recently published letters.[5] But, in what does the perfection of this film consist? Does it consist in the degree to which it perfects us? Or in the degree to which it provides us with an exemplar of perfection, which may lead us to perfect ourselves? Such I take to be your dangerous contention.

This view, I propose to say, is excessively theatrical. It could account for *The Philadelphia Story* as the play almost as much as the film that it became. That the theatrical spectacle could be a site of moral improvement is of course a highly Enlightened and long-disputed position. If a previous letter writer challenged that view purely with regard to the stage, then it falls to me to contest it with regard to cinema. There is indeed a lesson to be gained in understanding the uncanny power of this film, but it is not, I think, a lesson that will reconcile us to our democracy as you hope. Quite the opposite, I fear. While I would not say that the film degrades us, I would say that our attraction to it reveals our degraded condition and that it is in a sense this condition that binds us to it. What perfection the film embodies remains, therefore, out of reach for us and, as such, a hazard rather than a *telos*.

"The miracle at Philadelphia" was the old name for the process of remarriage that gave us the United States as they currently exist, that is, as the "re-United States." Having been brought into being only a few years before by the unmemorable and unloved Articles of Confederation, the Union, in 1787, was failing. To rebind it, its founders were recalled to the site of its inception for a repair that became, quite improbably, a refounding. They performed this act of reunion in less than four months, working in absolute secrecy. Is *The Philadelphia Story* a sort of re-enactment of this process? You, sir – planting the seed

4 Ibid., pp. 151–3.

5 Stanley Cavell, *Cities of Words: Pedagogical Letters on a Register of the Moral Life* (Cambridge, MA: Belknap/Harvard University Press, 2004), chs. 1–2.

for all that follows here – allude to this possibility but do no more.[6] But, I think it is the key point to understanding the film and, precisely, to understanding it *as a film*, and not as a play or as an adapted play.

* * *

It is instructive, in this respect, to begin our analysis by comparing the film with the play from which it springs.[7] As a play, *The Philadelphia Story* respected the traditional unities of time and space – the action takes place over twenty-four hours in a single house. The actions of the film, by contrast, are spread out over a weekend but also include a wordless prologue that takes place two years earlier, and the action moves up and down the Main Line with a brief excursion (it seems) to New York.[8] There are other differences: the heroine Tracy Lord's brother Sandy disappears in the film and most of his dramatic functions are taken over by C. K. Dexter Haven, whose role thus becomes even more substantial. But the most important changes are the ones that indicate both the political and the cinematic status, we might say, of the content of the movie. As a play, *The Philadelphia Story* is an elegant and hilarious drawing-room comedy. There is, as you have observed, an undercurrent of class resentment and reconciliation that also appears in the film, but it is not really emphasized in the play. Class serves more as an explanation of the characters' motives (specifically those of Mike Connor and George Kittredge) than as a dramatic theme.[9]

6 See Cavell, *Pursuits of Happiness*, pp. 153–4, and, even more briefly, *Cities of Words*, p. 40.

7 Why this has not been done more frequently is a mystery to me. Perhaps, on account of the widely known circumstances that the play was written as a vehicle for Katharine Hepburn, that it was a stage success and filmed very rapidly thereafter, it is assumed that there is little difference between the two versions. But there were, in fact, important changes made and, while the film version at times retains its stagey feel, the differences point to a layer of meaning in the film that is not available, and could not be available, on the stage.

8 In both the basic plot is the same: Tracy Lord, a rich Philadelphia heiress, having divorced Dexter Haven two years before, is set to marry George Kittredge. Haven shows up at her house, on the eve of the wedding, with two reporters (Mike Connor and Liz Imbrie) at the behest of publisher Sidney Kidd, who is blackmailing Haven so that he can procure a story on this high-society wedding. But Haven also has plans to win Tracy back and, by the end, after an extended flirtation between Tracy and Mike, he does so.

9 See Philip Barry, *The Philadelphia Story: A Comedy in Three Acts* (New York: Coward-McCann, Inc., 1939). There is a stark contrast here with the earlier *Holiday*, from the same author and stars, which I discuss below.

But the film insists, from its first frame, that politics are at issue. I mean from its very first frame, from the sadly neglected opening credits. As the film begins, the expected names and titles are projected over a series of sketches or reliefs: first, Independence Hall, the site of the Constitutional Convention and, earlier, of the Continental Congresses; then the Liberty Bell; then the statue of William Penn (Quaker, democrat, founder and "Absolute Proprietor" of Pennsylvania and Philadelphia) that sits on top of Philadelphia City Hall; then a brief panorama of the city, emphasizing its Grecian Museum of Art; and finally a return to Independence Hall. These are the only moments of the film that depict any part of municipal Philadelphia proper. And yet, so that we will not miss the point of what is at stake in the film, the final stencil of Independence Hall (where the final credit – "Directed by George Cukor" – has just been displayed) is replaced by the first live-action shot, an exterior view of the Lord mansion where most of the film takes place, the establishing shot of the first scene, but also, thereby, of the entire movie (it recurs twice more at least). The two buildings do not particularly resemble one another, so the transition mostly makes sense as a symbolic rather than aesthetic one, as if we are about to see into the temple of democracy.

But it is this very question of whether we *ought* to see into the temple of democracy that I want to claim is at issue here. For what the film adds to the play at this point is exactly a kind of discursus about the legitimacy of such a viewing, and especially the legitimacy of it in *photographic* form. In the play, there is only a brief mention of photography when magazine photographer Liz Imbrie (Ruth Hussey) says in an early scene that she is "quite a pest" with her camera and Tracy Lord (Katharine Hepburn), her photographic subject, replies, quite insincerely, that she hopes Liz will take lots of pictures. This exchange remains in the film version but photography, and the invasiveness of photography, have now become a major theme.

In an early scene at the mansion's stables, which has been added to the film, we are introduced, visually, to *Spy* magazine, which we see being read by Uncle Willy (he holds it, rather unnaturally, exactly perpendicular to the ground so that we can see the cover). Tracy looks contemptuously at the magazine, replete with photos: "Where'd you get this idiotic thing anyway?" When her little sister Dinah says "I love it – it's got pictures of everything," Tracy replies, with complete disdain, "It certainly has." And when her fiancé George Kittredge shows an unseemly interest in the magazine, Tracy gets positively upset. "Of all the filthy ideas! Coming into a private house with a camera!," she says, flinging the magazine to the ground and later having her horse stomp on it for good measure.

The title of the magazine, not incidentally, has also been changed. In the play it is called "Destiny" magazine, although it is also mentioned that Sidney Kidd owns magazines called "Dime" and "Spy." The stable scene ends with a dissolve from the stomped-on copy of *Spy* to a building engraving which announces that we have arrived at "Dime and Spy Incorporated, Sidney Kidd, Editor and Publisher" (an obvious satirical reference to what was once known as Time/Life International, owned by Henry Luce), presumably in New York, another setting that has been added to the play. In the scene that follows, we see Sidney Kidd, who does not appear in the play at all (though he is often talked about), set the plot in motion by blackmailing Dexter Haven (Cary Grant) so that he will arrange entry into the Lord house for the writer Mike Connor (Jimmy Stewart) and the photographer Liz, the results of which are to be published in *Spy*.

Haven, we learn, also despises the photographic invasion of private life. We are told the story of how he smashed the cameras of the paparazzi (including Liz) who tried to record his honeymoon (later paying for the cameras and writing letters of apology): "I had the strange idea our honeymoon was our own business." Connor protests against the secret, invasive assignment as degrading and undignified, while Liz shows no enthusiasm for it but says, "I can't afford to hate anyone, I'm only a photographer." But Kidd has determined their course of action and, thus, the course of the film. Unwilling as they are, no one has the power to resist him.

What has happened here? Around the core of a romantic comedy where the principals are the maiden and her suitors, the film version has added a conflict between the principals, who wish not to be photographed nor to be seen in public at all, and an antagonist who wishes to put them on film and expose them to the world. (That George Kittredge is the one principal who wants publicity, and wants to appear in *Spy*, is the repeated sign we are given of his utter unsuitability for Tracy and his general bad taste.) But, of course, we are already in the process of watching the film that will only show us more and more intimate moments. These early scenes are posing the question, however, of whether it is perhaps indecent that such a film should exist, and if it does exist, if it is decent for us to watch it. Again, sir, these are questions you raise momentarily, but decline to answer.[10] As much as we wish to identify with Grant, Hepburn and Stewart, the glamorous romantic leads, our position as the viewers of the filmed entertainment instead forces us to identify with Sidney Kidd.[11] While it is clear enough in the play that the off-stage Kidd wants to invade the privacy of the Lord family, the film goes out of its way, by all these devices, to emphasize that it is the *photographic* invasion that is the most important, "filthiest" element.[12]

We are forcibly returned to this theme at the close of the film when – his blackmail plot having been foiled – Kidd sneaks into the wedding himself (now the wedding of Tracy and Dexter, rather than of Tracy and George). In a remarkable sequence that ends the film – and which has no parallel in the play – the sight of Kidd drawing a small camera from his pocket and snapping a picture is the penultimate live-action shot we

[10] Cavell, *Pursuits of Happiness*, p. 160; Cavell, *Cities of Words*, p. 41.

[11] Liz takes the pictures but she's "just a photographer," a camerawoman, so to speak. It is Kidd who directs the action from offstage (and not, as you suggest, Dexter). Pushing the point a bit, one might add that Kidd is played by Henry Daniell, an actor who bears a pretty clear physical resemblance to the director George Cukor, and Daniell's performance has a slightly bizarre fey quality to it, which further associates him with Cukor, whose homosexuality was well known in Hollywood (Clark Gable had him fired for it), if not to the general public.

[12] I do not mean to obscure here the differences one might notice between still photography and motion photography. My point here is simply that the film itself uses still photography as a metaphor for film and thus comments on itself while appearing to discuss a magazine.

see. In the final shot, we see the wedding party turning toward Kidd's camera and freezing, with looks of surprise and displeasure on all of their faces. Were it not for the theme of invasive photography, it would be hard to explain this final shot, which otherwise spoils the happy ending of the lovers reuniting. What happens next is even more remarkable. This final image of the wedding party turns into a freeze-frame, which is then further transformed into a picture in a magazine. As the camera draws back and the page of the magazine is turned, we see various other wedding pictures with captions that we cannot make out (but which signal with absolute clarity that we are looking at a magazine, presumably *Spy*) and then a final picture of Grant and Hepburn kissing.

It is the classic final image of a romantic movie – it is the only time in the film that they kiss – but the kiss is transformed by appearing as a photograph in Kidd's magazine. And the effect of being photographed is pronounced: instead of being happy, Hepburn looks incredibly uncomfortable. Again, were it not for the running theme of photography, one might think that the director had made a mistake in choosing this image, or that somehow there had been a problem in production and no better shot existed. The closing credits follow, which return us to the sketches of civic Philadelphia, now unquestionably the subject of a photographic exploration.

* * *

At the American Constitutional Convention in Philadelphia in May of 1787, on the first day, the participants all swore an oath of secrecy. Although they could not agree on things like whether Africans or Native Americans were fully human, on this point there is no record of any disagreement. And during the Convention itself, secrecy was fully maintained. Indeed, so concerned were the delegates about their privacy that, even though Philadelphia is often very hot and humid in the summertime, the windows to the crowded discussion room were all closed and heavy drapes were put over them so that no one outside could hope to see or hear what was said. It must have been terribly uncomfortable, but everyone present agreed that the necessary negotiations could not be carried out in any other way, and certainly not in public.

There is something here about democracy that we do not like to acknowledge. When we describe the social contract in abstract forms, we tend to characterize it as a *public* promising or exchange (of rights for security, say, or for enforcement of authority). To be fair, or even meaningful, we are apt to say the terms of the agreement must be widely known and the transaction publicly witnessed. And, of course, we can rightly say that the rewritten Constitution could only take its validity from the public endorsement it received from the state conventions in the process of ratification.

What we do not like to say is that such an endorsement is only a public capstone to a secret process that preceded it, as a marriage ceremony is a public acknowledgment of a courtship that is generally not witnessed by anyone. The secrecy of negotiations is difficult to acknowledge in the political context because it seems to cut against the idea of a constitution as a document created by democratic means. It reduces the role of the validators of a constitution to that of mere witnesses to an *act* of which others are the author. In a wedding, of course, the secondary role of the witnesses is not such a problem, but, in a democracy of more than two, the situation is rather different.[13] If we merely *view* an act of union, if the ones who say "I do" are other than ourselves, then we are hardly the authors of that union or the authority over ourselves that it creates. If we are concerned that public power be only legitimated by the authorization of those it governs, then we can accept nothing less than an autonomous "I do" from every citizen.

In the case of a wedding, we understand that the passions which forge the union are only given a limited and ceremonial display in public. For most – but not all – cultures it would be obscene, for example (but why this is so deserves further consideration), to have the couple copulate in public, even though such physical joining is, in some sense, the acknowledged purpose of the ceremony. But what is the parallel

[13] The roles of publicity and secrecy in our democracy are canvassed, from a different perspective, by Jodi Dean in the thought-provoking *Publicity's Secret* (Ithaca, NY: Cornell University Press, 2002). Among other things, Dean calls attention to the way in which the era of the Founding was rife with conspiracy theory.

situation with a political union? Are these bonds so equally sexual that their public display is unseemly? That is unlikely. What then is their nature and why are they so fragile or intimate or shameful that it is difficult to make them public? Is there some cost or a danger here to the souls or individuality of those who enter into such unions? There is a famous painting of the Founders at the Constitutional Convention. You must know it as well as I. Would it have been wrong, if it were possible then, to have recorded a photograph of them at work?

When Tracy Lord discusses the photography of domestic life she calls it, with a great and unexplained vehemence, "filthy," but the specific photographs she is discussing are explicitly described as mundane (we do not see them). Tracy narrates (or perhaps reads the captions of) a photo-essay in *Spy*: "An average day in the life of a congressman (n. b.). The congressman's wife. The kitchen where is prepared one banana, sliced, two fried eggs. The congressman kisses his wife good morning." Regardless of what the camera sees in the congressman's kitchen, Tracy finds something pornographic about every published photograph of private life and, indeed, the phenomenon of certain kinds of "reality" television confirms that there is something titillating about the photography of even the most commonplace – I might say the most ordinary – elements of life in a famous household, as opposed to the direct experience of them. Were we actually in the congressman's kitchen – or the Kardashians' – we might get a kind of quick thrill being there, but what we saw would not be particularly exciting.

We generally use the term "pornography" to refer not just to any photography of private life, but to a specific kind: photography of the normally hidden act of procreation (and, I suppose we should add, of its endless analogs and debasements as well). Is there not a kind of likeness between the ordinary secrecy of procreation and that of constitution-making? Both, we might say, shield a bonding that requires the utmost in intimacy and trust for its performance, even if the *results* are publicly announced. These are acts both natural (if anything is natural) and elemental for the propagation of any society; and yet they are generally held, by diverse societies, not to be fit for public display, even when they and their results are celebrated. The secrecy of the Constitutional Convention, I would likewise maintain, is not just a veil of ignorance that one draws around horse-trading politics. It also reflects an ambivalence about the decency of the display of the act of conjoining that cannot be wholly explained by, say, embarrassment about logrolling (a term that, not surprisingly, has a sexual meaning as well as a political one).

The Philadelphia Story thus presents itself to us, rather self-consciously, as a kind of democratic pornography. It rewards our desire to see into the making of a bonding of equals even as it chastises us for having the desire. We see there the resistance of all the decent characters in the film to being photographed in their time of union and reunion and we nonetheless enjoy the fact that that resistance is overcome. Indeed, we rather luxuriate in it. Pushing the point a bit, sir, we might even say that there is more than a touch of masochism in the experience of the film. We hear of the filthiness of *Spy* magazine and its readers over and over and yet here we sit all along, the closing sequence tells us, with the magazine in our dirty hands! If we love the characters and events that we have just witnessed (as you and I, sir, certainly do), then we must also be enjoying in some sense the condemnation that those characters and events contain of the voyeurism we, as the surrogates of Sidney Kidd, are practicing. Surely it is not the happiness that results from the fulfillment of *this* desire that you recommend as the founding emotion of our democracy?

Confirming this view of things, I think, is the fact that there is one photograph which *disappears* between the play and the film. In the film, Dexter brings Tracy a wedding present (for her planned marriage to Kittredge) that is intended as an ironic reminder of their shared past: a miniature replica of the *True Love* "a boat he designed and built practically," a boat that only sleeps two and which they sailed together and alone on their honeymoon, unseen by anyone (the boat is a "haven" from the public). In the play, Dexter brings a *photograph* of the *True Love*, but in the film this has been changed into a working model that actually floats in the Lords' pool. The idea of the *True Love* is an important one (if a bit clunky and transparent) in both the play and the movie and several important conversations are centered around it, but these conversations are not changed by the presence of the working model (which itself appears only briefly). There is no reason, in other words, for Dexter to have brought a model *rather* than a photo *except* for the fact that the film evinces a loathing of the photography of love, which the play does not. Given the smashing of the paparazzi's cameras, there really should *be* no images of the *True Love*.

It is significant as well that the photo-essay which Tracy despises and which Kittredge defends concerns a congressman. Kittredge simply calls it "publicity" and says "some people like that kind of thing." When Kittredge asks Tracy, in the next moment, what would happen if he decided to go into politics, she says, brightly, "You'd be elected president!" But when he makes the obvious point that running for president might involve a certain amount of "publicity," she says, equally categorically, "Not in my house!" George then reminds her that, after their wedding, it will be "our house." Tracy sweetly agrees to this, and the point about publicity and politics is left temporarily unresolved between them. But Tracy's ultimate rejection of George means also a rejection of a political life, *if* such a life were to carry a requirement of "publicity."

What, then, are we to take away from this aspect of the film, which shows us an analog or simulacra of a political process we are forbidden to see? What is at stake here in this tension between publicity and its opposite? I hesitate, sir, to call that opposite "privacy" for fear of being misunderstood. For we are dealing here, I think, not exactly with something we hide or hoard from others, but rather with something that we hesitate to share with others but want to, something that can only be shared at the right time and in the right way, not indiscriminately. Food can be distributed from a warehouse, but a meal can be shared only around a table, even if that sharing involves an invitation to outsiders to join in. Although you can steal someone's food, you cannot thieve yourself a place at someone else's meal. Here, perhaps, we begin to see the difference between an intimacy which is shared publically but by invitation and an intimacy that is captured and distributed by a camera.

You have written, sir, that perfectionism's competitors "are the endless debasements of itself,"[14] but here it seems as if we, the observers of the film, are the debasers of all that is on its way to perfection.

But perhaps all this puts the wrong kind of emphasis on a word like "pornography," which I intend only as description rather than as criticism. Indeed, if we attempt to fill out the genre of democratic pornography, I think we would find some of the better films that are directly or indirectly about politics. I would nominate, for example, *The Man Who Shot Liberty Valance*, *Giant*, *Lone Star* and *The Dreamers* for starters – all films that attempt to make visible the elements of democratic politics that inherently resist "publicity." What is it, then, about politics that resists publicity of this sort, that finds it indecent? Surely not the intentions of our politicians, who are largely publicity hounds of the worst sort? What is it, then, that Kidd/Cukor sets out to document photographically and that the principals seek to hide? Is it really a striving for perfection that is so in need of a cloak of invisibility?

I reply, on the contrary, that it is weakness, vulnerability and finitude that are here put on display. I would contend further that all of these are related, in some sense, to the momentariness and fragility of intimacy and union that the film, *against* all of our desires for its permanence, manages to depict. It is this momentariness, I think, that the principals have an instinct to shield from public view, not because it is inherently shameful or disgusting, but because the visibility of it weakens the bonds of union which they are pledged to uphold. Allow me to explain.

It is indisputable, I admit, that *The Philadelphia Story* depicts a kind of growth in moral intelligence, an acknowledgment, as you would rightly call it, of the moral standing of others. This growth occurs principally in the character of Tracy Lord and, secondarily in that of Mike Connor. Both of them begin the film (and the play) as different kinds of moral prigs (she is intolerant of weakness; he is burdened with class resentment). And George Kittredge, who is equally priggish, despite

[14] Stanley Cavell, "The Good of Film," in *Cavell on Film*, edited by William Rothman (Albany, NY: State University of New York Press, 2005), p. 340.

his humble origins, is ultimately excluded from intimacy with the others for his failure to overcome this condition.[15] Nonetheless, I would say that were this merely a tale of moral improvement, it would be a dreary and dull afternoon special – *autant vaudrait aller au sermon* – and hardly the great film of America that it is.

What makes the film so magical and attractive, I would say, is not the outcome just described, but the way in which we get to see the radical contingency of that outcome. While the plot is not one of chance and misdirection (it is not a farce), neither is it one of fate and destiny (recall that *Destiny* has been *removed* as the title of the magazine we "read" – what we see is not what has been foreordained). The growth that takes place is both chancy and erotically charged – also alcohol-fueled. (One could almost interpret the film to say that no one who has not had a serious binge can be a moral person.)

What is it that we see – that we *actually see* in this film – that is at once both entertaining and dangerous? We see, I would say, the unpredictable and vibrant dance of Eros. Mike Connor is variously in love with Liz and Tracy. Tracy is variously in love with George, Mike and Dexter. All in the course of a weekend! Liz and Dexter are steadfast, but their wisdom in the film (born of experience) consists of their ability to let their desired mates pass through stages of erotic entanglement with others in order to find their way home. ("A little too rough?," says the manicurist to Liz at the moment she catches sight of Mike and Tracy chatting together. "A little," Liz replies, "but I'm used to it.") George lacks this ability (he is unable to forgive, but even worse, to understand Tracy's dalliances) and is thus morally obtuse. ("He's no tower of strength you know," Dexter quips, "he's just a tower.")

But the wisdom which Liz and Dexter share is not a guarantee of success. In the penultimate scene of the film, Tracy has broken off her

[15] It is rather a problem to your way of thinking, I believe, that the character of Dexter Haven undergoes no improvement but appears from the start as a paragon of moral perfection. Though it is made clear that in the past he suffered from alcoholism and has recovered (more or less through the force of his own will), in the story he is from first to last a moral touchstone that others refer to, but who never himself improves or changes in any significant way.

engagement to George and is pondering what to tell the wedding guests who have assembled in her living room. Mike impulsively proposes to her and, in the moment before she replies, the camera cuts briefly to both Dexter and Liz. Both look terribly anxious that she will accept. Although Dexter has sometimes seemed to preside over the events of the movie as a maestro, in this moment he is for once genuinely unsure of the outcome and it is important that he be so. For the path of love – and indeed of any political union – is not something guaranteed by good morals nor a reward for good behavior. Tracy chooses well but she could have chosen otherwise (and marrying Mike would hardly have been a disaster, merely non-optimal). Mike and Tracy have not merely flirted with one another but have shared something real, "the memory of which I wouldn't part with for anything," Mike says.

However, this acknowledgment is *only for us* to see. It takes place in an anteroom and cannot be seen by the wedding guests who will in a moment witness the reunion of Tracy and Dexter. Even this wedding, however, is not, the film insists, a part of destiny. After Dexter follows Mike's proposal with his own (or rather, in a classic act of ventriloquism, has Tracy indicate to guests that she will now marry him), the two have a simple exchange: "Dexter are you sure?", "Not in the least but I'll risk it, will you?" Tracy's agreement signals that this new marriage is to be different from the old one because it acknowledges the contingency of the feelings of both partners. Their marriage is at risk from the moment of its inception, but perhaps healthier for the fact that both are willing to recognize this fact.

When Tracy breathlessly promises in the next moment to be "yare," Dexter rejects the promise: "Be whatever you like, you're my red-head."[16] "Yare" is an ancient English adjective often used of ships. In an earlier conversation, Tracy gives a curious definition: "Oh, what does it

16 Dexter often refers to Tracy as "Red." He is the only one to do so. This element is present in the play and it is hard to know what meaning Barry intended for it, perhaps merely to highlight the special quality of their relationship. In the film, however, it takes on another meaning: it indicates to us that Dexter can see something about Tracy that the rest of us cannot, for the film is in black and white.

mean? … Easy to handle. Quick to the helm. Fast. Bright. Everything a boat should be … until she develops dry rot." She gives this definition in the course of explaining to George about the original *True Love*, a ship that all agree was quite "yare." It may seem that in remarrying Tracy and Dexter are merely reboarding the *True Love*, which they had somehow disembarked by mistake, but this is not right. Tracy at one point admits that she herself was not very "yare." In promising at the end to be so, she seems to be trying to correct this fault, but Dexter's reply indicates that it is not a fault in his eyes. He does not seek something "easy to handle," rather he seeks the unpredictability that is Tracy, the "human" Tracy (no longer a "Lord") that she always was but has become more fully now, now that she has rejected that status of "goddess" to which others and she herself were prone to assign her. However yare, boats always rot at some point.

Only that which is not fixed in form can avoid decay. Only as inconsistent, flesh-and-blood human beings can Dexter and Tracy have a relationship that might actually endure. Their union, even if it were like a ship, must still ply violent waters with an unruly crew. Tracy's moral improvement will not compel nature to reward her with a stable, happy relationship. At most, the change will be its own reward in divesting her of the belief that a stable, happy relationship is the natural recompense for her moral stature. In that sense, she now expects less of her second marriage than of the first, and likewise Dexter. Indeed, sir, I would say that they will be the happiest if they expect the least of it – nothing.

But the normal wedding ceremony that Dexter and Tracy, with the assistance of Mike and Liz, dutifully enact in public appears to deny all this. The event that we are shown (taking place, recall, in the Lord house, which parallels Independence Hall) is depicted as utterly traditional. The band plays the Wagnerian bridal theme. The surroundings are covered in crystal and lace; it is no Quaker wedding. Tracy wears white. The father gives away the bride. Every bit of it is a farce, given what has just occurred. And yet the witnesses are, in some sense, deceived. Tracy's little sister wrongly imagines herself to be the author of the happy turn of events ("I did it! I did it all!"). Kidd takes his candid photographs for *Spy* and, we assume, uses them to report a traditional high-society wedding.

Why go through with such a ceremony? Dexter and Tracy have been married and divorced before, by a judge. Yet their marriage will be all the more real now even as (perhaps because) the ceremony that marks its creation will be all the more phony. Around the reality of their contingent union, they draw up a show of its permanence and solidity. Is that not, perhaps, the meaning of all such ceremonies? And is not the political and social need for such an appearance of permanence and solidity the reason why "decency" – but perhaps we might say here, a generous desire that the benefits of union be liberally shared, like a great family meal – requires us to hide the contingency that precedes such a union? Mike and Tracy will remember their dalliance, as will Dexter and Liz remember it, *but it will not be publicly acknowledged.* Mike is best man both *because* he is part of the couple's erotic history and *because* he knows better than to speak publically about it. When one invites ex-lovers to a wedding, sir, one does so with the expectation that their good taste will cause them to refrain from speaking about a past relationship at any point during the proceedings.

Putting this point another way, we could say that intimacy and union are things that actually exist only from moment to moment, with no guarantees that they will continue steadily. And yet political life, no less than marriage, is formally and publically predicated on the idea that this is not so, that people can pledge themselves permanently, that humans, as someone once said, are animals that can make promises, promises which bind them forever. Experience shows this to be less than true.

It is often noted that modern, Western marriage takes place in the shadow of possible divorce and that it is thereby fundamentally changed. While this may be true and, indeed, a healthy change, it is not what concerns me here. Although divorce was still a scandal when *The Philadelphia Story* was made, Tracy and Dexter have nonetheless divorced and it would be obvious to anyone that they could divorce again. What the film points out, however, is not that one may love and then cease to love, it is rather that one's erotic attachments may be violently various, not just within a lifetime, but within a day or an hour. Yet Tracy is not a slut because she loves three men (and at least kisses them) in the course of two days – rather she is, as the film insists, "a human being" who has finally recognized her inability to control her own passions. Presumably, after remarrying Dexter, she won't do this sort of thing very often? But she is not promising that and Dexter is not asking her to promise. *Except in public.*

In public, we pledge our allegiance to an ever more perfect union. Each of us knows, or ought to know, that this pledge is a lie. Not in the sense that our intentions are other than our words, but in the sense that we know, or ought to know, that we cannot guarantee our own intentions, not by words, or ceremony, or law. With beings such as ourselves, there are no guarantees, but to publicize such instability on a daily basis is more than most of us can bear, and is probably counterproductive to the goal of union itself. To advertise the contingency of our union is not to uphold it but to accelerate its demise, to which end we are in no way obligated.

* * *

Yet, excluding this element of our erotic and political life from view ends up inexorably generating its own desire, a desire to tear away the veil of decency, which produces films like *The Philadelphia Story* as well as the audiences that so love to see them. It may be that such a pornographic tendency is an inevitable result of a democracy such as ours, which attempts to forge the bonds of union out of quicksilver souls. But, is it really, then, a desire for perfection that drives us to the cinema or do we rather go to the movies and their splendid common isolation in order to revel in what we cannot publicly acknowledge? Do we leave the show really edified or with palms that are a bit sweaty?

To ask if film is good or bad in itself is to pose too vague a question, as you well know. Films, like constitutions, exist in order to please and bind an audience and, unless they do both, they will certainly fail.[17] Yet what

[17] Thus the role that film might have in a dictatorship is a very different question that I do not address here.

pleases us about the film is precisely how it exposes us in safety to the danger we inhabit personally and politically. Should we call this our perfection or titillation? No doubt it is a noble undertaking to mark and remind us of our limitations. But *The Philadelphia Story* rewards, punishes and amplifies our desire to see what goes on within Independence Hall, our unrequitable desire to see the sources of our own independence, which we rightly fear is not ours because its originary moments are invisible. What would it take for us, instead, to live in a democracy that truly enacted the momentariness of our passions and attachments? Has the film been made which could show us *that*? And, if it were made, would *showing* it really help us toward such a democracy?

Once, in my youth, I took a bicycle trip through New England. I lost my way, at some point, in the vicinity of New Castle, New Hampshire, and presently found myself in a small village that seemed hidden in a valley. It did not seem unusual to me at first, since I had passed through many such villages on my trip, and I stopped at the general store for a soda and something to eat. I am sure there must have been a sign with the name of the village at the entrance, but I have long since forgotten it. It took me some time to realize what was unusual about the place. There was no movie theater – it would have been on the one main commercial street and there was none there. Nothing so strange about that, of course; it was a small village and no doubt there was some theater or other not far away. But most convenience stores in that area and at that time would have had a television going. There's nothing more boring than working in a small-town convenience store in the height of summer when the heat keeps most people in their homes. The clerks need something to pass the time. When I commented on this to whomever had sold me a soda, they told me that the position of the town in the valley meant that no television signals could be received without elaborate antenna equipment. A rich person could afford such equipment perhaps, but there was no one that rich in this little town. So they did without. This was in the days long before video recorders and cable and satellite television, mind you, which only came much later. There were simply no images to be seen there.

I will not contend that the people of this town were simple and virtuous. I will not romanticize, as it would be easy to do, New England in the 1970s or at any other time. Film and television are hardly the only media that could connect them to the outside world and, if they lacked these, they had all the others. But, they did seem a tad friendlier than those of the other towns I passed through that summer, a little more inclined to chat, to be sociable toward a traveling stranger who had come into their midst. Seeing that I was traveling alone and planning to sleep under the stars, a welcoming family invited me to stay in their guest room that night and enjoy their hospitality. I still remember the softness of the bed after many nights on the hard ground. The next day I rode away full of a sweet sentiment toward the family, a warm feeling toward the town, and a slightly improved appraisal of the species.

Now let us imagine that this isolated town were to be suddenly graced by the presence of a theater. Do we foresee that the character or the governance of the town would be thereby improved? Let us go further and imagine a cinema purged of its worst elements – careless violence, unfunny comedy and lifeless romance. It would therefore have to remain dark most of the time, but still we can imagine from time to time a film of quality would appear and, duly approved by the canons of good taste whom we would appoint, merit a screening. The prices would have to be fairly high, of course; without the subsidy of the normal dreck to subtend it, the few good films that played would have to support the whole cost of the institution. So, whatever good the films did would have to be weighed against what they subtracted from the budget of those who attend them. But, let us imagine what may not be true, that the cost is not prohibitive. What then? Would we expect the town meetings to be ennobled? The managers more responsible? The citizens more engaged? Would not the contrary be more likely? Would not the representation of a good conversation undermine the capacity to engage in one, as recorded music has undermined the ability to make music? Would a subtle depiction of intimacy really improve our capacity to engage in it? Or would it, on the contrary, deprive us of both the free time and the components of willingness to do so?

But what am I saying? Even if there is no theater there to this day, there is undoubtedly television via cable and satellite, and film via the various recording devices and internet streams. Geographic barriers have become as irrelevant to media as they have to armies and migrants. Nothing any longer stands in the way of good film, or bad, as it covers the globe. I must say, however, that we have yet to see the benefits of this blanketing of our culture with filmed talk in any improved conversations, marriages or political discourses. Would you not say, rather, that the opposite has occurred? What, then, would it take?

Perhaps, at a minimum, it would take an acknowledgment of the value of non-publicity, of not-open spaces, not as something that a polity must tolerate, but as something that it actually needs if it is to negotiate the delicate relationship between a stable *polis* and the passionate *pathē* that can either support or undermine it; non-publicity, not as something which negates or limits the public, but as something that supports and protects it. From this perspective, the boundary of public and non-public would not be marked by the door of the household, but rather by the ceremonies that acknowledge and stabilize the passions that can either support or undermine the polity depending on how they are negotiated.[18] But, going to the theater, I think it is safe to say, would not be one of these ceremonies. Schopenhauer said that the lesson we learn from experiencing life was not to want it. We might say the same of *The Philadelphia Story*: however pleasurable an experience it is, we can only draw the lesson that life examined by photography is not examined in the right way, for the *living* of a democratic life cannot be furthered by the mummification of it or by the violation of its fragility, however happy. *Neither the truest picture, nor the wisest teacher can substitute for the experience of the fragile moment.* Worse, insofar as we believe ourselves to be instructed in democratic life by its representations, we unknowingly deprive ourselves of the practice necessary to actually perform it.

[18] Far too late have I come to a fuller appreciation of my esteemed former colleague's reflections on these issues. See Debra Morris, "Privacy, Privation, Perversity: Toward New Representations of the Personal," *Signs*, 25:2 (2000): pp. 323–51.

I do not call this a defense of "privacy," because to frame the relation of the open and not-open as the opposition between public and private is to recreate or reinforce the pornographic tendency of contemporary democracy. It is also to impose a value hierarchy on these two elements of life that leads to an inevitable competition between them. It might make more sense to think of public and non-public as two states of matter through which a polity must oscillate, but by means of which oscillation it can achieve a kind of stability. Or, if that is too abstract, think of them as a structure with two rooms where each room is weighted to lean on the central wall so that the existence of each supports the other. Citizens, each at their own pace and on their own path, pass between these rooms as they do between the various rooms of a dwelling, each space hosting a function that is necessary for the life of the household. We cannot live entirely in the open or in the not-open, nor entirely in the erotic moment or the lawful union, and we cannot learn to balance the two except by the actual movement between them.

II

Every moment is as important as every other moment. By itself, this is an innocuous statement, as banal perhaps, if less common than, "every person is as important as every other person." Sentences like this only take on weight when they are put in tension with a countervailing value. For the latter, it might be something like "excellence must be rewarded; mediocrity held in contempt." But, for the first sentence, the counterweight is: no moment can have a meaning in itself, but only as part of a narrative.

That meaning is invested via narrative indicates that, as we experience each moment, we do not experience it in isolation. Each moment, for its content to be meaningful to a human being, must point forward to the future and backward to the past. Whatever is happening, we make sense of it and value or disvalue it with reference to our previous experiences and our hopes and expectations about the future. Even if we are consumed by immediate sensory experience, like eating or drinking, still we experience it with reference to our prior hunger or thirst, not to mention the meals we have had before and intend to have in the future.

People do, of course, claim to report moments that seem to them to be disconnected from the normal stream of time. They report them as moments of transcendence or rapture (not exclusively in a religious or theological sense), or of passion or boredom, or extreme abjection. Generally, they report such moments as unusual; no one claims to experience such moments constantly, though some claim (with little credibility, I think) to experience them routinely or predictably. You will forgive my tone of skepticism here. In my experience, even the most transcendent events (and it has been my blessing to have lived some) are deeply connected to the world and the relationships to it from which they emerge. Who could experience the divine without some prior notion of divinity? But, even if I am wrong or if there is a category of experience from which a malignant deity has excluded me, you will at least grant me that this is not the ordinary run of things.

Moments of transcendence aside then, how is the relation of moments and narrative accomplished? This is the question to which our consideration of the potential good of film has brought us. *The Philadelphia Story* gives us a kind of answer, an optimistic one, even if we can also discern in it some of the dangers of that answer. But here, sir, we must pause to take note of the dark twin that has not yet emerged in our story. For there was, indeed, *another* film of "national importance," released on the eve of World War II, that has the identical, very odd structure of the one we have been discussing: a woman pursued by three men, one of whom she has already married. Both films confront the passions of the moment with the political need for stability and constitution. In both films, the woman is estranged from her erstwhile husband, appears to be in love in turn with each of the two others, and ends up returned to her original partner, the man who loves her most sincerely. Yet, while in the *The Philadelphia Story*, which is about America, this is a happy ending – and so, you rightly term it, a "comedy of remarriage" – in Jean Renoir's *The Rules of the Game*, which is about France, the ending is anything but happy and we could, with some justice, term the film a "remarriage tragedy."[19]

What accounts for this difference? What indeed: a different mood perhaps, a different director? A closer proximity to the impending war? The different histories of America and France? All of these, no doubt, but something else as well: a fuller sense, I think, of the destructiveness and volatility of eros and the danger that it poses for any polity. The difficulty of reconciling a democracy of moments to a republic of laws is here on full and honest display. In the end, I fear, the plot and characters of *The Philadelphia Story* rely on luck and a sort of superhuman forbearance that it has not yet been my pleasure to experience in my fellow citizens. The characters of *The Rules of The Game*, though often aristocrats like those of *The Philadelphia Story*, are to me more ordinary and therefore more illustrative in their attempts to navigate the difficult time between the moments of passion and the persistence of marriage and state. Their failure is therefore more poignant and more instructive than the successes of their Main Line counterparts. And it instructs us thus: not to expect instruction from that which cannot share our experiences. It is no failure of film if it cannot provide us with what we should never have asked of it. Nor should we be surprised if a film of honest pessimism fails to reach its audience, and thus fails to instruct them. But, I am getting ahead of myself.

* * *

Please have patience with me for a moment while I catalog some of the extraordinary resemblances in these two contemporaneous films,

[19] The exact parallel of structure between the two films was obscured for a long time by the editing history of *The Rules of the Game*. The true original release form can no longer be seen. The film was famously denounced as unpatriotic and a slander on the French bourgeoisie (which it certainly was, although that was hardly the point) upon its debut in a Paris on the edge of war with Germany. Director Jean Renoir recut the film, eliminating one entire romantic subplot in the process (the one with a character played by Renoir himself). In the subsequent wartime chaos, the original version was lost. For many years, only the shorter version, distributed internationally after the war, was known. But a restoration effort has produced a version that is much closer to the original and which includes the third romance.

each witnessed originally by separate audiences, and only shown in the other country after the war.[20]

Each film is structured by its heroine's trilemma. Each, thereby, signals its distance from the common tropes and genres of the day: simple romantic rivalry and class polemic. The classes are indeed visibly opposed to one another, but their virtues and vices are not reduced in either case to an emblematic hero and villain. Neither are the romantic rivals simply good or bad; all have some legitimate claim. Indeed, compared with their creators' previous work, both films mark a conspicuous shift to a less stark relationship with class issues. Two years before *The Philadelphia Story*, the same writers and director, and many of the same actors, made *Holiday* (1938). Despite its impeccable Hollywood pedigree, that film *is* a class polemic: the working class characters are all witty and virtuous; the rich are stuffy and morally bankrupt. The crossover figure (played by Katharine Hepburn) must, in effect, be a class traitor to be a decent person. In *The Philadelphia Story*, by contrast, decency and indecency are distributed indifferently across the classes. Connor sums this up when he says, toward the end of the film, as if a revelation: "I made a funny discovery. In spite of the fact that somebody's up from the bottom, he can still be quite a heel. And even though somebody else is born to the purple, he can still be a very nice guy."

Likewise in Renoir's earlier works, for example, *Bondu Saved from Drowning* (1932), the simple and natural poor are contrasted with the overcultured and contemptible bourgeoisie. Whereas *The Rules of the Game*, though full of sharp observations about class, is careful to give us imperfect characters on all sides and no simply virtuous figures at all. No doubt the French film is far more pessimistic about relations between the classes (and between the sexes) than the American one. But this, I want to claim, has more to do with its general tragic themes than with a specific indictment of the venality of the upper classes.

[20] According to the Internet Movie Database, *The Philadelphia Story* was released in 1940 in the United States and in 1947 in France. *The Rules of the Game* was released in 1939 in France and only in 1950, in a shortened version, in the United States. (See www.imdb.com/title/tt0031885/releaseinfo and www.imdb.com/title/tt0032904/releaseinfo.)

There are a few uncanny parallels. In an early scene in *The Philadelphia Story*, Dexter Haven explains his continuing relationship with Tracy Lord by declaring "You might say we grew up together." In a comparable place in *The Rules of the Game*, a similar phrase – "I spent my whole youth with her" (*j'ai passé toute ma jeunesse avec elle*) – is voiced by Octave (Jean Renoir), in explaining his love for Christine (Nora Grégor). What is more, in neither case is it literally true: Haven and Lord are from the same town but not the same household. Octave, as a young man (but not as a child), was treated as a son while studying with Christine's father. However, both films use the phrase to indicate that at least one of the lovers comes to his passion from a familial origin. On the one hand, this origin provides insight: both Haven and Octave claim to know their beloved best, and there is some evidence that this is true, but both also come to their love with a kind of oedipal debt hanging over them, Octave to Christine's dead father, Haven to Tracy's family (indeed Haven acts to protect Tracy's father from blackmail).

In each film, the husband represents wealth and stability. Each husband, however, also has a flaw that threatens to undermine that status unless it remains ignored: Robert is descended from German Jews; Dexter is an alcoholic. Each husband is confronted by two rivals. In each case one is an artist (Octave is a musician in *The Rules of the Game*; Connor is a writer in *The Philadelphia Story*), but an artist who has found no commercial success and who therefore lives by his wits. The second rival in both cases is someone who comes from a modest background but has made a name for himself and even become famous for his accomplishments (in *The Rules of the Game*, André is a celebrated aviator; in *The Philadelphia Story*, George is a prominent businessman and budding politician). There is no point in reducing the characters to types – both films make a point of, and benefit from, the individuality of their characters – but it is not a mistake to say that in each case the woman faces a choice between (roughly) status, determination and creativity; one could also say between an insider, an outsider and a liminal, border-dwelling *arriviste* or *homo sacer*. And, in both cases, in the end the woman does not choose but has a choice thrust upon her, though with differing degrees of force and compliance; while the *homo sacer* is banished or killed without being murdered or sacrificed.

Further parallels of plot and character could be pursued: both films, for example, have a scene at their center in which the erotic ties which have supported the society of their members are blown apart (in *The Rules of the Game*, the hunt; in *The Philadelphia Story*, the party) and need to be subsequently reconstructed. Equally, of course, one could point to a thousand differences between them; most importantly, perhaps, to the parallel set of romantic entanglements among the servants that exist in *The Rules of the Game* without any equivalent in *The Philadelphia Story*. However, I hope what I have set out thus far is enough to convince anyone that there are important formal and thematic similarities here that would attract the attention of any observer.[21]

Most importantly, though, both films depict a marriage bond, in a substantial house symbolic of the nation in which it resides, under strain from the passions of the moment and ask what will have to happen for that bond of union to survive. Since in each case three men confront one woman, this turns out to be a question of what it will take for the woman to remain with the man to whom she is already pledged.[22] But while viewers of *The Philadelphia Story* are led to believe that these burdens are, in the end, quite minimal, those who see *The Rules of the Game* learn that the price to be paid is nearly unbearable. Let us see, then, which film will really instruct us in democracy and which will merely be popular there. For the difference between the films that is

[21] There can be no real question of influence between the two films. *Rules* opened first, in August 1939, but ran for only three weeks in Paris and was hardly seen by anyone. In any case, *The Philadelphia Story* had already premiered as a successful Broadway play earlier in 1939 and was in the process of being quickly transformed into a film when *Rules* had its limited original run.

[22] While one could take the framing of the question as sexist – and find many sexist moments in the films to support this thesis – I think in fact both films use the woman's trilemma (and, given the social conventions of the period, it really could only be the woman's) to ask what the cost to a human being would be of an imperfect union. In other words, it is the women who, for better or worse, run the risks and bear the burdens of the democratic citizen here and it is in their fates that the films locate whatever lessons for democracy they have. Certainly, the women in both films are not passive; although, as we shall see, in *The Rules of the Game* the heroine is reduced to passivity by the end, a conclusion clearly depicted as tragic.

truly important is this: *The Philadelphia Story* was a great commercial success that revived Katharine Hepburn's career and made a great deal of money for its producers, whereas *The Rules of the Game* was so hated by its original and intended audience that objects were thrown at the screen and it was quickly withdrawn from circulation and remained unseen for years. Intended, perhaps, to provoke its audience against a failed and phony nationalism, as we shall describe below, it only provoked its viewers against itself and its makers. If it is a famous film today, it is only because it has been championed by later generations of critics and other filmmakers; in its own time, it was not just a commercial flop, but a treasonous failure, just as *The Philadelphia Story* was a patriotic success.

* * *

Sir, my French is poor, but even I can see that Renoir's title – *La Règle du jeu* – is always mistranslated as *The Rules of the Game*, a common English idiom. "La règle" is singular. Renoir's title is "The *Rule* of the Game." *Règle*, like "rule," is a flexible word that can be used in a variety of contexts to mean a ruler (the instrument), a measure, a regularity, a pattern or a model – or so the dictionary tells me. But *règle* can mean "rule" in a more political sense (*la règle de Louis XIV* means "the rule of Louis XIV") and it is easy to understand why. To rule a game, or a people, can mean not just to measure or to bring order but to have the authority to do so. To ask what the rules of a game are is also to ask "what (or who) rules here?"

What is the game, then, and what is the rule? What *does* rule here? Certainly none of Renoir's characters are rulers of the game in which they are all enmeshed, though some are clearly more adept than others. Nor is it clear that they all understand themselves to be playing a game, or playing by the same rules. Certainly, they play many games, some more explicit than others: cards, hunting, table manners, adultery, marriage and propriety in general are just a few of these. But are these all part of one game, with one rule or ruler?

A game, we might say, is a series of moments held together by a set of rules, just as our narratives hold together the moments of our lives.

Such was, as you know better than anyone, Wittgenstein's insight into games and the reason for his obsession with them. The position of the pieces on a chessboard at any one time cannot be understood without also understanding their original positions, their permitted movements from that point, how games are won and lost, and so on. Even the most well-regulated games are capable of being disrupted from the inside, as it were, by moves that destroy the embedded narrative.[23] How much more delicate, then, is the balance between moments and narrative outside the context of a well-established game, where no rule book provides us with an agreed-upon framework within which to operate.

However, were such a rule book to exist (and a referee to enforce it), even then a final (or prior) mystery would present itself. The rule of all rules – *la règle* – cannot be given, it can only be experienced:

> I cannot describe how (in general) to employ rules, except by *teaching* you, *training* you to employ rules.[24]

In a political context we might say: a people have laws, rules which serve a publically enunciated end, and then they have a constitution which authorizes those laws. But what is the law that binds them to this ultimate law? Rules can be described, but *la règle* cannot be described, it can only be shown as it is shown to the characters in the film and as Renoir purports to show it to us. It turns out to be a harsh lesson. One may know many games without yet knowing what games one is involved in or what fidelity one will ultimately owe to *la règle*. For there is an authority involved, though not a political or theological one.

Moments may be related to narrative by many different rules, but the attempt to break this relation, to escape, provokes a harsh response, it would seem, from the rule itself. There is no person or clique who rules

[23] Wittgenstein: "I give the rules of a game. The other party makes a move, perfectly in accord with the rules, whose possibility I had not foreseen, and which spoils the game, that is, as I had wanted it to be. I now have to say: 'I gave bad rules; I must change or perhaps add to my rules' … So in this way have I a picture of the game in advance? In some sense: Yes." Ludwig Wittgenstein, *Zettel* (2nd edition, Oxford: Basil Blackwell, 1981), p. 53.

[24] Wittgenstein, *Zettel*, p. 58.

the game and yet, Renoir will say, we are not free to change the rules that govern it. If *The Philadelphia Story* suggested that the balance of moment and narrative might be accomplished simply through friendship and goodwill, *The Rules of the Game* shows us, if it shows anything, how an absence of malice on the part of everyone is utterly insufficient to regulate the pluralism of erotic attachment.

The "game" of erotic attachment might appear – to a teenager perhaps – to be one with a fixed end, but any mature reflection on the matter – and *The Rules of the Game* is nothing if not that – will tell us that desire is more complicated and multifaceted than the juvenile understands. Indeed, it is not a single game at all but a series of interactions governed by competing sets of rules. People who speak and act by different rules may understand each other, after a fashion, and may even interact as if they are playing together. However, they constantly run the risk, not surprisingly, of *misunderstanding* each other, because they speak the same language but do not play the same game.

An example of this situation, and of its implications, appears in the very first scenes of *The Rules of the Game.* André Jurieux, the aviator, has landed in Paris after flying solo across the Atlantic – a feat of skill and endurance for which he is instantly famous. But, he is disappointed because the woman he loves, Christine (who is married to the Marquis), has not come to meet him at the airfield. He voices his disappointment to a radio reporter and it is broadcast live. Christine, in Paris, hears the broadcast as she prepares to go out for the evening. Although André does not use her name, she knows it is she whom he accuses. She is perturbed, but not overly so, and engages her maid, Lisette, in a curious exchange.

Christine asks Lisette, who has recently married, about her lovers: how they behave, what they want and what they do together (it sounds like they flirt a lot and kiss, but not much more). Finally, Christine, now looking pained, asks whether these relationships have any friendship in them (*l'amitié*). Now Lisette looks shocked. "L'amitié avec un homme?" she says incredulously. Then she uses an expression which the subtitlists translate as "when pigs fly!" but which is actually more like "that's like talking about the moon in broad daylight" (*autant parler de la lune en plein midi*).

Although she is not sleeping with her lovers, Lisette does not pretend that these are friendships. There is no game of friendship with men for her, but she does not view this as a personal preference. The very concept makes no sense for her. The expression she uses indicates exactly that Christine has made some kind of *grammatical* mistake. André feels quite the same: he has spent many hours with Christine, talking intimately and perhaps embracing occasionally, but nothing more. It does not occur to André that Christine is anything but his lover and when his lover does not support his efforts, he accuses her of disloyalty.

However, Christine, as this scene and others demonstrate, is not (yet) playing this game. In speaking to André, she has been speaking of something else. She has embraced him, it is true, and held his hand. But, as she explains elsewhere, these are to her gestures of affection that she might bestow on anyone she considered a close friend. She does exactly the same with Octave, whom she has known in a familial way for many years. Since they grew up together, he understands the meaning of these gestures very well. But, he instructs her in a later scene, not everyone else will. Christine is from Austria and many characters point out that French is not her native language and Paris not her native milieu. Octave emphasizes that while he, from experience, will not be confused by her open Salzburg habits, others will:

OCTAVE: You throw yourselves around men's necks like you are twelve years old!

CHRISTINE: So in Paris, you cannot show a man affection without …?

OCTAVE: No. (He says all this with his arms around her.)

CHRISTINE: Ah, no. Then I'm to blame for everything?

It is one of the originating points of the tragedy in *The Rules of the Game* that Christine is not playing the same game as the others. She has not grasped the rules that govern social life in Paris. But because she *seems* to and speaks French well, she can make moves in the game that are meaningful to others in different ways from the ones she intends. Christine is not uneducated in the ways of eros; she has just been educated differently. She is deeply committed to her friendships and is upset that André has misunderstood her intentions, which were not at all frivolous, even if they were also not romantic.

As those educated in the ways of theater know, misunderstanding makes for a farce, but not (normally) for a tragedy. And, indeed, it takes some time before the tragic element in the film becomes visible. The drawing-room comedy in *The Philadelphia Story* is framed by a larger question of visibility. Here, too, a drawing-room comedy is framed, but then displaced, by a larger issue that Renoir displays in a way that Wittgenstein cannot: is it love at all – is it life at all – if it is governed by strict rules? Apart from the conflicts that the principals have with one another, is the conflict that they all have with *la règle*. Once again, the woman is the heroine of this battle and once again her transformation is the key development in the story. But instead of changing from a statue to a human being, she moves in the opposite direction. Starting the movie full of life, she ends it nearly lifeless, a ghost of her former self, defeated not by any other character but by a nemesis, a necessity of obedience, that she will never fully understand.

Removed from her native land, where all her customs felt natural, Christine lives in a place that seems to her filled with rules that appear arbitrary. However, she never expresses a desire to return home; instead, she longs for a life that does not feel rule-bound at all, where emotions can be expressed spontaneously. She is not a hedonist or even a sensualist, but she is, in this sense, a romantic and a partisan of the democracy of moments. Her idea of love is that it should be something that escapes rules entirely and is not governed by them. One by one the men in her life disappoint her when, though they love her intensely, they refuse to take this view and subordinate their passions to established norms. When she submits to her fate at the end of the film, the tragedy is not that she has lost her freedom to a man, but rather that she has lost it to *la règle*. Rules can rule with no less cruelty than a tyrant, and with even less feeling.

Let me briefly trace how this occurs: at the estate where most of the film takes place, Christine learns that her husband, whom she has always trusted, has been carrying on an affair for the entire period of their marriage. (In fact, he has just ended this affair, out of renewed devotion to Christine, but she never learns of this.) Dismayed, she attempts to accommodate herself to these Parisian rules by chatting about the affair in an open and blasé manner with her rival, but this proves too excruciating. She then turns to André and wants to take up his passionate offer to elope. What happens next is both painful and hilarious. In the most explicit discussions of rules in the film, André explains that he will be delighted to run away with Christine, just as soon as he and the Marquis can sit down and discuss it like gentlemen:

> ANDRÉ: I must tell La Chesnaye [the Marquis].
>
> CHRISTINE: Why?
>
> ANDRÉ: But Christine, because that is what is done (*parce que ça se fait*).
>
> . . .
>
> CHRISTINE: But since we're in love, what difference will it make?
>
> ANDRÉ: Christine, all the same, there are rules (*tout de même, il y a des règles*).

André's use of the objective tone of voice here indicates just how completely he (the supposed outsider) feels bound by these rules, even in the middle of an act which, on its face, would seem to violate the norms of propriety. But, Christine's love for André was predicated on the hope that he could liberate her from the demands of such rules, which, among other things, demand that she tolerate her husband's affair with good humor. She insists that they leave at once or not at all. What she wants is to inhabit the moment of their passion without regard for how it will fit, or not fit, within the larger social narrative. She is not so much angry with her husband's affair as she is dismayed by a society where such actions are normal and, indeed, regulated by a set of rules. Her desire for André is really over the instant he decides to delay their departure for the sake of such rules, the author of which he does not (cannot?) name and yet the authority of which he will not question.

André appears to be the rebel – he is young, impetuous and physically courageous – whereas Christine seems to be only a well-bred, slightly naive lady of society. Yet, in the end, it is André who is more deeply committed to the rules and integrity of the society of which he has only recently become a member, while Christine is more devoted to the erotic urge to break free from that society. Even the Marquis, once he gets over his initial anger at potentially losing his wife, expresses his gratitude to André for playing by the rules. If his wife is going to leave him, he says, he is glad it is with "one of our set" (*quelqu'un de notre milieu*). As he says this, to reinforce the point, he helps André back into his tuxedo.

True erotic conflict, the film seems to say, must be in conflict with a rule-bound society. André wants to make a radical move in a game of chess, but still a legal one. Christine, quite differently, wants to play another game, or no game at all. However passionate lovers may appear, when they submit to the rules, they sacrifice whatever spontaneity and individuality their love appears to possess. From Christine's perspective, the very phrase "love by the rules" can make no grammatical sense. Love, in one of its senses at least, indicates a relationship of such particularity that it cannot be duplicated. Rules, as Wittgenstein well describes, and as you yourself have elaborated, can only be said to apply to an activity that takes place repeatedly.[25] Just as there can be no private language, there can be no game that is played only once. The relations between rules and love would, then, appear to be two opposed logics of binding: one singular, intense and unrepeatable; the other repeatable, regular and orderly, or at least capable of being so.

Yet romantic love and bureaucratic routine are merely two ends of a spectrum. In-between them lie families and nations, familial love and patriotism. Can these two opposed logics be made to cohabit? Yes, *The*

[25] See James Conant, "Stanley Cavell's Wittgenstein," *The Harvard Review of Philosophy*, 13:1 (2005), pp. 51–65.

Rules of the Game seems to say to us: Yes, they can, at *enormous* expense to the former. At the end of the movie, the rules have been kept, passion destroyed and a man is dead. But the family which represents the erotically bound nation continues. The optimistic *Philadelphia Story* ends with a photographed kiss, but it is still a kiss (and a happy wedding) after all. *The Rules of the Game* ends with no kiss and no joy, but instead with a brief conversation between two minor characters, witnesses to what has just happened, about how, after being threatened, propriety has been well maintained. *La règle* has spoken and it has had the last word. How can remarriage be a comedy when it is so neatly scripted? How can it be a comedy when so much is sacrificed for the sake of a perpetual union? Remarriage, in both films, means the reassertion of the normal and necessary and the demise of the spontaneous and the momentary. Eros has not been destroyed, but it has been tamed. One film, sir, is honest about the cost of this process, though it is not the one you champion.

* * *

One of the curiosities of the *The Rules of the Game* is the Marquis's hobby: collecting and fixing mechanical musical objects. Wind-up figures – birds, men and machines – populate his home and are the object of his constant attention. He accumulates, repairs and displays them. In the climactic party scene, after various guests at his house have performed elaborate skits and songs, the Marquis makes his contribution: he unveils an enormous calliope that he has just purchased and restored. Renoir pans carefully across the machine so that we can slowly take in its many moving parts, which contribute various sounds to its overall tune. No one else in the film shares the Marquis's interest in these objects and, despite being featured prominently in several scenes, they play no obvious role in the story. If the Marquis had another hobby, or no hobby at all, nothing else of the plot would need to be altered.

What significance, then, do these many musical machines and toys have? One scene, I think, gives us a clue. About halfway through the film, Marceau, the poacher, has entered his short period of domestic service in the Marquis's household. He has begun flirting with Lisette, the gamekeeper's wife and Christine's maid. She happens upon him as he is shining some shoes. She is friendly but, when he tries to embrace her, she pushes him away. Puzzled, his eye alights upon one of the Marquis's mechanical dolls. He puts his hand behind a doll and winds it up, leaving his hand there afterwards so that he appears to be cradling it. The doll begins to move its head back and forth and plays a tune. The camera cuts from the doll's impassive, moving face to Lisette's. She is very prominently holding a bitten apple that she continues to chew. As the music plays she begins to smile (at Marceau). The camera then cuts back to Marceau and the doll, framed together. Marceau also begins to smile. As the music continues, he begins to move towards Lisette in a sort of mechanical dancing motion, as if he too were a wind-up toy. When the music ceases, he pounces. This time Lisette laughs and, although she tries halfheartedly to escape him, it is clear they are now playing the same game and they end up in an embrace that is only prevented from becoming more intense by the arrival of Lisette's husband.

My description is clumsy. All this takes place in a wordless pantomime and seems effortless to the viewer. But what have we witnessed here? A kind of erotic display certainly. But what kind? Does Lisette recognize herself in the musical doll and smile in recognition? Perhaps it is better to say, given the framing choices Renoir makes here, that the doll helps Lisette to recognize herself by recognizing Marceau. When she smiles, first, we are shown the two figures she is smiling back at: Marceau and the doll framed as a pair. By standing where he does with his arm around the doll, Marceau is saying who he is: a man no freer to control his actions than a mechanism. Put a beautiful woman in front of him and he will pursue her, whether or not it makes any sense or is safe to do so. And Lisette, smiling at this, is acknowledging that she is much the same: when an attractive man flirts with her, she will respond, married or not. It confirms, besides, her earlier stated view of the uniformity of male desire: *les hommes sont comme ça*, "men are like that." Men chase women; women tease men.

An early treatment for the film by Renoir bore the title *Les femmes sont comme ça.*[26] So, women are like that and men are like that. People are like that. So when the Marquis confronts his collected guests (collected, perhaps, like his hobby objects) with the massive calliope, he is confronting them, in effect, with an image of themselves as mechanically predictable erotic beings. They spend the party chasing after one another in just as inevitable a way as the calliope plays its music, making the same motions and striking the same notes over and over again. And, though the Marquis presides over this as a kind of master of ceremonies, owner of both the calliope and the house in which the music is made, he is no more immune to this than anyone else. All the humans here are dominated by their passions as by a mechanistic fate. It is this world of regulated eros that Christine finds unbearable and seeks to escape. But, within its limits, this system "works" very well: the music plays splendidly (for a time) and the guests play their erotic games in the prescribed manner. It is Christine's unregulated desire that disrupts the harmony.

Here Eros rules with the force of natural law, not as a force of spontaneity but subordinated to *la règle*. Eros rules because her unruliness has been tamed to the point where the energy she provides, like that of avarice, can be ordered and produces disciplined music, like the Mozart melody which opens the film and which Renoir described as one of his inspirations.[27] This is the pathetic Eros that Genevieve, the Marquis's lover, refers to when she invokes Chamfort early in the film: "Love, *in society* [my emphasis], is the exchange of two fantasies and the contact of two skins" (*l'amour, dans la société, c'est l'échange de deux fantasies, et le contact de deux epidermis*). Love outside of society conforms to no grammar and, to sophisticates, sounds like so much noise.

The Rules of the Game, like *The Philadelphia Story* then, contains an internal metaphor for film itself. The calliope is a reproduction of life

[26] Jean Renoir, *La Règle du jeu: Scénario original*, edited by Curchod et Faulkner (Paris: Édition Nathan, 1999), p. 8.

[27] German Dance No. 1 in D Major. See Jean Renoir, *My Life and My Films* (New York: Atheneum Press, 1974), p. 169.

like photography, and in this sense both are akin to film. But the calliope is a mechanical technology of life, and an even starker indictment of that technology than the use of photography in *The Philadelphia Story*, which is dark enough. It reduces life to mechanical movement, a narrative without any moments, as it were, whereas photography gives us a moment without a narrative. While the tendency of the latter toward pornography is regrettable, it is not as dangerous as the tendency of the mechanistic life toward violence and death.

If *The Philadelphia Story* questions itself as a piece of pornography, *Rules* questions itself as an exercise of political power, the power to force an outcome onto other humans at the potential cost of their lives. As the party progresses in the culminating scene, things get out of hand and the music becomes discordant. What seemed a polite game and dance becomes impolite when one of the characters (the gamekeeper) becomes so jealous that he introduces a gun, a real one, into the proceedings.[28] Some of the other guests imagine that it is all part of the show and carry on in a lighthearted fashion, while others realize that they are threatened with death and become terrified. Even the Marquis loses his cool and punches André. Renoir has famously said that he could not decide, as he made the film, whether it was a comedy or a tragedy. In the party scene, we see that the difference is really just a matter of degree. The free play of eros animates both, but in a comedy, this seeming disorder is happily managed by rules, while in a tragedy it is brutally policed by them.

In an early scenario, Renoir described his characters thus: "In this film, everyone is sincere. There are no villains." This sentiment is expressed by Octave's famous line of motivational equality: "Everyone has his reasons" (*tout le monde a ses raisons*). If there are no villains, then why does it all end so badly? The tragedy, in fact, is not caused by any subjective evil, but by the conflict between the democracy of

[28] Although I do not have space to discuss it here, the gamekeeper (Schumacher) is Christine's double in the servant group that mirrors the bourgeois. Like Christine, he is a foreigner of a kind with a German (Alsatian) name, whose desire for a relationship with his partner unbound by society's rules violently disrupts the regulated dance of eros to which the other characters are accustomed.

moments and the republic of laws. Who was it that said that the rule of law means the law of rules? Rules give meaning to our moments, but their existence also makes moments of true individual experience harder to come by. Violence here is not the result of any original viciousness on the part of the characters, but rather their recurrent dissatisfaction with the rule-bound life to which they are largely, but not entirely, accustomed. It is this conflict that sends them on their various paths that end in dissatisfaction, jealousy and, finally, death.

At times, various characters in the film speak wistfully and hopefully of friendship (*l'amitié*), as if it represented some alternative logic of human relation. Christine, as we have seen, speaks of her friendship with André. The Marquis, much later in the film, also speaks of his friendship with André – a friendship that he apparently hopes will survive an exchange of spouse! But none of the action of the film supports this possibility. Instead, Lisette's sense of *amitié* between the sexes as a preposterous, utopian dream is borne out. While there are friendships within each sex and between the classes, they are utterly inefficacious in preventing or containing the chaos produced by the erotic relations between the characters. Order, such as it is, is restored at the Marquis's chateau by rules and the violence that enforces them. If it is self-consciously a facade, it functions no less effectively for that. Friendship plays no part in it.

Wittgenstein returned habitually to the game of chess when he was attempting to explain rule-bound behavior. But no one plays chess here. They play cards, and they hunt. The hunt (*la chasse*) is regularly invoked, both by the characters and by the film itself, to explain the goings-on. Like a duel or a bullfight, a hunt is a highly ritualized (that is, rule-bound and time-ordered, pre-narrativized) activity with many symbolic elements, but also with a real death at its center.

The film depicts this violence with an almost documentary-style detachment. The hunt scene that appears at the center point of the action begins lightheartedly enough. All the guests at the mansion proceed happily to the hunting grounds. Some are more interested than others, but all participate without objection. At the signal, the servants begin to flush out the game and the aristocrats take aim. All that happens next is that animals (mostly pheasants and rabbits) are killed, on-screen, over and over. The actual shooting only takes about a minute but, to the viewer, it is a very long minute. We see a dozen or more animals killed before our eyes, some of which die less than instantly. By its own standards, the hunt is a success: there is much game and everyone has a trophy for his or her efforts. And yet, everyone's mood has become foul. Friends accuse one another of poaching. Lovers bicker. They have all become infected by the violence they have enacted. However ritualized, hunting is a brutal business and its brutality spills over into the society that makes sport of killing.

Every commentator has remarked on the brutality of the hunt scene, but in fact nearly every scene in the film is, in effect, a hunt scene. Every scene depicts a rule-bound ritual with a hovering danger and implicit violence. The hunt fails to satisfy, even when the game is plentiful, because hunting, as a sport, is not about the provision of food but about competitive killing in an endless cycle, a game that pauses but never concludes. To succeed in the hunt is not to be rewarded, but simply to have taken a temporary advantage in a sort of economy of violence that masquerades as a social order.

Is it an order that can command our loyalty? In *The Philadelphia Story*, order is restored in a form to which we can easily consent. Lovers are paired off with their appropriate mates and the only one painlessly sacrificed is the philistine. The practical and affective ties of the individuals overlap and reinforce one another, creating a community that is both stable and happy. But, no such happy ending or happy polity is available to us in *The Rules of the Game*. The fate of the animals in the hunt scene presages what will happen to the humans. After quickly tiring of André's rule-bound love, Christine just as quickly agrees to run away with Octave, whose love, he suddenly decides, is not so fraternal after all. But it is not to be. Through a series of misunderstandings and misidentifications, the artist (who is, after all, played by Renoir himself) is excluded and André is killed. He dies, we are told (though accidentally) just like an animal in *la chasse*.

Worst of all, perhaps, is the crushing *inclusion* of Christine that follows this death. Having attempted twice to run away with two different men, she is now symbolically re-incorporated into the family and nation of rules that she was attempting to flee. Nearly lifeless with grief, she is marched back into the house she was attempting to leave, welcomed warmly but quite formally by her husband (with a handshake, not a kiss), all the while with a look of absolute expressionless abjection on her face. Her spirit has fled and only her near lifeless body remains for membership in the polity.

In *The Philadelphia Story*, Tracy is not just the central character – the plot turns on the nature of her subjectivity. Will she be a "goddess"? Or a "first-class human being"? Christine faces a romantic trilemma equivalent to Tracy's and she is possessed of a strong passion and will as well. Yet her fate is the opposite: she ends the film less human than she began it, but neither is she a goddess. Christine's absence from the center of the film, where she should have a presence, strikes one more and more as the film goes on. Indeed, rather than growing through her adversity as Tracy does, Christine seems to shrink. In the opening scenes, she may be an outsider, but she is poised and confident. Throughout the film she becomes increasingly desperate until, at the end, she passes beyond desperation and appears numb to her fate. She ends, as do the hunted (and mechanical) animals, as a lifeless prize to be displayed in a rich household.

While she has returned to the family and, indeed, become more fully bound to it, the cost is that the essence of her personality – her strong will and desire to escape the rules – has been effaced and her relations of *amitié* (with André and Octave) have been destroyed. All she has left is her membership. And this is an indictment not so much of sexism or bourgeois manners but of political membership per se, democracy not excepted. If there were only the death of André and the exclusion of Octave, one might conclude that, although something had been sacrificed, something had also been gained if the love of Christine and Robert continued to animate their marriage. But the crushing of Christine indicates that the family is incompatible, not just with certain individuals or with a certain number of individuals, but with individuality itself. It is more brutal, in its way, than the death of André, which seems merciful by comparison.

Renoir's indictment of France is not merely an indictment of its bourgeoisie. It is not, at the end of the day, even merely an indictment of *France*. It is simply an expression of pain at the cost of association, of the self-constitution of a group of animal individuals as a society. We need eros to bind us together, but, in its undiluted form, the instability and intensity of eros is destructive to any household and any state. The lover must die so that the family and state may live. If the only cost of this exchange were the proliferation of pornography, as *The Philadelphia Story* implies, we might find the bargain an acceptable one. But Renoir filmed the actual death of animals, and killed off his most democratic character, to remind us that the cost is in fact much higher.

No doubt *The Rules of the Game* is a better, more honest teacher of social reality than *The Philadelphia Story*, but we cannot draw the conclusion, on this basis, of the instructive capacity of film. We should instead wonder why such a noble story was banned by both the last French government of the Third Republic as well as the Nazi regime that succeeded it, *and* shunned by the immediate audience of filmgoers whom it initially confronted. To be banned by the fascists is, of course, a great honor, but the democrats received it with no less discourtesy.[29] This latter hostility is often explained by the film's supposed assault on the French *haute bourgeoisie*. But, unlike some of Renoir's earlier works, *Rules* is not really about relations *between* classes at all. Rather, there are two social worlds in it, visible to one another and, indeed, reflective of one another. No character here is *defeated* in an attempt to cross class boundaries; no such attempts are made at all. While it is possible to view this as Renoir's indictment of the stratification of French society, I find this implausible. The fact that he goes out of his way to depict the two social sets as mirror images of one another points to the opposite, and darker, conclusion that nothing in particular would change were

[29] Renoir himself testified to this; see *My Life and My Films*, p. 169ff.

class boundaries to be dissolved. The two groups are already too much alike; bourgeois and servant already live by the same rules. *The Rules of the Game*, then, is not so much pessimistic about class relations as it is about *human* relations.

It is this pessimism that explains the universal hostility with which the film was greeted at its debut. If it became popular with critics after the war, it is only because the intervening catastrophe so distanced the events and context depicted from their later viewers that they came to be viewed across a comfortable temporal divide and were no longer experienced as a direct indictment of the audience. What better evidence could we have, then, of the commercial necessity of flattering the audience than the universal rejection of a work, however intelligent and moral, which fails to do so? An honest misanthrope cannot succeed in Hollywood, nor, it appears, in Paris. We see here the fundamental problem with the idea of film as an instructive democratic medium: when the lesson displeases the audience, they can shut their eyes against it, and they do. I see nothing in your presentation of the joys of remarriage comedy that could solve this problem or even address it.

* * *

The Rules of the Game was made as the happy family of European nations were about to plunge themselves into the most violent conflict imaginable. Everyone involved with the making of the film well knew that war was approaching. What good, one might ask, is the sacrifice of eros that binds us into nations if the nations themselves simply renew the disorder at a level well beyond the control of any person? Renoir could not have known, of course, about the extent of the violence in World War II, but he had lived through World War I, which had been more violent than any conflict known on Earth before. Perhaps there would be no families and no nations if eros were given free reign, but then perhaps there would be no Verduns and no Shoahs either. Surely a trade-off worth pondering.[30]

[30] See Jacqueline Stevens' *States Without Nations* (New York: Columbia University Press, 2009).

Critics routinely refer to the hunt scene as the central scene of the movie and many of Renoir's main themes are certainly found there in concentrated form. However, there is another scene that is, in essence, repeated several times, which perhaps gives another important perspective on these questions. It is also a favorite point of critics to note Renoir's use of deep focus in this film to show action simultaneously in the foreground and background. The hunt does not make particular use of this technique. However, at several points in the film, Renoir trains the camera down a long hallway off which the guest rooms of La Colinière are arranged. In various planes of action, the characters go back and forth between the rooms, sometimes chasing one another, sometimes making music, joking or flirting, sometimes interacting or changing directions, often moving at a very high velocity. It is a repeated scene as lighthearted and unrealistic (training a camera down an actual hallway would never result in such images) as the hunt scene, which directly follows one of these shots, is brutal and realistic (shooting rabbits really does look like that).

What is it that animates the characters as they bounce back and forth with great energy even as they are supposedly about to bed down for the night? The energy of eros, no doubt – the characters are animated, but not quite like billiard balls. They move at similar speeds, but not all in the same way. Why choose to depict eros in this way? The poet Anne Carson has written that we are wrong to think of eros as a dyadic relationship. Eros, she claims, is a "three-point circuit": the lover, the beloved, and that which separates them. When lover and beloved are finally united, erotic feeling is at an end; it exists only so long as they are kept apart (by a rival, happenstance, time or anything else).[31] Here the hallway is what separates the various characters in their rooms. They keep attempting to cross that space and make contact with someone else. Each one has his or her own particular beloved, but together the scene shot down the hallway makes a kind of music that is, I think, intended as a reminder of the possibility of an amiable erotic

31 Anne Carson, *Eros: The Bittersweet* (Princeton, NJ: Princeton University Press, 1986), p. 16.

community – before that community is torn apart by the hunt and the violent emotions which it harnesses and magnifies. Each person pursues his own erotic object (love, friendship, music, fun) and, if there are jealousies under the surface, everyone seems amused enough by the situation to keep it going.

What happens, by contrast, in the hunt scene, is that the space between the individuals, which fuels their erotic energy, is collapsed. Hunters take hold of their prey by killing it and, in so doing, they destroy the social fabric that sustains their relations. At the end of the hallway scene, nobody has what they want and everyone (more or less) is happy. At the end of the hunt scene, everyone has what (they thought) they wanted and they are all miserable. But, more importantly, their relationships have been put out of kilter and will not be put back into a kind of order until André is dead, Octave banished and Christine neutered.

Remarriage – the reaffirmation of the set of relations that are threatened with erotic disorder – is a tragedy here, not just because someone dies, but because eros is tamed to the point of suffocation. Tracy Lord was lucky, but families, and nations, are not built on luck but on bonds that the inconstancy of eros cannot bear. Christine by contrast is not extraordinarily unlucky. What happens to her is more like the ordinary passage from inconstant adolescence to an adult responsibility and a formalized place in a social structure. The price that she pays is one that we all share in as a cost of the social union; she merely pays in a more concentrated and vivid way.

The entire film is prefaced by a set of lines from *The Marriage of Figaro* (the play by Beaumarchais which became the basis for Mozart's opera):

> *Est-ce un crime de changer?*
> *Si l'Amour porte des ailes,*
> *N'est-ce pas pour voltiger?*
> *N'est-ce pas pour voltiger?*
> *N'est-ce pas pour voltiger?*

Is it a crime to change?
If Love has wings?
Isn't it to flitter?
Isn't it to flitter?
Isn't it to flitter?

Isn't eros naturally inconstant? Aren't our affections routinely in motion? Is it a crime to change? Not to Renoir, perhaps, but to the family and the state, yes. That is why *The Philadelphia Story* can only legitimate marriage with sleight of hand and blind luck, as if living by the rules were no more costly than miming one's way through a wedding ceremony. In *La Règle du jeu*, eros and union are locked in a perpetual struggle; anyone friendly to both can only view the situation with pity and pessimism.

III

We seem to be at a deadlock. Two views of remarriage, symbolic of democratic union, equal and opposed. In both, the variability of erotic life is in tension with the bonds of union. But in one, this tension is happily mediated by friendship and pretense, while in the other a balance is maintained only by violence and an ugly decorum. What instruction can we find in these antinomies? In viewing them, are we denizens of the grindhouse on our way to being better citizens? Where you find enlightenment, I find only a repulsive clarity.

Perhaps we must ask the question in another way. I hope I will not have to convince anyone that this disagreement goes far beyond the individual films in question and will not be resolved by some discovery about the particular intentions of their creators. Rather, our two opinions about which film is more exemplary of the relation of the medium to a living community derive from something more fundamental. "In a movie house," you have written, "the barrier to the stars is time."[32] But I do not

[32] Stanley Cavell, *The World Viewed: Reflections on the Ontology of Film* (Cambridge, MA: Harvard University Press, 1979) p. 155.

believe we have yet really settled on the time of film, if there is such a thing, and what kind of connection or barrier it creates with its audience. I believe that it is here that we will find the key to our difficulties.

Let us begin where the water is shallowest and one can pretend to swim while still standing on ground that is relatively firm. Since nearly the beginning of the era of film and of writing about it, it has been recognized that the distinctiveness of film has something to do with time. Film is a form of photography that captures or reproduces, as still photography does not, something more than a moment, some stretch of time. But film proceeds by means of photography, the rapid succession of still photographs which make visible a moving image. Beyond these elementary points, it is difficult to produce concurrence.

A long debate has taken place, which I do not pretend to recount, about the time of cinema to which we are both latecomers. Whether we should lay emphasis on the frozen photo frame on the filmstrip or on the perception of movement in the eye; whether film is more natural in displaying movement, or less natural in preserving it against a natural destruction; whether, in short, film in its essence is a medium that brings us closer to life or takes us further away from it constitutes a question that has been often asked and contrastingly answered.[33]

To solve these paradoxes is well beyond my ability, as others will not hesitate to point out. But to ask these questions in an absolute way is to make them all but unanswerable. Closer to life? What is *that*? Whose life and which moment of it? Who will name for us the universal generic qualities of life or experience to which we can compare the cinema? However, perhaps we can put these paradoxes to use in another fashion by asking a more particular question, one more relevant to our shared concerns with film's contribution (or lack thereof) to our freedom. We can ask whether and how popular or commercial film supports or impedes the democracy of moments and the republic of law. Is the experience of

[33] One would begin, perhaps with Henri Bergson and André Bazin and continue at least through Christian Metz, Siegfried Kracauer, Jean-Louis Baudry, Pier Paolo Pasolini, Laura Mulvey and Gilles Deleuze, to name just a small selection in a large debate, an excellent discussion of which is in Mary Ann Doane, *The Emergence of Cinematic Time* (Cambridge, MA: Harvard University Press, 2002).

film an active or a passive one? Ask, rather, whether it makes for active or passive citizens. Of course, particular films and directors will have their own perspectives, but here the question is whether they (we) are constrained by the medium and the audience in some direction. Godard (very fond of pronouncements), in a letter, called *The Rules of the Game* "the film of films," meaning perhaps that it was a movie that somehow exemplifies the quality of the medium. But in what way?

Perhaps, too, we can make some headway by contrasting cinema with television, which shares with film the quality of being a mechanical reproduction of images in time while remaining, at least so far, a distinct medium. Originally, of course, the technology of television did not allow for any kind of recording and broadcasts could not be repeated except by re-enactment. Television was live television or did not exist. Later, the development of kinescope and then videotape made possible the recording and replay of television programs. But "live television" is still a substantial subcategory of what we see on television, while "live cinema" cannot exist.

We can agree, I suppose, that there is some sort of difference between the time of film and television. You yourself have called attention to it, although not in a way that I can fully endorse.[34] Film always presents itself as a recording, that is, as a reproduction of something that exists in the past (even a future past, "A long time ago in a galaxy far, far away"). Film is always in the perfect tense, we might say, while television is far from perfect. So, although this limit is not an insurmountable one, each medium has a dominant tense, so to speak, built into its grammar.

The liveness of television is much more, however, than a residue of the history of its technology. For decades there has been nothing technologically necessary about the liveness of television and yet it persists. A great

[34] See Stanley Cavell, "The Fact of Television," in *Cavell on Film*, pp. 59–86. Some today, seeing technology erode the divide between film and television, have come to maintain that it was never that significant to begin with. I do not have the space here to directly rebut this plausible view, but my reasons for disagreeing should become clear in what follows. See Jacques Rancière, *The Future of the Image* (London: Verso, 2007), ch. 1.

deal of what we watch on television remains live[35] (news, sports, some comedy, chat and quiz shows, and talent shows including, of course, the most popular kinds like "American Idol"), despite the fact that there might be some considerable advantages to having the opportunity to edit or shape what is broadcast. More significantly perhaps – or what shows the significance of it – much of what is not live on television goes to great lengths to present the *illusion of liveness*. Shows that are taped (I will not say filmed) are taped in front of audiences or have audience-reaction tracks added to their audio so that they have the feel of a live transmission. Others are filmed in a pseudo-documentary style that, although edited, strives to appear unedited. Yet no one, so far as I know, has ever added a laugh track to a film or proposed filming in front of an audience, although, again, the technology obviously exists to do so.

Although we think of television as the venue of constant repetition, this is something of a mistake. Only certain television programs – generally the filmed ones – bear repeating and their capacity to be repeated bears an inverse relation to their liveness. News and sports cannot be repeated at all – no one wants to hear yesterday's news today and no one wants to watch sporting events the results of which are already known.[36] The same holds, to a lesser degree, for chat shows as well as other shows that hold a contest or a secret. When the result is known, the precedent events become inherently boring. A talk show may be shown a second time for those who missed the first broadcast, but it is not repeated a month or a year later. Television seems so repetitive because very little of what is broadcast actually bears repeating at all, and what remains is therefore pressed into double and triple duty while the networks display

[35] Or nearly live. I leave aside here such deviations from liveness as the seven-second delay that networks use to purge words they deem unspeakable, the later rebroadcast of live television in other time zones, etc. Since this involves no editing or shaping of the material involved, I treat it, perhaps contestably, as "live."

[36] I realize that in recent years some channels have tried to defy this law by rebroadcasting "classic" sporting events, but I have never met a human being who has actually watched such a rebroadcast and their scheduling late at night and early in the morning only reflects the network's desperation to have something on the air at an hour when no sporting events are actually taking place. This is the case of the exception proving the rule.

a voracious appetite for new material of any kind to fill up the hours which they feel obliged to broadcast. The present tense of television means that as soon as the events depicted retreat into the past, their transmission is pointless.

With film, by contrast, it is all different and nothing is in the present tense. From the beginning, film was a medium of repetition and not only because a film that is worth watching once is generally worth watching again (and only a small number are really "spoiled" by knowing the ending). While it is certainly true of any narrative that knowing how it will end changes one's perspective on the whole, good films are like good novels (which is not to say films are like novels) in being endlessly repeatable to those who love them. Even when films affect an aspect of "liveness" (as in cinema verité), they do not escape from this, nor do they really pretend to be live in the way that television sitcoms, for example, pretend to be live. While it used to be that most people would only view a film once, that is no longer true and everyone can (and does) see their favorite films over and over.

Films have this capacity for repetition precisely because they are never present in the first place. They are always preterit, have already gone by. They endure because they were never subjected to the flux of living temporality with its routine passage from possibility to oblivion. It is only the mildest symptom of this difference of tense that historical films are far more common than historical television shows. These categories are far from absolute, of course. One can always speak in a language the grammar of which is unfamiliar; one merely speaks awkwardly. Historical television has surely been made. Equally, one can easily show a film on television and television shows (but usually the more "filmlike" ones) are available for purchase and repeated viewing. But, surely, the distinction I have made tells us something about the nature of film and indicates to us that film is distinguished from television either by lacking the quality of liveness that the latter possesses or by possessing some other quality that overshadows the liveness. This, I think, rather than the mechanical quality of photographic reproduction is what is important here.[37] Photographs, television and film all share this latter quality, so it cannot explain the differences between them.

I have avoided calling the liveness of television "presentness" because I think it is the nature of presentness that is precisely at issue in this distinction. Certainly, it should not be denied that television's liveness has a certain power. When I viewed the first moon landing, for example, or the destruction of the Berlin Wall, or the collapse of the World Trade Center towers, as each of them happened I had an experience that cannot be resurrected either by viewing those events on videotape or in any kind of dramatic recreation. But events like these are exceptional and certainly do not give us an understanding of what goes on in the *five hours every day* that the average American still views television.[38] If the unrepeatable moment seems essential to my citizenship, is the other its complement or its opposite?

Films, on the other hand, never have the quality of liveness. We never suppose that what we see is taking place simultaneously, as we can do with television. As a result of this, we might say, whatever claim to veracity that film might have, it is of a different order from that of television. A temporal distance is always open between a film and its audience, just as you say. But what sort? What is the reason, for example, that the dominant commercial mode of film is fiction, while television is dominated by so-called "reality" shows which at least pretend to documentary status? Documentary film exists, of course, but is only rarely popular. Is documentary perhaps more naturally at home on television, where it sits with its cousins news, sports and chat? We often say that a film "loses something" when seen on television rather than at a theater.

[37] That "mechanical" quality is, in any case, breaking down as the technology of digital editing and animation increases in its ability to alter, extend and manipulate what is "photographed" in the traditional sense. We may rapidly be reaching the point where it is considered normal for every frame of film to be something other than a photograph in the traditional sense.

[38] Nielsen Company, "Comparable Metrics," Q4 2015, pp. 6–9.

Does anyone say this of documentary film? Surely this cannot be simply a matter of the size of the screen or the beauty of the images; there are all kinds of documentaries. Perhaps it is rather the case that television has a generic documentary quality, its liveness, that makes that category of films that we call "documentaries" seem more at home there.

When a certain type of critic bemoans the fact that modern humans watch so many hundreds of hours of television in a month, a certain type of reply is often made that we are not really watching at all. The television may be on, but that does not mean we are paying heed to it; we may get up and do something else for a while, our attention may wander, the television may be background noise as we prepare food or converse or otherwise go about our business. But no one would claim that we routinely watch films this way. People do not get up and wander around a theater; while the film is running, people generally attend to it. Sometimes people talk in theaters, sometimes not, but if one can really draw oneself away from a film long enough to turn around in a theater (and what does it say if you have never done this before and if it feels unnatural to do so?) you will see, I wager, well over 95 percent of the eyes firmly fixed on the screen. We go with others, but we hardly see one another when we are there.

Rather than look for a magical quality that film has that causes us to pay attention to it, I think it makes more sense to seek the quality in television that allows us *not* to pay attention to it, and I would nominate for this the very quality of liveness that I have been discussing. It is frequently said that people turn the TV on (as they do with radio) for its quality of "keeping company" rather than for its specific content; but nobody goes to the movies for the company. Or, rather, it is uncomfortable to go to the movies *without* company – that is, without other people in a group – because the film itself provides no company. Only someone as depraved as a critic goes to see films alone. Yet a modern citizen may spend many hours alone with his or her television and not think this incident worthy of explanation. Seeing someone alone at the movies is like seeing someone alone in a restaurant: one can feel simultaneously embarrassed for them and ashamed for the reaction.

Television functions as a kind of substitute for our attention, a substitute for our minute-to-minute consciousness in a way that is different from film. The evidence? That we can pass into and out of attention with television in a way we generally do not with film. We find television and waking life to be easily interchangeable. With film, by contrast, we isolate ourselves in a theater to give it our full attention and, when we do so, we generally do not intend for our mind to wander.[39] If it does, we blame the film for being boring or ourselves for lacking focus, but whoever sought to allocate blame for not paying attention to television?

It is a mistake, then, to exaggerate the realism of film; it is certainly less present to us than television. What explains its immersive qualities? The photography of film is no doubt impressive, but one day it will surely be exceeded, for example by virtual reality.[40] What, then, is film if not a substitute for our waking consciousness? The question of course contains its own potential answer, one that has been offered many times: a substitute for our non-waking consciousness, that is, for our dreams. Only in dreams are we enveloped in an unreal experience the way we are in cinema. Only in dreams do we devote our full attention to a spectacle without prospect of diversion. And only dreams repeat without the repetition feeling unnatural. When dreams repeat, we do not call it, as we might, déjà vu.

What effect does this have? I think there is no fact more important in understanding cinema than that it is an experience that produces emotions that exceed or extend (rather than mimic) those of ordinary daily life. There is an entire population that cries only at the cinema and rarely or never outside. Even for those not in this category, surely all but the most hard-hearted have had the experience of being swept away by an emotion at the movies while knowing full well, upon reflection, that a similar experience outside the movie house would produce nothing like it. How many have come home from a good cry over a

[39] Perhaps this distinction explains why there is a large population that never goes to the movies at all, but only a tiny one that never watches television.

[40] There is even an interesting film about this prospect: *Strange Days* (1995), directed by Kathryn Bigelow.

sentimental film to watch the evening news, which is full of real death, disease and suffering and yet produces no similar response? Where else is it in our lives that we experience emotions in excess of our regular ones on the basis of illusory stimuli?[41] The answer can only be in our dreams: arousal, fear, sadness, anger, embarrassment – we experience all of these in a way that is often more intense than when conscious. The most direct example is also the most irrefutable: one can have an orgasm in one's sleep, but I defy anyone to reproduce the result through pure conscious imagination.

I do not claim originality for this thought. It is a commonplace of course that the best film experiences are "like a dream" and many more serious reflections than that have been made on the likeness of films and dreams. But so many of the latter have been made within a Freudian framework, where the unconscious "knows no time," that they have had to settle for an account of film that finally ends up merely repeating and relying on a vocabulary that, in the end, settles nothing.

What *are* dreams, after all, that the likening of films to them may produce some insight? When Baudry spoke of the cinematic apparatus as producing a dreamlike effect, it is not clear that he had any time in mind at all but rather the undivided space of the infantile imagination that experiences all of the world as part of itself.[42] Surely, there is an important point here, but we cannot really understand the cinema merely by referring it to a category of experiences that we label as primitive narcissism. What does this really mean in any case? Again, how much will this entail insisting on the necessity of a large screen and a darkened room?

It makes no sense, I think, to ask whether the supplementary emotions of the cinema are true or not true, any more than those of dreams. I do not

[41] There is, I admit, a population that can also be moved to tears by novels and poetry. But these exquisitely sensitive souls, though precious, are so few that we can safely leave them aside here. Do I need to add that no one has ever cried over a book of philosophy (though many have wished to and even pretended to)?

[42] See Jean-Louis Baudry, "The Apparatus: Metapsychological Approaches to the Impression of Reality in Cinema," in Leo Braudy and Marshall Cohen, eds., *Film Theory and Criticism* (6th edition, Oxford: Oxford University Press, 2004), pp. 206–23.

know any grounds on which one could distinguish here between reality and simulation. Certainly, it is possible to imagine a world without cinema and without these emotions, but that hardly proves anything. It is also possible to imagine a world without dreams but, however appealing such a world might be to our rationalist friends, it is not one we are ever likely to inhabit nor, for that matter, would there be anything more real about it. Indeed, it would be profoundly unnatural, if anything is.

Some filmmakers, of course, have attempted to reproduce the experience of dreams (Wim Wenders' *Until the End of the World* (1991) is an important example that demonstrates the contradictions involved). But this too does not really speak to the issue at hand. When people talk of the "non-linear" time of dreams, they are apt not to indicate a true alternative time, but just a random passage from moment to moment with no logical connection between them. What, after all, could be farther from that than the "ordinary" linear storylines of movies like *The Philadelphia Story*? But dreams are not really non-linear, at least in the sense usually meant. Freud was right about that much: dreams generally make sense, even if we do not always perceive the sense. Nor are their moments randomly connected.

Freud, in any case, was only following Nietzsche in arguing that the experience of the dream was entirely the creation of the dreamer, or perhaps a vast phantasm of commentary on the extremely minimal text of the bodily impressions we receive when asleep: the cool breeze from the window blown up to a narrative about a ship sailing through arctic waters.[43] How can we square this with an experience of cinema where we know, before anything else, that something we have not conjured

[43] Friedrich Nietzsche: "*Dream and Responsibility*: – You are willing to assume responsibility for everything! Except, that is, for your dreams! What miserable weakness, what lack of consistent courage! Nothing is *more* your own than your dreams! Nothing *more* your own work! Content, form, duration, performer, spectator – in these comedies you are all of this yourself" (*Daybreak* (Cambridge: Cambridge University Press, 1982), p. 78). C.f. Sigmund Freud, *The Interpretation of Dreams* (New York: Avon Books, 1965), chapter 3, "A Dream is the Fulfillment of a Wish," *passim*; and "Some Additional Notes on Dream Interpretation as Whole," in *Complete Works*, vol. 19 (London: Hogarth Press, 1966–73), pp. 123–8: "Obviously one must hold oneself responsible for the evil impulses of one's dreams. What else is one to do with them? Unless the content of the dream … is inspired by alien spirits, it is a part of my own being."

is put before our eyes? Do we really want to say that this is a fact we perpetually forget? The pleasure of the cinema must surely include the pleasure of the unexpected and, again, Freud is right to say that, at some level, nothing unexpected can occur in a dream, since it is all our own work. What can the two phenomena really share?

We do not yet have an adequate set of names for the variety of temporal experiences, which is to say that we have only begun to map the terrain in this area. Film has a presence that is not liveness; at least, it does not threaten to substitute for our ordinary consciousness and we do not usually mistake it for that (as we do mistake television when we allow it to occupy our consciousness, for hours on end, without making the slightest impression). Most of our daily thoughts are transient and forgettable, like television.

Rather than mistaking film for an element of our own consciousness, I think it is crucial that we know that it is not. If anything, we make the opposite mistake: part of the power of film's presence lies in our mistaking it for something that is eternal. Film's presence is not fleeting but lasting, but how and why? What is it that film shares with dreams if not the egoism?

Perhaps they share the sense of being a revelation that is, at the same time, a recovery. When dreams are powerful, it is because they are both strange and familiar. Strange in the sense that they reveal to us something we did not know, but familiar in the sense that, in fact, this something is something we knew all along. In the Freudian view (and I think, in this matter, the Lacanian view also), this must always be something about the self, that is, something that is rooted in the individual ego. That is why so much film interpretation in the psychoanalytic tradition always turns films into events of self-revelation (or, alternatively, of revelation about the *auteur*). But, if we relax the rigid bounds of Freudian egoism, we can learn to view the familiarity of film in a different way, one that does not pretend that viewers forget that films come to them from the outside.

In the Nietzschean view of dreams, they were the creative act par excellence. But when Nietzsche referred to Homer as "the dreaming Greek," he meant this to go hand-in-hand with his statement that "three-quarters of Homer is unoriginal."[44] Why unoriginal? Because, in Nietzsche's view, Homer's creativity lay in synthesizing existing myths, stories, songs and legends into a whole that was greater than any of these. The Greek world, then, recognized itself in Homer not only, or not merely, on account of his virtuoso originality, but because they themselves had already lived the experiences (heard the myths, sung the songs, etc.) that became part of this greater whole. When we recognize ourselves in a story, this does not have to mean that we suddenly have access to some isolated nugget of our individual unconscious that no one has ever seen. It can also mean that we see the identity between ourselves and elements of the world that are in some sense exterior to us.

What Homer actually accomplished to make this possible was to put these elements into a narrative. That is the "Apollonian" talent that Nietzsche celebrates in the first half of *The Birth of Tragedy*. It is the creation of a time scheme out of the timeless primordial Dionysian chaos that he describes as the core of human imagination.

Putting these points together, we might say that the power of filmic presence derives from its revelation of hidden or lost time, rather than from any particular temporal scheme or structure. Films, after all, have many time schemes. Most follow everyday linear time, sometimes adding flashback or, less commonly, flashforward. Some scramble time or show things out of sequence – *Pulp Fiction* (1994), *Amores Perros* (2000) – and a few attempt to work backwards – *Memento* (2000), *Betrayal* (1983) – though in practice this amounts to merely reversing the order of scenes which are themselves shot conventionally. But, whatever it is we want to say about the power of film and time, it needs to apply to all of these and not only to those that get a narrative jolt by disrupting our expectations about linear time.[45]

[44] Friedrich Nietzsche, *Human, All-too-Human* (Cambridge: Cambridge University Press, 1986), p. 339.

[45] Not forgetting, of course, that great monument of comic Nietzscheanism, *Groundhog Day* (1993). I do not know whether it is right to say that any films at all are "about" time, but I would nominate *Citizen Kane* (1941), *Unforgiven* (1992), *Voyager* (1991) and *The Dreamers* (2003) as films which have something important to say about time, but which follow a perfectly ordinary linear sequence.

To say that film shows us a hidden or lost time, then, is not to say that a particular film shows us a particular temporal structure. It is to say, instead, that a film holds our attention by showing us something about ourselves that brings together novelty and memory in a temporal-visual matrix. It is this matrix that puts the film in the presence of our minds, from which point we can accept or reject it (I do not mean that this is a voluntary choice, but simply that not all films that reach us actually remain with us). This is not a matter of recovering experiences we have had and suppressed (*Spellbound*, I think, is a rather dull Freudian exercise). Rather, it is a matter of taking some or several elements of our unprocessed past and placing them in a context which gives them a new meaning, a meaning which nonetheless draws some of its force from the way in which it evokes an element of our own identity. So it ought to be no surprise when televised news of actual tragedy leaves us dry-eyed while filmed melodrama executed with a modicum of skill makes a puddle, for the latter can mimic the qualities of being that daylight renders invisible.

This process need not, in a general way, be exclusive to cinema. My language here is meant to point to our countryman Proust. What, after all, was his famous book intended to accomplish? In recovering lost time, he obviously did not mean that he could have experiences for the second time *as if* they were the first time. The person who dunks his cookie in tea is a middle-aged man remembering his past. Nonetheless, the emotion that is generated by this recollection is *more* intense than the original experience, even though the second experience is the "passive" one of recollection. The recollection, then, can be more intense the original. Is it always so? Certainly not, but, he hopes, the experience he had spontaneously with the madeleine is one that he can reproduce in his novelistic reproduction of the past. But he did not write the novel so that *he* could have this intense experience of recollection. He wrote it so that *we*, who had not experienced any part of his life, could now experience it as he did, *as a narrative recollection*, with all the accumulated intensity and meaning that it lacked as an original experience. We are, so to speak, the subject and object of an event of witnessing (a word which brings together the acts of seeing and knowing).

Just as we, who have not had Proust's life, can nonetheless experience his memory in a fictional recreation of it, and thereby have a more intense emotion, so can a film produce for us a revelation which we may experience in part as a memory even if it is not our own. (Is this not the power of *Citizen Kane*'s "Rosebud"? Is this not why so many consider this film as some kind of ur-phenomenon?) Indeed, film may have more tools at its disposal for achieving this aim than Proust had at his, even including the darkened room and the large projection screen. Yet, the grounds on which we distinguish an artform as a genre do not require that its aim be utterly counterdistinguished from that of all other art objects (and not all novels, after all, are Proustian).

Saying, then, that the time of cinema is a dreamtime is not an attempt to ascribe to the cinema mystical powers, nor is it to give sway to the authority of Freudian categories (the two most common mistakes, I think). It is rather an attempt to account for the strength of film's presence in such a way that makes sense of what we know about the phenomenological aspects of the film experience and to relate those to the closest analog possible in an ordinary human life. Dreamtime, in my Nietzschean account, is not a specific temporal structure. Rather, dreamtime is the narrativization of the past in a way that endows it with a novel meaning without destroying the trace of the original experience. Furthermore, we should not say that dreams do this "internally" or "intrapersonally" while films do this "externally" or "interpersonally" – that already puts a certain kind of egoistic characterization on what a dream experience actually is, that is, a distortion. Another person cannot experience my dreams, it is true (but, again, see Wim Wenders' *Until the End of the World* for an imagination of the reverse); but dreams are from the start not a "merely" personal experience but a reinterpretation, not of my inner life, but of my whole life, a life that I share with other people. We should not believe people who say they have identical dreams, of course, but we should not dismiss people who report similar dreams, since it is not surprising that people who share a world, experiences and emotions should similarly reconfigure these in nighttime interpretations.

Time, therefore, *is not the barrier – as you say – but rather the medium by which we receive the force of the filmic experience*, which is to say, the force of the film as opposed to the photography. It is the transmissible template by which representations of being can pass from mind to object and back again. It is, therefore, also the point of ontological contact between the film object that is available to us and the human subject that constitutes that availability. It is, of course, true that the movement in time of a film is an optical effect (let us not say "illusion") created in the eye or the brain from a series of still images. Since neuroscience seems increasingly set to tell us that ordinary seeing consists of this same effect, there is no cause to indict film (on this point, at least) as being any more deceptive than the world it views. We might do better to say that film as a medium emphasizes the burdens of temporality that it shares with ordinary life, the burdens of impermanence, contingency and chaos forcibly subordinated to an ordered narrative.

How does it do this? Not as a human would. Film is not a mind but a technology and we must take a moment here to appreciate this element of its nature and add it to the picture we have been building. I do not say it is a technology in order to dispute its status as an art. Film is undoubtedly an art, the dominant art of our times, but we cannot understand its qualities and political effect simply through aesthetic categories. Of course, there is a component of technique in the painting of pictures and the printing of books, but books and painting existed in other forms before their modern technological incarnations. Film did not. Film is a spectacle but plays are not pre-cinematic films in the way that cave drawings are pre-modern paintings. It took so long for film to be recognized as art, in part, because it was the first new art form in generations, but also because it was obviously a technological innovation with little connection to previous aesthetic media (photography, at that time, was hardly recognized as an art either). When the first cinema opened, it was a modern marvel, not the rebirth of some ancient art. Film theorists, having struggled for so long to establish the aesthetic seriousness of their subject, are now in danger of forgetting its technical character.

Film is an art that required, from the start, and as with no other, complicated machines, not only for filming but for editing (and then for adding sound), and for reproduction and display. What does this mean? First of all, that we must treat film, not only in relation to other art forms but also in relation to other technologies like television, computers and telephones. All of the political innovations of the twentieth century (fascism, communism) have disappeared as quickly as they have emerged, while the technics of that period structure almost every moment of our daily life. It is surely the technology of the twentieth century rather than its art or politics that will be remembered in a thousand years.

It has been argued that all technology betrays an origin in a certain picture of the world;[46] and to the extent this is true, there must be a special account of the technology that ends up producing its own pictures. But this need not mean, as Baudry maintained, that the cinema is primarily a certain kind of apparatus. What matters is that technics like film, as we were saying above, can only emerge on the basis of a certain relationship between humans, nature and time, a relationship that precedes any kind of apparatus. We may be born *to* a mediated relation with nature, but we are not born *in* one, so the manner in which we enter this relation makes all the difference.

In this view, we must not think about the technology of film simply as this or that machine, but as something that mediates our relation to the world in a way that is unavailable to the animals. What separates us from the animals is not our intelligence or our sympathies (animals have some quantity of both, it would seem), but simply our availability for this kind of temporal mediation. In order to see a picture, that is, one must first have the ability to see it *as* a picture and not simply as another piece of the world. The apparatus of cinema has changed and

[46] Martin Heidegger, "The Age of the World Picture," in *The Question Concerning Technology* (New York: Harper & Row, 1977), pp. 115–54.

will continue to change (soon there will be no film or tape at all), but the picture-sight that gives the apparatus its function is not subject to that kind of technical evolution.

The animal does not lack for intelligence, or not only. It lacks, as I have claimed elsewhere, the human experience of time. What does this mean? We might just as easily say that it is humans who lack something here; they lack a connection to the world that captivates them such that time stands still for them. The animal is not a machine – not in the least – but it interacts with the world according to patterns that do not change from day to day or year to year, or, for many species, from generation to generation. It sees the world in a way that does not change and it cannot be brought to see the world in a different way. It cannot have one picture of the world because it cannot have two pictures of the world; it simply has the world, picturelessly. If it is true that technology has a picture of the world or produces one, that is only possible as a result of its human origin and does not subsist in the physical properties of the machine.

A human sees the world, but also sees others seeing it and thus begins to admit to the possibility of seeing the world differently. It is not as if time invades the human mind and takes root there as an alien force. Time has no force and cannot force anything to happen. It is better to say that the ontological barrier between the animals and time is dismantled or collapses by the same process that makes us visible to one another as humans, that is, as individuals who share a collective identity as humans. That Aristotle, Linnaeus and others later projected the concept of species back onto the world of differentiated animals means only that we see them through the lens that we use to see ourselves. A mediated relation to time and nature becomes possible when the space between individuals acquires an erotic significance as a space that could be closed, that is, as a space whose closure would be meaningful. Animals have eyes as we do; their sight lacks nothing physical (indeed, it often exceeds ours) but only the longing to see the world as others do, to share a vision. That is, they lack the erotic distance that is the basis both for disruptive politics and for a genuine pluralism of perspectives and minds.

The signal difference between dreams and waking life is not in what or how we see – that is, there is *no specific difference of content* between them – but rather in the fact that in dreams, as in cinema, we see *without being seen in return*. Normally, to see something that appears, one must also stand in some place in the world and appear oneself at the same time that one sees others. Consciousness is something we must share with others. In conscious perception, seeing and being seen go together. Alone on an island, we would never know whether we were asleep or awake. But, in dreams, as in cinema, we are the seers that do not reveal ourselves to anyone in seeing. In exchanging social appearances for filmed pictures, we trade a kind of seeing that requires that we participate with others in a moment of exchange of visibility for a viewing that isolates us from others and gives our seeing a sense of false control. In so doing, we return, in a sense, to the captivation of the animal in a world without sociality.

We imagine that cinema extends our vision. Does it not let us see things that are far away? In the sky? Under water? In fact, it restricts our vision, not as to what is in the field of view itself, but in the sense that we see as if absent from the public moment of seeing. Our vision is restricted not in terms of space and time but reciprocity. We have the vision of the animal, which sees everything except another perspective.

We believe ourselves in control of our experiences at the movies. Have we not paid to see the film and chosen it? But, just as in our dreams, the opposite is the case: we are captivated by these images we do not control. Just as in sleep, we generally cannot choose to wake up from a dream that displeases us, so in a film we are locked in to an experience which we only judge, if we judge it at all, when it is over. Can we not walk out of a film that displeases us? In principle, yes. Yet how many times have you done it? How many times, instead, have you endured a film that you knew to be pointless or even degrading and satisfied yourself with a negative judgment as you left the cinema. As if that weak reply made you the master of the experience! I have woken myself out of an unpleasant dream at least as often, perhaps more often, than I have taken myself out of an unpleasant film. And yet, in only one of these situations am I supposed to be unconscious! Why do we not demand a fast-forward control in a cinema, like the one that we use at home with the television? Foolish media executives who think that consumers want control of their media! Control of their money, yes! Of their films? You have missed the point of the cinematic pleasures of captivation.

By contrast, in the waking world, the democracy of moments is something that can at least be experienced. You can and do experience each moment separately, let it find its purchase in a variety of narrative possibilities rather than being yoked to a story given in advance that you passively accept. This is not to say anymore that you are a master of your own experience. Let us thank the heavens that we are not! To be a master of your experience would mean that you were limited to your own imagination, the pitiful singular imagination of a single human. Instead, we routinely have blessed moments that transcend our imagination not because they are visibly (or visually) spectacular, but because they exceed our available interpretations (and thus simultaneously rely on them). An animal is subjected to no political power and yet this democracy of moments is not available to it because the sociality of consciousness is not available to it either. The animal can never exceed its own imagination. In compensation, you could say, the animal will also never experience all the deprivations of consciousness and eros that humans are subjected to.

The artful technology of cinema is not generically pleasing because it provides us with something new or some narcotic, but rather because it subtracts from our experience, however temporarily, a source of our suffering, our decaptivation. That is why one can enjoy the basic experience of movie going, even when the film itself is awful. We relax into the comfort of a prehuman isolation only to enjoy the spectacle of human travails. We enjoy, that is, a deprivation of community and citizenship that we would protest loudly if it were forced upon us by some political power.

Why is the language of friendship unavailing in *The Rules of the Game*? In place of this question, ask instead whether you have ever made a friend in a movie house. I wager, and this is my last wager on your experience, that you have not. Before a film? Yes. After a film, talking about it? Yes. Waiting on line or in the restroom? Why not? But *during* a film? Never. We go to films with preexisting friends precisely to compensate for enduring the loneliness of the experience. For, however marvelous an experience, it is a lonely one, not one that can be truly shared. Are we not afraid to go to sleep precisely because we cannot bring others along with us to share our dreams and nightmares? Do you fear the content of your nightmares or the fact that you must endure them alone?

Friendship arises from shared activity: walking, talking, building, destroying, learning, parenting, eating, drinking, fighting, hiding, even philosophizing – there are endless examples – but what does it say that film-going is not one of them? It does not impede friendship certainly and so may be an inert part of an ongoing relationship, but if all you can do with another person is see movies together, you must know that the relationship is at an end, or never began. To share someone's perspective, you must first acknowledge its difference from your own; cinema affords no space for this experience.

An experience of citizenship is surely one that can be shared, that indeed must be shared, and which therefore makes a friendship (and an enmity) possible, though certainly not necessary. Citizenship, like consciousness, is a social activity. However much I have learned about friendship from film, however many friends I have made through and around film, I have never yet made a friend *in* a film, and I expect I never will. Friendship does not avail in *The Rules of the Game*, "the film of films," because it cannot really exist in that world any more than love, citizenship or any other joint experience. You might as well expect to make friends in your sleep.

The experience of film, taken in through the medium of narrative, does not put us in the presence of another mind, but, because it *seems* to, we are apt to let it take the place of those more truly democratic experiences, until the day arrives when we have lost our ability to tell the difference or, worse, when we prefer the dream, which we think we control, to the waking life, which we know we do not. The reciprocity between individuals, like the oscillation between moment and narrative or public and not-public, must be free and uncontrolled if it is to serve its purpose of creating and sustaining a union of democratic experience. This experience may be terrifying, and it is understandable that we would shrink from it and seek alternatives, but it is also ultimately sustaining and conjoining – the alternatives are isolating and deadening.

In film, we always see the democracy of moments subordinated to the republic of laws. It can either pretend that this subordination is free and costless, as in *The Philadelphia Story*, or it can display the costs vividly, as in *The Rules of the Game*. But which of these films was met with an adoring audience? And which nearly instigated an armed revolt? Film succeeds commercially when it disguises the subordination that it embodies, and, when it reveals it, it fails. So, if *The Philadelphia Story* instructs us to be happy and claims this as a democratic emotion, it is an instruction as profoundly false as the phony wedding which Tracy and Dexter stage for the guests. It is a myth of optimism that happiness and freedom walk hand in hand. No, freedom is not a guaranteed tragedy, but it always risks one, and an honest account or remarriage will have to risk it too.

IV

Let us waken, then, from this reverie and return to Philadelphia. It will be asked how a man who so loves the cinema can stage a criticism of it. I ask in return whether any of us really has his or her loves and ideals in perfect alignment? Must a cinephile be a bad citizen? Let us just say that I am a very bad citizen and leave it at that.

Is there no place at all for cinema in a democracy? In democracy, we fetishize the publicity of politics and insist upon the openness of political institutions. But, since perfectly transparent institutions, like perfectly transparent personalities, are impossible, we inevitably lapse back into episodes of secrecy. Our refusal to accept this necessity means that the boundary between the open and the not-open cannot be a stable division but rather an endless provocation to our imagination. Instead of a division of labor between public and not-public we have instead a tortured dialectic in which we repeatedly seek both to construct walls around certain behaviors and to tear those same walls down with excessive relish. The endless political cycles of "scandal" and "reform" that have been with us, it seems, since the first days of modern democracy are the mildest incarnation of this pattern. It is only natural, then, that film, with its propensity to show us lost or hidden time, will easily become recruited into this dialectic and produce the genre of democratic pornography (among others, of course).

In a country such as ours I would deny to no woman or man the pleasures of cinema, but neither would I imagine that we could build democratic institutions on such pleasures or that they might instruct us on such a project. Cinematic pleasure is as real as any other, but it is not freedom. The tension between the two is the essence of the pessimism to which Rousseau committed himself in his *Lettre à M. d'Alembert*. Pleasure is our attachment to objects which can have no permanence in this world; freedom is our actions and experiences in a world that are autonomous in that they refuse enslavement to such object-desires (which does not mean that we must ignore them). Dreams can tell us what we want, but the daylight world outside the movie house tells us we cannot hold on to such things. The pleasures of a Philadelphia story end when the story ends; they cannot be preserved, anymore than we can hold on to our dreams. When the moving pictures turn into a static arrangement, they bring joy neither to the participants nor to the audience (the joy of the climactic moment is immediately followed by the disappointment, the little death, at the end of the show). Likewise, we cannot as public democratic citizens enjoy the heady transient exercise of constituent power that the framers shrouded in secrecy.

More important, though, is our continuing ambivalence about this chance and contingency that are hidden at the root of our union. This, it must be admitted, is something that film has the capacity to show us in a way that few other art forms do. Films like *The Philadelphia Story* get their charge in part by satisfying our desire to observe this phenomenon, but to observe it in such a way that it remains contained within a dreamlike experience, one we enjoy in isolation from other citizens. It is indeed a sweet dream, but do such dreams make better citizens? I have given the reasons why I believe they do not. One learns to have sex very badly from pornography.

A phrase that is repeated several times in *The Philadelphia Story* is that what is necessary to be fully human is "to have some regard for human frailty." It is a wise maxim. "Frailty," which can indicate a fragility both physical and moral, is our fate, but naming a disease makes us no healthier. Worse, we may be deceived into thinking that our reception of wisdom is the same thing as our display of it, or as an action predicated thereupon. "The time to make up your mind about people," says the drunken Tracy, "is never." Nothing could be truer, but the time to act is always now. The dreamtime of film is always closer to never, the viewer, like the dreamer, held quiescent by an image of beauty. No one learns to act in a dream; one watches and perhaps learns how to watch better. If the very best of films teaches us not what it is to be better, but only how to watch it, what can we hope for from the rest of them?

If we leave the theater exhilarated by a display of warm chaos, are we really motivated, thereby, to introduce such a form of life into our waking existence? Or are we simply motivated to return that much more quickly to the world of dreams? Are we motivated to effect political change or are we sated by a discharge of psychic frustration that might otherwise find its way into the political realm? It may well be that, with real national politics at such a remove from the life of the individual, we should blame neither filmmakers for making such works, nor citizens for enjoying them, if there is no other option. But would anyone really believe that, even if our multiplexes were filled with films as edifying as *The Philadelphia Story* (which they most certainly are not), our nation was thereby being repaired? To ask the question is to see its absurdity. It may, indeed, be a loss to our imagination that we are now more likely to spend our days watching television than our nights watching films, but our imagination is not the same thing as our polity and from that perspective neither medium seems like a path to perfection, Emersonian or otherwise.

As I peer out of my window here in Los Angeles – that city of breathing, speaking people that provides the geographic surround to Hollywood, and which partakes of Hollywood only as a consumer – I see the students making films in the garden beneath my office. Shall I pretend that they are thereby being trained to be better citizens and teachers of their fellow citizens? Even they, I think, would not dare to claim so much.

Rather than seeking to educate the city, they are attempting to leave it, to leave the actual place of spontaneity, luck, eros and disorder that is their home with others for the world of beauty and permanence where their films will stand as monuments to their solitary selves. If there is a generic criticism to be made of pornography it is that it has the effect of eternalizing what should be momentary. If we are to experience a democracy of moments, we can never learn to do so from an art that exists to subvert them.

Sir, you have proposed a solution fit for the smallest of republics at a time when the size of nations has never been larger! Where would a film like *The Philadelphia Story* do good? The Geneva of the eighteenth century, perhaps, with fewer than 50,000 souls, fewer by far than walk the streets of your own city of Cambridge on any given day. A tiny republic with a small population, secure defensible borders and limited contact with the outside world. Here, it might be appropriate to imagine every adult having some nodding acquaintance with every other adult. It might be appropriate to imagine a form of friendship and personal trust, however limited, among the citizens, which could mediate all the conflicts created by other emotions and interests. Though the Genevans were Calvinists, we can at least imagine them becoming a Quakerly Society of Friends and carrying on their politics under the watchful eye of William Penn.

However, even the smallest of nations today, leaving aside a few islands and emirates where perhaps these ideas could have purchase, is composed of millions of people. We distort the concept of friendship beyond all recognition if we pretend that it can apply to such large polities. Such a people may (or may not) share laws, culture and history but they cannot share a friendship. Friendship and love require some kind of appreciation of particularity and the sheer size of today's nations absolutely precludes this. If we recognize no other fact about modern life as relevant to our political theory, we must at least recognize the scale and scope of modern states – they are gargantuan.

Here is a final place where we must fault your comedies – and your celebration – for a political optimism that cannot be sustained. For in "solving" the erotic problems of citizenship through the mechanism of remarriage they might lead us to believe that the violence of eros can be tamed once and for all. That is, in essence, what happens between the principals in these films, whose irregular hearts might cause them to hate one another were it not for the new constellation of relationships that they come to share. But the friendships of *The Rules of the Game* fail to stem the violent tide. If this seems like happenstance or bad luck when the two films are compared as household dramas, it seems more like a point of realism in *Rules* when viewed as a national epic. For, in truth, no single household could contain the general erotic conflicts that a modern state must manage. What is finally inimitable politically about films like *The Philadelphia Story*, then, is not the chaos of its emotional conflicts but the miniature solution of them. The microcosm cannot become the macrocosm and so remade families such as these cannot teach nations how to endure, they can only teach the limits of their endurance, as *Rules* does.

Is there no place in the modern world, then, for a comedy of remarriage? In totalitarian nations, perhaps, they may do the most good. In those places where friendship itself is in danger of extinction from a government that turns citizen against citizen until no trust between them is possible. The descriptions of Soviet Russia and Maoist China that we have, where spying and denunciation were ubiquitous features of everyday life, sound like this. Belarus and North Korea still have such systems in place. Here a defense of friendship is needed, as a minimal condition for a human life. Here an appreciation for the micro-foundations, as our political science friends like to say, of decent daily interaction with our fellow citizens may be required. Indeed, in any modern society where humans are tempted to dispose of friendship, to view it as a luxury, as we are sometimes persuaded to do, they may do some good. However, the good they do will not form the basis (or at least cannot form anything like a full basis) for political renovation. For that we must look elsewhere.

The terror of wideawake relationships, of citizen interactions that are fully reciprocal and uncontained, needs an institution that can be scaled to something approaching the size of modern states. Friendship is open-ended; it has no *telos*, and although it cannot bear *anything*, it can certainly tolerate more variation, more turbulence, than other erotic relations. Since friendship has no goal, it need have no end; it never fails from want of achieving something. We cannot expect of citizens that they will all be friends with one another, however irreplaceable the experience of friendship may be in itself. Friendship is a localized bond and, even in small states, a politics of friendship inevitably morphs into cronyism and exclusion. Film, at least, is mass entertainment – mass friendship seems a contradiction in terms.

If a community of friends cannot sustain itself, how could it sustain a state? Through its representations? Do we really think our state could be improved by the institution of film festivals? I have given my reasons for thinking otherwise. But, I will be asked, what shall we have in their place? Every society needs festivals, no doubt. What action or institution is there that can unite a people while respecting their freedom? Where shall we look for it? Could there be any festivals in the democracy of moments? Is there any way to bind moment and narrative without destroying the one or reifying the other? Can the movement between public and not-public be stabilized in a fruitful oscillation? Or is this only possible at the microscopic level?

In response to these questions, I ask: what would it mean to approach our shared life together through the logic of a quest? This is not the occasion, nor have I the ability, to give a full account of a pessimistic public life. But you would think me ungenerous to have emptied your cup of optimism and to have left you with nothing in its place. You sometimes refer, wistfully, to that time in American history, before television, when fully half the population went to the movies every week. And, as the release of films was then controlled by the studios, the choice in any given week was small, so many millions of people saw the same film.

I can think of a moment when even more people saw the same thing and saw it together. On July 20, 1969, at least 500 million people saw earthmen land on the moon and later walk upon its surface. I, myself, recall being woken out of a sound sleep by my parents for the first extraterrestrial steps of mankind, which took place long after my normal bedtime. It remains perhaps the single greatest simultaneous gathering of human attention. No human could be indifferent to such an event, an event that nonetheless altered almost no one's material circumstances. So nothing changed, and yet too everything did and I doubt whether you can find a living human being with a memory of this moment who will say that he or she was unaffected by it.

We can think of the quest for space as relatively small government program, begun on a certain date, with certain resources and discontinued once its goals were met. But I do not think that the world's attention focused on this event from that perspective. Here was a real-life drama, centuries in the making, which organized the efforts, in fact, of millions of people over many generations. Indeed, a great many people continue to this day to make sense of their world from the perspective of this quest and its offshoots. This is not mass entertainment, but it is an example of a large-scale civic enterprise to which citizens can contribute without captivation and with reciprocal engagement. It may not appeal to everyone, but perhaps there are other equally modern-sized projects that might, for example, the curing of disease or the restoration of the planet.

To view the world as it may best be seen, is that not the goal that our rival inquiries, after all our disagreements, still share? Isn't it only from space that the world can be viewed, really and fully viewed? All but a tiny number of humans, therefore, have never viewed it and never will view it except in filmed or televised images. What if we set the goal of giving every soul the chance to view Earth as a whole, an opportunity, therefore, to encounter it and to consider and render judgment on the whole. What would that be like? To truly view the world, we must have the opportunity to leave it, to look back upon it in retrospect. We can worry that, separated from Earth, we would lose all basis for judgment, all affection for terrestrial life. I, for one, would wager that the sense of wonder which we are so apt to lose in front of the screen, but which is excited even in high-altitude aircraft when the world begins to bend beneath you, would be empowered and emboldened by such an experience, and that we would return to Earth better citizens of our respective countries and of the Earth for having, for once in our lives, viewed the world.

Nothing, you will agree, compares with the excitement of making a country; certainly not the boredom of having one. So inconsiderate of the founding generations of our modern states to keep the honeymoon to themselves and to leave the dotage to others! But, we must not look to recover youthful passions in dreams of the past but rather seek outward, toward new democratic vistas, even vistas of the whole world, to stimulate our wonder and affections. A vista occurs when the world presents itself to us and when we put ourselves in a position to receive its presentation. It does not occur when we represent the world to ourselves; that is when we avoid its presentation in favor of our own recreation. To see a vista is to be awake; otherwise, in representing ourselves to ourselves, we dream. The best thing to be said about film is that it is a captivation we can emerge from. We can leave it and leaving it is liberating. (With television, as we know it, there is no escape.)

It is the logic of exploration, then, the logic of the quest, the search for new vistas, and not the logic of the story with an ending, that combines moment and narrative in a way that preserves the openness of both, a friendship with the world and not with a single other person. The moon shot, whatever its base motives, was such a quest, a worthy festival for democracy. Obviously, there was a goal involved, but perhaps it was just a stepping stone, the first island in an archipelago of discovery. Is it so hard to imagine others? Having viewed one world, should we not seek others? Please forgive my foolish enthusiasm. No doubt I have seen too many movies. But, if you ask me what I would put in the place of remarriage, I say: in a quest, we can meet each other as citizens and share a moment without the associated narrative dominating or captivating us and yet embracing the open-endedness of our association, its contingency and its dangers. It is a mutual vision that is, potentially, reciprocal and uncoerced. That is a citizenship I could embrace. It would make a terrible movie.

A democratic vision is a vision of others and of the Earth, a shared moment, however difficult, of seeing and being seen. In dreams and cinema, no one sees us, which means that, in the end, we see only ourselves. To dream is human, but to extend that human capacity by prosthetic means until it displaces all others is to fall, with Narcissus, in love with our own reflections. It is to lose the democracy of moments and to gain only some pretty stories in return. We learn to dance by dancing, not by watching Fred Astaire. We learn to explore by exploring, not by watching documentaries. Likewise, we learn to politick by politicking and we learn to democratize by democratizing. If our cinema does no harm to this process, let it flourish in all its beauty! But, if it impedes us or retards us on our quest, well … let us at least refrain from recommending it lest more terrible measures become a duty.

Part II

Responses

2

Emancipated perfectionism – or, In praise of dreaming

Clare Woodford

> [T]he issues raised in these films concern the difficulty of overcoming a certain moral cynicism, a giving up on the aspiration to a life more coherent and admirable than seems affordable after the obligations and compromises of adulthood begin to obscure the promise and dreams of youth and the rift between public demands and private demands comes to seem unbridgeable.[1]
>
> In the logic of emancipation … there is always a third thing … The same applies to performance. It is not the transmission of the artist's knowledge or inspiration to the spectator. It is the third thing that is owned by no one, whose meaning is owned by no one, but which subsists between them, excluding any uniform transmission, any identity of cause and effect.[2]

I imagine that democracy without dreams would be a rather dull place. If we accept Dienstag's argument that "the time of cinema is a dreamtime," then I would suggest that dreaming, both with and without films, is not merely a pleasurable distraction but a valuable pastime for democratic citizens. I take this stance in response to Joshua Dienstag's brilliant "remake" of Rousseau's *Lettre à M. d'Alembert* in the form of his "Letter to M. Cavell." There is much to ponder in this rich

1 Stanley Cavell, *Cavell on Film, edited by W. Rothman* (Albany, NY: State University of New York Press, 2005) p. 11.

2 Jacques Rancière, "The Emancipated Spectator," in *The Emancipated Spectator*, translated by Gregory Elliott (London and New York: Verso, 2009) pp. 14–15.

and thoughtful letter, which argues *contra* Cavell that, although enjoyable, film does not teach us "what it is to be better" and that to claim that it does and that it is therefore beneficial for democracy is "dangerous," (pp. 75, 10). Although I admire much of Dienstag's analysis, I am bound to defend film as a possible source of fruitful and inspiring dreams and hence seek not to go so far as to champion film-watching as a necessary democratic activity, but merely to suggest that watching films can be beneficial for democracy. In making this argument I wish to emphasize that this requires us to focus our emphasis less on the vision of the world (or beyond) that is portrayed in film and more on the relationship between the film and its audience.

I will begin my response by briefly examining differing alternative interpretations of *The Philadelphia Story* to defend its use as a fruitful exemplar for my understanding of democratic relationships. I refer to my own interpretation, not in challenge to Dienstag or Cavell, but to engage them in conversation, and indeed will then draw on Cavell's work on exemplarity to remind us that, for moral perfectionism, the act of interpreting is prioritized over the interpretation. By, then, reading this claim alongside the work of Jacques Rancière, I will emphasize his claim that spectators are always already engaged in such interpretation, but too often do not trust the legitimacy or authority of their own interpretation over that of others. Rancière suggests that in learning to accept one's own authority, and in being recognized as doing so, the role of spectator is emancipated from the unequal hierarchies of knowledge, giving us a more democratic model of the citizen. I will consequently argue that we can read Cavell and Rancière together to establish an idea of an emancipated perfectionist society in which citizens as spectators are seen to acknowledge the authority of their own thoughts. With this in mind, I will turn back to Emerson to discuss how the perfectionist commitment to self-reliance is cultivated through "aversive thinking" and the positive role of dreaming within this. Finally, I will explore Dienstag's wider claim about the value of films for democracy in general. Here I suggest a symbiotic relationship between eros and stability and defend moral perfectionism as the compass with which we can navigate the winding path between the anarchy of eros and the order of stability to enable us to draw on both without losing the other.

Yet, as I begin, it is important to note that I admire Dienstag's vision of democracy as a quest. On this quest he envisages that we "meet each other as citizens and share a moment without the associated narrative dominating or captivating us and yet embracing the open-endedness of our association, its contingency and its dangers" (p. 81). It may perhaps seem strange that this quest is not very different from the way I have always conceived Cavell's work on perfectionism, as an unending ateleological search in the company of others, each for our unattained self that always remains one step ahead of us on the path of life.[3] Because of this, I see Dienstag's essay as a puzzle to solve, forcing me to return throughout this chapter to how it is that his reading takes Cavell's work on film to give us something rather different from this quest.

Two models of exemplarity

In much of Cavell's writing on film he seeks to show us that the protagonists of the films he terms "remarriage comedies" live a form of perfectionism that he upholds as desirable for contemporary democratic society: moral perfectionism. However, there appear to be two ways in which we can interpret exemplarity in Cavell's writing. One, I suggest, may be more valuable in helping us understand the perfectionist register than the other.

The first type of exemplarity is found in the understanding that the central couple in the remarriage comedies exhibit desirable qualities, as if Cavell is then indicating that we would do well to imitate them.[4] Indeed,

[3] See Stanley Cavell, *Pursuits of Happiness: The Hollywood Comedy of Remarriage* (Cambridge, MA: Harvard University Press, 1981), p. 29, where he claims that life is a journey, and Stanley Cavell, *Conditions Handsome and Unhandsome: The Constitution of Emersonian Perfectionism* (Chicago, IL, and London: University of Chicago Press, 1990), p. 56, where he emphasizes the ateleological commitment of perfectionism.

[4] As may be interpreted by his claim that the films can "instruct" us (Cavell, *Pursuits of Happiness*, p. 7).

it is this model that Dienstag is concerned about, suggesting that, for Cavell, *The Philadelphia Story* "provides us with *an exemplar* of perfection, which may lead us to perfect ourselves."[5] Dienstag opines that this is a "dangerous contention." Instead, he suggests that our attraction to this film "reveals our degraded condition and that it is in a sense this condition that binds us to it. What perfection the film embodies remains, therefore, out of reach for us and, as such, a hazard rather than a *telos*" (p. 10).

In contrast to what he finds in Cavell – the idea that this film shows us how to be more perfect democratic citizens – Dienstag's counter-reading comprises the following argument: *The Philadelphia Story* provides us with a model of behavior that hypocritically seeks to keep the difficulties and troubles of life private, hiding them behind a public veneer of perfection; it reveals to us that, for the protagonists, publicity and therefore democratic scrutiny is dirty and voyeuristic and, therefore, if their behavior and opinions were copied it would lead us to a questionable type of happiness that is far from suitable for a democratic way of life. Enjoyable the film may be, but exemplary of ideal democratic relationships it is not. To take it as so is at best misleading and at worst dangerous.

Consequently, although Cavell has claimed that we have a responsibility to be happy in a democracy,[6] Dienstag is concerned that the happiness of the film is the happiness of a masochistic voyeur who finds *Spy* magazine in their hands at the end of the film. Thus, to argue that this film is an example of a more perfect democracy is shown to propagate a myth: democracy is capable of synthesizing our private loves with our public responsibilities in a way that leads to happiness only if we accept that this happiness depends on us denying the unruly extent of eros, and therefore pretending that we are happy when in actual fact we have to repress our desires. Thus, after this reading, we are left rather confused about the so-called happiness which Cavell wishes us to pursue.

5 See above, italics added.

6 Cavell, *Cavell on Film*, p. 348.

In contrast, I wish to share a third interpretation of *The Philadelphia Story* that incorporates elements of both Cavell's and Dienstag's readings. Let us begin with Dienstag's concern that the hypocrisy of the public wedding is different from what he sees to be the "true" state of affairs behind the facade: the pretense that we can happily control our erotic attachments, when in actual fact we cannot. I would suggest that if the couple had not opted for a traditional white wedding then this would uphold the idea that a second wedding is in some way inferior to the first: that the "failure" or imperfection of the first has tarnished the couple and that society no longer deems them capable of the lofty ideals and control of eros implied by a traditional marriage. However, Tracy and Dexter's wedding is, as Dienstag observes, like a rerun of the first, with lots of guests, crystal and lace decorations, Wagner's bridal march and the bride in a traditional white wedding dress. I took this to imply that Tracy and Dexter are having a go at the whole thing again, in all its romantic glory. Acknowledging, at least to the film's audience if not to the wedding guests, that, despite social pretenses, behind *every* wedding – not just second or third weddings – is the reality of imperfection, contingency and possible heartbreak and infidelity. The wedding scene appears as a challenge and reinterpretation of the traditional view of marriage, seeking to reform the very view of the institution itself, not merely propose an alternative. If, conversely, Tracy and Dexter had opted for a smaller "second" wedding, the film would be condoning the social idea that there are two types of wedding and therefore two types of possible relationship: the traditional white wedding for perfect relationships and the non-traditional or smaller wedding for imperfect relationships. This contains within it the assumption that perfect relationships can and do exist. Instead, the film shows that all marriages are imperfect despite the promises we make, and thereby acknowledges the contingency in every promise: the ability to fail and the ability to try again, expressed in the bittersweet phrase "for better for worse." The human condition is to aspire to perfection whilst always falling short. This, for me, was the beauty of this hopelessly romantic, yet wonderfully idealistic finale.

Yet, alongside these initial concerns, Dienstag observes throughout *The Philadelphia Story* the repetition of the claim that "what is necessary to be fully human is 'to have some regard for human frailty,'" yet then notes that "naming a disease makes us no healthier," (p. 75). This is interesting, because it reveals Dienstag's more cynical view: his disappointment in the human condition and his desire to act to overcome this. But, for Cavell, perfectionism is about accepting (to the point of happiness) our frailty at the same time as seeking a little more strength.[7] It is about smiling at the challenge that adversity brings rather than recklessly seeking to eliminate it, for it is this adversity that denotes our humanity; we cannot overcome it, but we can face it head on. Such a realization may understandably provoke cynicism or even despair, but Cavell's strategy is not to give in to this, but to instead be happy that we have the chance to engage in the challenge, and to enjoy the journey. Consequently, at this point I would claim that *The Philadelphia Story* is not so much about hypocrisy and privacy, but about the acceptance of imperfection without accompanying this acceptance with cynicism. Instead, it finishes on a positive note, that we can always work to attain something better. Thus, the couple have a traditional wedding ceremony not *in spite of* their acknowledgment of their imperfection and the contingency of the relationship, but *because of* this: to reveal to the viewer the contingency behind every agreement, ceremony and promise, and the fact that acknowledging this is OK and need not undermine its seriousness, but instead underlines the need for all involved to continue to accept their unavoidable implication in the relationship, and the perfectionist requirement to work at it continually, summed up in Cavell's phrase "as if all genuine marriage is remarriage."[8] Thus, perfectionism, as Cavell explains in the quote that opens this chapter, is about overcoming the usual cynical reaction to human imperfection with a commitment to seeking happiness regardless.

[7] Cavell, *Conditions Handsome and Unhandsome*, p. 110.
[8] Cavell, *Conditions Handsome and Unhandsome*, p. 104.

Furthermore, with respect to Dienstag's concern about the voyeurism of the viewer-subject, the uncomfortable "magazine photograph" kiss at the end of the film alerted me, as viewer, to every audience's voyeurism, but not to simply reward it, as in Dienstag's reading. In showing Hepburn as uncomfortable it emphasized that it is our voyeuristic desire to watch and comment on others' lives that puts pressure on others to not admit their imperfections and to sweep their troubles under the carpet of privacy. From the early discussion of *Spy* magazine, through the comments about Tracy being a "goddess" to this final frame, the film reveals the damage that we "the public" do through our taste for tabloid scandal and celebrity worship. We set up heroes to live our lives for us and then wait like vultures for them to fall, rather than attend to our own troubles. The moral of this viewer relationship could be interpreted as implying that our desire and enjoyment to be the passive viewer rather than the active critical thinker invests our political and civil ceremonies with more importance and permanence than they should really have. Our dysfunctional society forces the protagonists to seek privacy (whilst they may be wrong to do so, this becomes more understandable given such a society). If we readjust the balance so that we focus more on our own lives than those of others then perhaps we can all admit our imperfections a little more and loosen the pressure we all feel to keep our troubles private and put on or receive a show of perfection intended to impress others. So, although Dienstag is right to suggest that in today's society we may expect that the visibility of our frailty "weakens the bonds of union which they are pledged to uphold," (p. 20) it strikes me that a perfectionist society would be one in which such expectations are lowered and that visibility of frailty could strengthen such bonds, revealing that their maintenance requires constant attention and thereby inspires people's motivation. In the same way that any grand structure built on slender foundations would likely take our breath away, recognition of frailty could increase our awe.

In this interpretation, Cukor's film inspired me to reflect upon the extent to which we could engage in our relationships, both intimate and political, in an open non-finite manner to live in a forgiving and open way in our lives, as the protagonists learn to do in theirs, rather than to focus on watching and gossiping about others. This involves a much deeper interpretation of democratic relations than that found in much political thought today. With relation to the political analogy discussed by Dienstag, the moral would be to stop watching others making a constitution and then limit our involvement to merely moaning about it, but to get involved in making our own constitution, to push democracy to a fuller definition. Hence, *The Philadelphia Story*'s ending seems to moralistically say that we should not have enjoyed it in the way that we did (letting it just wash over us as entertainment), that we need to work on ourselves to interact more actively with everything around us to learn from the relationships rather than just watching them. In this way, I interpreted the film as seeking to inspire the viewers to think more carefully for themselves. Yet, this is a different model of exemplarity from that encountered above, for it does not imply that the protagonists are to simply be copied or imitated in any particular way, but instead it inspires us to be more active viewers and citizens ourselves.

Indeed, if we return to Cavell for a moment, we find a more predominant role for this second model of exemplarity as inspiration – in the sense of inspiring one's own thoughts and responses[9] – rather than the previous imitation model. In the essay "Aversive Thinking," Cavell draws on Nietzsche's paraphrasing of Emerson's work on the exemplar relation. In Nietzsche's talk of consecrating oneself to culture and attaching one's heart to great men,[10] Cavell reads the imperative to be inspired by one's heroes, not to copy them, but in a way that leads us to hate one's own meanness and be inspired by the way that these great men lived for themselves, and therefore to aim to do the same, to take their work as stimulus for our own.[11] Cavell also notes the call in Emerson to never be content with oneself and always to be

[9] Not in the sense of a film director controlling inspiration, merely as impulses that stimulate thought.
[10] Cavell, *Conditions Handsome and Unhandsome*, p. 53.
[11] Cavell, *Conditions Handsome and Unhandsome*, pp. 49–54.

inspired by others, not to do as they do, but to live for oneself: "Each philosopher, each bard, each actor has only done for me, as by a delegate, what one day I can do for myself."[12] This model of exemplarity is not a model of imitation, but one of inspiring a passive observer to become the active doer.

It is necessary to note at this point that although Dienstag does not seek to distinguish the two models of exemplarity discussed in this chapter, and although he does at times refer to film "instructing" or "teaching" us, at other times he seems to wish to focus more generally on the interplay between possible interpretations. Without explicitly acknowledging this distinction between the two models of exemplarity, and in some ways bound to the first through his invocation of Rousseau, Dienstag seems to predominantly read Cavell's use of exemplars in the imitative model. In this sense, then, he is right to question Cavell's reading of *The Philadelphia Story*, and many of the other remarriage comedies that Cavell draws upon, because, despite my interpretation, the protagonists do seem to portray characteristics that may not be desirable or possible for all people in a democracy, such as a privileged, often aristocratic upbringing, privacy from the public gaze, a life together away from society, a life of leisure, and in many cases the patronizing and subjection of the female role by the male. Nevertheless, more often than not, when Cavell talks about the way that films interact with our society, it is this deeper understanding of exemplarity that he seems to be drawing on.[13] But, as seen in Dienstag's interpretation, Cavell does not often make this explicit, instead perhaps assuming his readers will already be aware of his discussion of exemplarity in *Conditions Handsome and Unhandsome*, and does not always practice a completely consistent application of this model himself. It is thus maybe rather too easy to read the imitation model into his work, since this has always

[12] Cavell, *Conditions Handsome and Unhandsome*, p. 54.

[13] Indeed, I cannot find any place in Cavell's writing where he is explicitly drawing on the first model, although at times it may be implied. In particular, in *Cities of Words* he notes how these films "manifest" something to us, rather than evoke us to imitate (Cambridge, MA, and London: Belknap/Harvard University Press, 2004), p. 9. See also note 35 below.

been so dominant in Western thought.[14] According to this model, the spectator is educated (whether for good or ill) by that which he sees portrayed, because it is assumed he will seek to imitate it (or, in the situation of a negative example, to refrain from imitating it). Indeed, such a view appears to be echoed in Cavell's invocation of "good film" in the quote chosen by Dienstag at the opening of his letter.

However, I am not discussing this in order to take a side in history with Voltaire and d'Alembert against Plato and Rousseau for, upon examination, we see that d'Alembert's claim also invokes the imitation model, believing that, with better regulation concerning both the conduct of actors and the theaters themselves, the presence of theater in Geneva could have a moralizing influence on society.[15] Instead, I want to draw upon Rancière's essay "The Emancipated Spectator," in which Rancière claims that both sides in this debate are based on an inaccurate picture of the relationship between art and the spectator. Even with regard to recent postmodern forms of art, Rancière suggests that artists "always assume that what will be perceived, felt, understood is what they have put into their dramatic art or performance,"[16] and thus think that they can control to some extent the effect of their art upon its audience.

In contrast, despite the aspiration of artists, playwrights and writers, Rancière suggests in the epigraph above, that they can never control the influence of their art because the contingency of meaning cannot be controlled once it is let loose into the social world.[17] Thus, the

[14] In particular, in relation to the impact of art on democracy, Plato's concerns about the negative effects of art on political society, voiced by Socrates in *The Republic*, filtered down via Rousseau into the concerns of newly emerging representative democracies of the modern age in the writings of eighteenth-century French Revolutionaries (Susan Maslan, *Revolutionary Acts: Theatre, Democracy and the French Revolution* (Baltimore, MD: The Johns Hopkins University Press, 2005) esp. ch. 2). From there it can be traced into the ideas espoused by radical playwrights who seek to orchestrate their audience's response by promoting "good" art over "bad" art, perhaps most familiar in the writings of Brecht, but also more recently in Augusto Boal, *Theatre of the Oppressed* (London: Pluto Press, 2000).

[15] D'Alembert, cited by Jean-Jacques Rousseau, *Politics and the Arts*, translated by Alan Bloom (Ithaca, NY: Cornell University Press, 1968) p. 4.

[16] Rancière, "The Emancipated Spectator," p. 14.

[17] Rancière, "The Emancipated Spectator," pp. 14–15.

aforementioned imitative model of the relation between art and its spectator is revealed as illusory: the relation of imitation that so concerned Rousseau and Voltaire from different perspectives is thereby revealed to be a useful myth to propagate the status of intellectuals (philosophers, playwrights, authors, etc.) as society's interpreters.[18] Instead, according to Rancière, such a role is unnecessary, as all spectators already do and will continue to interpret for themselves in ways that are beyond the control of any director, playwright, actor or artist.[19] Thus we see Rancière drawing on the model of the audience-spectator relationship as being always to some extent inspirational rather than imitative.

More work needs to be done if we are to be able to read Rancière and Cavell together on this, for, at present, it seems that some important differences remain between the two thinkers. First, in contrast with my explanation above, Rancière states that this insight means that it is wrong to assume that spectators are passive until awakened by the knowledge imparted to them by others. Instead, he claims that the condition of the so-called passive spectator is our normal condition[20] and, furthermore, that such viewing is also an action.[21] In the act of viewing, we link what we see and understand to what we have already seen and said, done and dreamed to weave it into the web that is our own individual life course.[22] Furthermore, to see spectators as such is undemocratic, as it is based on an inequality that establishes two camps: the knowledgeable from the ignorant who are in need of this knowledge; the active thinker who must educate the passive spectator. This can become clearer if we supplement it with Rancière's *The Ignorant School Master*, where he suggests that such a division between the ignorant and the knowledgeable is the basis for all traditional pedagogy. This conveniently masks the inequality of power that it maintains between the two groups and thereby ensures the dominant position

18 Rancière, "The Emancipated Spectator," p. 8.
19 Rancière, "The Emancipated Spectator," pp. 14–15.
20 Rancière, "The Emancipated Spectator," p. 17.
21 Rancière, "The Emancipated Spectator," p. 13.
22 Rancière, "The Emancipated Spectator," p. 13.

of the knowledgeable. To make this argument, Rancière draws on the writings of nineteenth-century French pedagogue, Joseph Jacotot,[23] who, whilst in exile during the French Restoration, developed a method called "universal teaching" whereby illiterate parents could teach their children to read. Following Jacotot, Rancière uses this method to challenge the traditional explicative teacher–pupil relationship, suggesting instead that teachers should not be conceived of as passing on knowledge, but of merely creating the conditions for students to learn. The success of this method is based on the assumption that all people are equally capable of learning for themselves, because "all men have equal intelligence."[24] This can be used to challenge the inequality inherent in traditional teaching methods and thereby emancipate people without formal education from their dependence on "intellectuals."

The use of the term "emancipate" is important here. Rancière claims that when someone acknowledges the legitimacy of their own thought rather than that of another, this is emancipation.[25] He later adds that emancipation can therefore be understood as the following: "that every common person might conceive his human dignity, take the measure of his intellectual capacity, and decide how to use it."[26] If we take this back to the spectator relationship, then we see that if we are to be emancipated as a spectator then here too we need to trust our own judgment and not defer to another's interpretation.[27] We need to be willing to accept our own translations of what we experience not by preventing film or other art forms from telling us stories, for "an emancipated community is a community of narrators and translators," but by all acknowledging their own ability to be "active interpreters, who develop their own translation in order to appropriate the 'story' and make it their own story."[28]

[23] Jacques Rancière, *The Ignorant School Master: Five Lessons in Intellectual Emancipation*, translated by Kristin Ross (Stanford, CA: Stanford University Press, 1981).
[24] Rancière, *The Ignorant School Master*, p. 18.
[25] Rancière, *The Ignorant School Master*, p. 13.
[26] Rancière, *The Ignorant School Master*, p. 17.
[27] Rancière, *The Ignorant School Master*, p. 13.
[28] Rancière, *The Ignorant School Master*, p. 22.

It is interesting to note that this would consequently indicate that, where Cavell mainly focuses on the value of remarriage comedies for democracy, Rancière leads us to be less restrictive, indicating that all films and all types of performance can play their role in our journeys of self-reflection. Indeed, if I turn back to my interpretation of the relationship between viewer and film above, we can see that in the final wedding scene of *The Philadelphia Story* the viewer is looking in on other viewers, the guests at the wedding. Although the guests only see the "perfect" wedding ceremony that Tracy and Dexter present to them, the viewer of the film sees more. The viewer's privileged position could be interpreted to mean that in all of life's experiences we can gain something from appreciating our perspective as onlooker on our society; by viewing the experience as if watching a film, looking on from a distanced perspective, we can think and reflect on our lives together from a critical distance. Hence, the practice of being a spectator engaged in the watching of a film, or viewing any work of art, is an exemplary relation (not necessarily the best, but a useful one) for our day-to-day lives that not only can but will inspire us in critical reflective thought.

Rancière further translates what this practice of emancipation entails, suggesting that, as emancipated spectators, we link what we see to that which we know in order to learn something new, "if we refuse, firstly, radical distance, secondly the distribution of roles, and thirdly the boundaries between territories."[29] Ultimately, then, we are emancipated if we reject the vision of the world that we are told about by others and instead listen to our own thoughts.[30] In noting this, I do not intend to go out of my way to read Rancière back to front, for I am aware that he is using the assumption of equality to challenge the notion of division of the social. I too share this aim, although by focusing on this passage it may seem I am trying to overturn it by substituting the division between the ignorant and the knowledgeable with a division between the emancipated and the unemancipated. However, there is a crucial

[29] Rancière, "The Emancipated Spectator," p. 17.
[30] Rancière, "The Emancipated Spectator," p. 22.

difference here, for the emancipated are not in a relation of power over the unemancipated because what they recognize – that all men are of equal intelligence – unites rather than divides. Yet this does mean that there are two ways of being a spectator. In neither is the spectator passive in the sense of not thinking. The crucial difference instead is whether she respects (and is expected to respect) the authority of her own interpretation or whether, in the unemancipated model, she submits her own interpretation (and is expected to do so) to the authority of others. Consequently, we perhaps need to revise the use of the terms "passive" and "active" above, such that, if perfectionism is to respect the logic of emancipation, we see the exemplar relationship as one that not only inspires response (for this will always be the case), but also encourages and accepts that the observer will trust her own thought rather than seek to imitate what is being shown.

Rancière refers to the state whereby we refuse to trust our own thoughts as one of "stultification" and "routine"[31] and identifies a task for us in overcoming this in ourselves as well as in others: "any individual can always, at any moment, be emancipated and emancipate someone else, announce to others the *practice* and add to the number of people who know themselves and who no longer play the comedy of the inferior superiors."[32] He thereby acknowledges a role for those he refers to as "the disciples" of universal teaching, who "announce to all individuals … the way to teach what one doesn't know on the principle of the equality of intelligence."[33] Such a disciple "does not teach a pupil his knowledge, but orders them to venture into the forest of things and signs, to say what they have seen and what they think of what they have seen."[34] Although such a program of radical pedagogy and emancipation may at first appear to emerge from quite a separate tradition from the ethical focus of Cavell's moral perfectionism, it does not take much to find echoes of this emancipatory task in the writings of Emerson that

[31] Rancière, *The Ignorant School Master*, p. 108.
[32] Rancière, *The Ignorant School Master*, p. 98.
[33] Rancière, *The Ignorant School Master*, p. 105.
[34] Rancière, "The Emancipated Spectator," p. 11.

Cavell draws upon. In this sense, I see Emerson as one such disciple of universal teaching, and thus Rancière's work on emancipation supplements Cavell's moral perfectionism, suggesting that the latter model of exemplarity – whereby art inspires you to think for yourself – is more instructive than the former imitative model, not because it is a *better* way for people to act but because it is a *more accurate* description of how people already do relate to art. If we realize this, we understand better the role that films, as art, play in our social world.[35] It is important if we are to draw parallels here, however, that I emphasize that, for Cavell, this holds as long as we do not understand Cavell, along with Emerson, telling people to think for themselves as opposed to not thinking, but understand that these passages summon people to trust their own thoughts rather than defer to the thoughts of others. This is invoked in Emerson's claim that "Man is timid and apologetic; he is no longer upright; he dares not say 'I think,' 'I am,' but quotes some saint or sage."[36] Thus, in relation to Rancière's understanding that an emancipated spectator relates everything they see and experience to the narrative of their own lives, it is important to return to Cavell's aforementioned discussion of exemplars[37] to emphasize that perfectionism places less emphasis on the content of the interpretation of any film than on the act of interpreting itself,[38] because each film can prompt independent reflection and thus will bring this value to the life of the person experiencing it.[39]

35 This is summed up in the sentence: "Truly speaking, it is not instruction, but provocation, that I can receive from another soul" (Cavell, *Conditions Handsome and Unhandsome*, pp. 37–8, citing Emerson's *Divinity School Address*).

36 Ralph Waldo Emerson, "Seal-reliance," in *Selected Writings of Ralph Waldo Emerson* (New York: Signet Classics, 2003), p. 279.

37 Cavell, *Conditions Handsome and Unhandsome*, p. 53.

38 I am not implying that interpretations are not of interest for what they can prompt in us, merely that I do not intend my interpretation of these films to be seen as rivaling Dienstag's or Cavell's, but to be complementary. Indeed, Cavell notes the importance of the interplay of interpretations for a person, interspersed with her own experience (*Pursuits of Happiness*, p. 36).

39 "[T]o examine and defend my own interest in these films is to examine and defend my interest in my own experience, in the moments and passages of my life I have spent with them" (Cavell, *Pursuits of Happiness*, p. 7).

For both Rancière and Cavell, interpretation of film is seen as an exercise in self-reflection and conversation with oneself, with one another and with one's society, where film is one inspiration amongst many that can be of use to us as we continually engage in the practice of revising and reapplying interpretations of the social to our own lives every day. Rancière's work has been useful in helping us to understand the power relations at stake in the two exemplar models encountered in this essay, to reveal that the model of imitation belongs to the explicative order of traditional pedagogy and unequal intelligences, whereas the inspirational model belongs to the emancipated order of universal teaching based on an assumption of equality. Furthermore, Rancière helps us to challenge Cavell's desire to draw only on "good" film[40] and instead shows that all film is of value to the moral perfectionist life.

If we are to accept Rancière's suggestion that trusting the authority of our own thought will help us avoid reifying the inequality of intelligences, we nevertheless find little suggestion of how to cultivate such a practice and guard against accepting the authority of others' thoughts. Indeed, Rancière can be criticized for not thematizing democratic subjectification more thoroughly and so Cavell's work can be useful here to supplement Rancière.[41] In particular, it is useful to return to the Emerson essays Cavell uses to thematize in more detail what it is that reflecting on films and other exemplars is meant to add to our lives and whether it is important for democracy.

Dreaming for democracy

> In times when we thought ourselves indolent, we have afterwards discovered, that much was accomplished, and much was begun in us.[42]

[40] Cavell, *Cavell on Film*, p. 334.

[41] I develop this argument more in Clare Woodford, *Dis-orienting Democracy: Aesthetics, Knowledge and the Subject After Rancière* (London: Routledge, 2016), ch. 3.

[42] Ralph Waldo Emerson, "Experience," in *Selected Writings*, p. 351.

> [A] dream may let us deeper into the secret of nature than a hundred concerted experiments.[43]
>
> A strange process too … by which experience is converted into thought … The manufacture goes forward at all hours.[44]

I wish in this section to revise why accepting the authority of one's own thought, hereafter referred to as "aversive thinking," is of value for democracy in order to defend the view that film, inasmuch as it is important for such thought, is therefore significant for democracy. It is first useful to recall, albeit briefly, what it is that aversive thinking comprises and how it can be accomplished. To begin with, Cavell argues that Emerson's writing shows how conformity captures our thought and expresses the claim that we need to become self-reliant by practicing an aversion to this, which will lead us to greater freedom.[45] In Emerson's language, we each have an inner "genius," which we have to cultivate and follow rather than merely imitate others.[46] By following our own genius and thinking aversively, we are enabled to conceive of life as an open-ended journey during which one is always seeking to develop the self, by never accepting the self as it is (the attained self) and always looking to the future to the next self, as yet unattained. When engaged in aversive thinking, it seems that the self is never satisfied and is always restless to develop; yet this state of affairs cannot come about in isolation, but relies on the perfectionist community of exemplars. Thus, this is not a solitary journey and can be achieved only through living "in conversation" with others both living and dead through the aforementioned consecration of one's heart to great men[47] and also through conversation with one's own contemporary society,[48] where conversation refers not just to speech but to a "way of life together."[49] The figure

[43] Ralph Waldo Emerson, "Nature," in *Selected Writings*, p. 218.

[44] Ralph Waldo Emerson, "The American Scholar," in *Selected Writings*, pp. 233–4.

[45] Cavell, *Conditions Handsome and Unhandsome*.

[46] Cavell, *Conditions Handsome and Unhandsome*, p. 25.

[47] See Cavell, *Conditions Handsome and Unhandsome*, p. 53.

[48] See Stephen Mulhall on the role of friendship for Cavell: *Stanley Cavell: Philosophy's Recounting of the Ordinary* (Oxford: Oxford University Press, 1994) p. 269.

[49] Stanley Cavell, *Cities of Words: Pedagogical Letters on a Register of the Moral Life* (Cambridge, MA, and London: Belknap/Harvard University Press, 2004) p. 173.

of the exemplar is central to this conversation where we learn from all others around us, be they friends, family, fellow-citizens, strangers, artists, authors or anyone; and, also, we need to remember that we too should live as exemplars to others to inspire them to be true to themselves. Further, it is clear that for Emerson the exemplar figure need not restrict us – indeed, it would seem that we can take instruction (on our own) from anything and everything – and every part of our lives is instructive since "the scholar loses no hour which the man lives."[50]

Although Emerson seems to prioritize the lessons we can learn from the natural world over what we can learn from other humans, he does think that human exemplarity has its place. Consequently, we can articulate this relationship between one's thought and the arts as exemplar more precisely, in this passage from Emerson:

> Man Thinking must not be subdued by his instruments. Books are for the scholar's idle times. When he can read God directly, the hour is too precious to be wasted in other men's transcripts of their readings. But when the intervals of darkness come, as come they must, – when the sun is hid, and the stars withdraw their shining, – we repair to the lamps which were kindled by their ray, to guide our steps to the East again, where the dawn is. We hear, that we may speak. The Arabian proverb says, "A fig tree, looking on a fig tree, becometh fruitful."[51]

Thus, we can conclude that films can be a useful tool, but that is not to say that they are the best tool, nor that they will always be of value to us, but neither is it to say that we can overrule their potential to impart a valuable experience.

Consequently, it is important to remember that Cavell has argued that moral perfectionism is essential "training" for democracy.[52] If we accept this argument, then seeing as we need exemplars to prompt us to always continue on this journey, and given that films can act as exemplars, it follows that they can comprise part of our training. Yet there is

[50] Emerson, "The American Scholar," p. 236.
[51] Emerson, "The American Scholar," p. 231.
[52] Cavell, *Conditions Handsome and Unhandsome*, p. 56.

a wider issue here beyond the issue of whether the comedies of remarriage, or film in general, may have some benefits for democracy, because Dienstag turns in the last section of his letter to express unease about the negative effects film may have on democracy. Before continuing, it is worth noting that Cavell has also noted that the type of cinema-going he invokes for moral perfectionism is a practice of a bygone day, and in many ways may not relate to the way in which we now frequent cinemas.[53] In this respect, it may well be that Cavell would share some of Dienstag's unease. However, in relation to my argument that all film could in some small way be of value for democratic life, I would suggest that these concerns can be responded to from within the moral perfectionist register by turning back once more to Emerson.

In particular, Dienstag raises a few interrelated concerns in the final part of his letter with respect to films promoting a kind of dreamlike state which takes us out of our time and also out of our community, and thereby fails to enhance the important perfectionist quality of friendship and instead violently subordinates the unruliness of eros and passionate desire to a stifling order. In response to these concerns, I emphasize that the perfectionist practice of aversive thinking is a return to one's previously rejected thoughts.[54] It is a reflective engaging practice in which the mind is *never* still. Thus, the time spent dreaming need not, and perhaps cannot, be neatly separated from our waking activities. Indeed, Emerson notes that our idle times[55] and our dreams[56] can often be more fruitful for perfectionism than time spent in other activities. Consequently, with respect to Dienstag's claim that our minds do not wander in the cinema, I can only claim from personal experience that this is not the case. Often the escape of the cinema provides a space away from the frantic hustle and bustle of daily life, where, whilst our bodies unwind and our buzzing minds start to slow, the deeper levels of

53 Stanley Cavell, *The World Viewed: Reflections on the Ontology of Film* (Cambridge, MA: Harvard University Press, 1979) p. 11.

54 Cavell, *Conditions Handsome and Unhandsome*, pp. 54 and 59.

55 Emerson, "Experience," p. 351.

56 Emerson, "Nature," p. 218.

our unconscious can also unfold to reflect upon our own interpretation of the events we see unfolding before us. Indeed, there is little chance in ordinary life today, beyond time spent in front of a screen, that allows time for such deep and reflective thought; yet, for the aversive way of life, time to think is clearly essential. In this sense leisure-time is necessary for aversive democracy and watching films is one of many forms of leisure activity that provide space for this. Accordingly, I wish to suggest that dreaming need not be quite as separate from democracy as Dienstag professes it to be.

However, Dienstag is also worried that such solitary leisure-time takes us away from our wider commitments to society and community-spiritedness. Yet, with regard to the solitude that we may encounter whilst in the cinema, it would seem that this can provide valuable space for somebody to develop their aversive thought, for "in the solitude to which every man is always returning, he has a sanity and revelations, which in his passage into new worlds he will carry with him."[57] Hence, this activity should not be seen in competition with our commitment to society, for the physical time-out that it provides may re-energize us, give us time to think things through and therefore make us better citizens when we leave the cinema and re-enter the social world.

Furthermore, in the model of exemplarity that we find in Cavell, such solitude in the company only of exemplars need not take us into ourselves, but instead encourage us to be more than we are. Cavell contends that the exemplary films he writes about encourage us to have deeper, more responsive, relationships. Indeed, when watching films we get to see the perspective of others whose lives we can never share. We are made aware of other lives beyond our knowledge and understanding by these stories that take us beyond the confines of our own. Although it is true that we could well settle for the belief that we have experienced others' lives because we have watched a film about them which could limit our sensitivity to the concerns of others, such an

[57] Emerson, "Experience," p. 374.

assumption does not fit with Cavellian perfectionism. This is made clear from Cavell's engagement with Rawls' *Theory of Justice*,[58] in which Cavell notes that the perfectionist life is never "above reproach": one can never sit back and assume that one's democratic duty of responsiveness to others is fulfilled. Instead it requires that we see this responsiveness as an open-ended and never completed task.[59]

In this vein, although Dienstag is concerned that perfectionism stretches friendship beyond the possible, this does not mean that using friendship as an analogy for citizenship is a bad idea, for although it may be something we can never fully live up to, it does express the depth of the relationship that Cavellian perfectionism asks of democratic citizens, setting up such friendship as a valuable ideal to seek to attain, if only ever in part. Furthermore, if there is a possibility that access to cinema can be detrimental to our community-spiritedness, but films are simultaneously a valuable tool for democracy, then perhaps we need to ask more of ourselves and seek to be as friendly as the villagers that Dienstag encountered on the cycling holiday of his youth, whilst also having access to cinema.

Finally, then, to respond to Dienstag's concerns about eros and unruliness, it is helpful to begin by turning to his discussion of *La Règle du jeu*, which, he argues, is a "better, more honest teacher of social reality" (p. 49) than *The Philadelphia Story*. In his interpretation, this film reveals to us what happens when we try to control eros by subjecting it to a stable institution, in this case the institution of marriage: it leads to violence, anger, frustration and the final subdued scene of the Marquise, forced back to her husband's side with no hope of future escape. This leads him to suggest that the desire to control eros in any social institution, including democracy, can be dangerous, for it leads to suppression of people's spirit rather than the happiness called for by Cavell.

[58] Cavell, *Conditions Handsome and Unhandsome*, ch. 2.

[59] See also Clare Woodford, "From Nora to the BNP: Implications of Cavell's Critique of Rawls," *British Journal of Politics and International Relations*, 15:4 (2013): pp. 586–609.

However, this is not the only interpretation of this film. It could alternatively show us the confusion of a woman so restricted by her own willingness to submit to social rules, despite her lonely marriage and confused feelings. Shocked awake by her husband's infidelity, she tries to rebel against the social order by throwing herself at anyone to find comfort and simultaneously settle the score with him; first setting her sights on her preferred accomplice (St. Aubin), whom, she confesses to her maid, she rather likes; when that fails, in panic she first takes advantage of André, who would do anything for her (although she thought he was boring), and then Octave, whom she knew cared deeply for her as they had been friends for so long. This film made me reflect on possible responses to betrayal. It indicated that any attempt at further manipulation and deceit can spin drastically out of control with disastrous consequences. It seemed to imply that it can be worth working at your relationship from the inside, rather than seeking to abandon it in the face of trouble. Consequently, for me, the principal difference between the two films was that, in *The Philadelphia Story*, the characters, especially the principal pair, communicate and learn together, whereas, in *La Règle du jeu*, the principal characters do not seem to think they have anything to learn, and certainly not to learn *together*, and thus play out their charade by destroying the lives of others around them. Hence, contrary to Dienstag, I would not argue that either film is "a better, more honest teacher of social reality," nor, in light of the above argument about imitation and inspiration, that either film is a more fruitful source of inspiration, for, as these counterinterpretations show, they will speak to people of different things in different ways.

However, I share my interpretation for a further reason, as Dienstag argued that film in general seeks to subdue eros with stability, to subordinate the democracy of moments to the republic of laws. It can portray this trade-off as inconsequential or costly, but will do so at its own risk. However, in my reading, film will only reflect the dance between eros and stability that underlies all of our social lives, yet it also reveals that there are various different ways to cope with this potentially antagonistic relationship: engage with it or ignore it (at your peril).[60] In contrast, Dienstag suggests that, by giving eros free reign, we may be able to avoid the symbolic and often actual violence that emerges from the forced and cruel imposition of social order: "Perhaps there would be no families and no nations if eros were given free reign, but then perhaps there would be no Verduns and no Shoahs either" (p. 50). But, whilst admiring the sentiment behind this claim, I feel that it is to miss the symbiotic relationship between the two: we could not have the enjoyment of the disorder that eros brings if we did not know the sometimes stifling extent of a stable order, nor could we ever hanker after such stability if we had not experienced the confused exhaustion and insecurity of eros. Indeed, if eros were given free reign, what is to say that it would not become mundane and we would lose on all fronts. Instead, there is no easy way out of the conundrum. We have to learn to manage the relationship between the two and still avoid the violence that comes with either when pushed to extremes. We cannot avoid the need to work at our relationships, and it is here that I would suggest moral perfectionism can guide our way.

Returning Cavell to Emerson via Rancière helps us to reveal moral perfectionism as a compass to chart the path between eros and stability without stumbling too much toward either extreme. In each life the struggle between eros and stability is different. Furthermore, it is important to emphasize that the burdens and price one will pay to pursue this happiness and to live the perfectionist life will vary depending on one's material position and psychological disposition in a way that is often far from just, and in many cases requires urgent attention and action in the name of a responsive perfectionist citizenship. But this

[60] The reasons why *La Règle du jeu* "nearly instigated an armed revolt" are, for me, more likely tied up in the context of wartime France in 1938, where the protagonists are unpatriotically seen to represent desperate European countries, all leaping in and out of bed with one another in last-ditch attempt to avoid calamity. In the end, calamity strikes (André is killed) but the target (Marceau) is not hit; instead a more innocent victim (André) suffers, whilst the privileged instigators of the situation get off scot-free and survive to cause more disagreements in the future. Not a wonderfully patriotic picture to comfort a nation on the brink of war.

is not to say that a flight of fancy, daydream or moment of realization whilst watching a film will not be of use in helping us imagine better worlds – in order to inspire us to work for them – where the obstacles to the pursuit of happiness are not so unequal.

Conclusion

At first, perhaps, it would appear that I do not agree with Dienstag. I do not think that instead of disappearing into the nearest multiplex to watch remarriage comedies, tragedies or other films we would necessarily always do better to envisage ourselves engaged in an open-ended citizenship quest that keeps our focus on the world around us rather than distracting us with "pretty stories," (p. 81). However, this is not because I think that Dienstag is wrong, merely that I think the terms of the debate needed to be clarified, for I do not believe we can separate the first activity so clearly from the second, nor that these stories can ever be *just* a distraction in the sense that they *prevent* us from thinking for ourselves. Instead, I think that time spent in the cinema can be of value to democracies in that it may, as may other leisure pursuits, help us to slow our thoughts and engage with our democracies more deeply by giving us time to pause and reflect on our own views, and perhaps become more emancipated citizens in the process.

It has, therefore, been suggested that the difference between Dienstag's and Cavell's readings come about in part because of the fact that neither distinguishes clearly between the imitative and the inspirational models of exemplarity, to emphasize that it is the latter that may be more beneficial for democracy whilst the former can be detrimental. This means that the differences in their readings of film are then *compounded* by Dienstag's more cynical outlook in contrast with Cavell's insistent commitment to happiness despite the way that our "obligations and compromises of adulthood begin to obscure the promise and dreams of youth and the rift between public demands and private demands comes to seem unbridgeable."[61] But, this is to be celebrated rather than bemoaned for, in questioning Cavell's unstinting commitment to happiness, the limits, burdens and responsibilities of moral perfectionism are revealed and laid open to scrutiny and assessment, which help to clarify what it can offer our democracies today. Thus I am able to suggest that by choosing the aversive path, but with a more precise understanding of the role of exemplarity within this, we may begin to address the disadvantages and inequality of burdens in the deep and ever more responsive way that perfectionist democratic life entails. And so, taking moral perfectionism as our compass and pausing to dream as we travel, I hope we can embark on Dienstag's quest, navigating our way between eros and stability, in pursuit of the happiness that is the promise of an emancipated perfectionist democracy.

[61] Cavell, *Cavell on Film*, p. 11.

3

The phenomenology of the political: a reply from Saturday Night to Mr. Dienstag

Tracy B. Strong

> τὸ μέντοι κεφάλαιον, ἔφη, προσαναγκάζειν τὸν Σωκράτη ὁμολογεῖν αὐτοὺς τοῦ αὐτοῦ ἀνδρὸς εἶναι κωμῳδίαν καὶ τραγῳδίαν ἐπίστασθαι ποιεῖν, καὶ τὸν τέχνῃ τραγῳδοποιὸν ὄντα καὶ κωμῳδοποιὸν εἶναι.
>
> But the substance of it was, he said, that Socrates was driving them to the admission that the same man could have the knowledge required for writing comedy and tragedy – that the fully skilled tragedian could be a comedian as well.
>
> Plato, *Symposium*, 233D

I confess, my dear friend, that I am unable to find the appropriate disguise in which to respond to you. That of, shall I say, "Monsieur"? No, "Mr.," for he writes in his native tongue. That of *Mr.* Cavell himself is too seductive, and too dangerous: one false word and the whole matter implodes. And that of your erstwhile friend and editor to whom the quasi-eponymous you addressed a famous letter is also just slightly discordant. Indeed, M. d'Alembert seems to hold a position such as that which you think Mr. Cavell is advocating when he says, responding to your quasi-eponymous predecessor's letter: "According to you, when one goes to a spectacle, one goes forgetting those to whom one is close, one isolates oneself from one's fellow citizens and one's friends. On the contrary, a spectacle is of all our pleasures that which calls us the most to others; it does so by the image that it gives us of human life, by the impressions it makes on us and that stay with us."[1] There may be some truth to this,[2] but the problem with any association of this particular judgment with that of Mr. Cavell is that M. d'Alembert also thinks that "all music that depicts nothing is only noise"[3] and places music in "the last place in the order of imitation"[4]; whereas, as voice, Mr. Cavell thinks music does not represent and places music highest of the human arts, perhaps ironically, for I note that so does M. Rousseau, whose voice you have assumed. The question of voice and music will return.

Let me rehearse, therefore, what Mr. Cavell thinks the place of film in our lives should or can be. His first claim is that there are films the viewing of which can or should be thought of as part of an education. Here "education" has resonance to the German *Bildung*, a formation of self and character. His second claim is that those films that can be thought of as part of an education are precisely those films that can stand up and respond to as rigorous a criticism as anyone is able to bring to them.[5] Note that not just anything will count as a criticism, one must make available something that is there and was not available before. Note also that it does not in some sense matter if those who "made" the film had explicit conscious intentions to include all that

1 Jean d'Alembert, *Lettre de d'Alembert à M. J.-J. Rousseau sur l'article "Genève,"* from *l'Encyclopédie*, vol. 7. Online at: http://fr.wikisource.org/wiki/Lettre_de_d%E2%80%99Alembert_%C3%A0_M._J.-J._Rousseau_sur_l%E2%80%99article_Gen%C3%A8ve (accessed January 19, 2016): "On va, selon vous, s'isoler au spectacle, on y va oublier ses proches, ses concitoyens et ses amis. Le spectacle est au contraire celui de tous nos plaisirs qui nous rappelle le plus aux autres hommes, par l'image qu'il nous présente de la vie humaine, et par les impressions qu'il nous donne et qu'il nous laisse."

2 C.f. Guy Debord, *Society of the Spectacle* (New York: Zone, 1995); Jean Baudrillard, *Simulacra and Simulation* (Ann Arbor, MI: University of Michigan Press, 1995).

3 Jean d'Alembert, *Discours préliminaire de "l'Encyclopédie."* Online at: http://fr.wikisource.org/Discours_pr%, p. 17.

4 D'Alembert, *Discours préliminaire*. See my "Music, the Passions and Political Freedom in Rousseau," in Stanley Hoffmann and Christie McDonald, eds., *Rousseau and Freedom* (Cambridge: Cambridge University Press, 2010); see also "Rousseau: Music, Language and Politics," in Keith Chapin and Andrew Clark, eds., *Speaking of Music* (New York: Fordham University Press, 2013), pp. 86–100.

5 Stanley Cavell, "The Good of Film," *Cavell on Film*, edited by William Rothman (Albany, NY: State University of New York Press, 2005).

criticism can reveal. Whatever the intentions of the film are, they are in the film itself and one need not search outside it.[6]

A third claim is that film functions in our contemporary lives much in the manner that opera functioned in the nineteenth century.[7] There were, even in America, opera houses or performances in most towns of even a middling size.[8] Literally hundreds of operas were written and produced, most of them now forgotten, much in the way that most films have been forgotten. Attendance was regular and high.[9] I doubt that you have ever heard/seen *Emilia di Liverpool*, an opera that Donizetti cranked out in 1828, one of the *seventy* he wrote in under thirty years, roughly the rate at which a director might turn out B-movies. There are, however, great films, just as there are great operas. How did/does opera function? What is it about music and voice?

Mr. Cavell's last claim – one we have known since Plato – is that the interplay between the "personal" and the "political" is such that they cast light on each other and show what possibilities for each – at first unrealized – exist in that interaction. Film can thus be a key conveyor of both the individual and political perfectionism that Cavell finds at the center of his thought. Here the model is already found in Milton:

> He who marries, *intends as little to conspire his own ruin, as he that swears Allegiance: and as a whole People is in proportion to an* ill Government, so is one Man to an ill Marriage. If they, against any Authority, Covenant, or Statute, may by the sovereign Edict of Charity, save not only their Lives, but honest Liberties from unworthy Bondage, as well may he against any private Covenant, which he never enter'd

6 This position Cavell holds from his earliest writing. See his analysis of *La Strada* in "A Matter of Meaning It," in *Must We Mean What We Say?: A Book of Essays* (New York: Scribners, 1972), pp. 230–6.

7 See Stanley Cavell, *A Pitch for Philosophy* (Cambridge, MA: Harvard University Press, 1994), p. 136.

8 See John Dizikes, *Opera in America: A Cultural History* (New Haven, CT: Yale University Press, 1995).

9 And it continues. There are at present approximately 125 professional opera companies in America; annual admissions are estimated at 20 million (about the number that attend NFL games). See Jonathan Leaf, "America's Opera Boom," *The American* (July 20, 2007). Online at: www.aei.org/publication/americas-opera-boom (accessed January 20, 2016).

> to his mischief, redeem himself from unsupportable Disturbances to honest Peace, and just Contentment: (Address to the Parliament).
>
> From which words so plain, less cannot be concluded, nor is by any learned Interpreter, than that in God's intention a *meet and happy Conversation* is the chiefest and the noblest end of Marriage: for we find here no Expression so necessarily implying carnal Knowledge, as this prevention of Loneliness to the mind and spirit of Man. (I, 2)[10]

I have italicized the words that are of note here. I know you resist this conversation of public and private. The first paragraph legitimates the possibility and necessity of divorce on a model drawn explicitly from the political, and of the political as modeled on a true marriage. The second suggests that a true marriage, and therefore politics, is that of a conversation. The question has to be how these elements are related to each other in film and what the relation of the film is to those who view it. The "remarriage comedies" to which Mr. Cavell draws our attention, and the intention of which you wish to contest, are thus presentations of the achievement of a "meet and happy" marriage. They show us perfected marriage, not in the sense of the best of the best, but in the sense of having become more of a true marriage. There is no Platonic *agathon* here.

Perfectionism, it should immediately be said, thus does not hold that we are ever to move higher to the single best self or solution, nor recover a lost "true" self. Rather, perfectionism thinks that we can learn – only a piece at a time – that what a transformation would make of us is a bit more of what it is ours to be. Mr. Cavell calls this "philosophy" or "the education of grown-ups."[11] These films are thus about adults growing

[10] These citations from John Milton, *The Doctrine and Discipline of Divorce: Restor'd to the Good of Both Sexes, From the Bondage of Canon Law* (1643, 1644). Online at: www.dartmouth.edu/~milton/reading_room/ddd/book_1/index.shtml (accessed January 19, 2016). Is it worth noting that Milton's wife, Mary Powell, left him shortly after their marriage? He had, however, been thinking about divorce before his marriage. See James H. Hanford, "The Chronology of Milton's Private Studies," *PMLA*, 36 (1921): pp. 268–9, 272–4.

[11] Stanley Cavell, "Philosophy as the Education of Grownups," in Naoko Saito and Paul Standish, eds., *Stanley Cavell and the Education of Grownups* (New York: Fordham University Press, 2012), pp. 19–32.

up, with the implication that most of us are most of the time not grown up and have to learn to be such. As Mr. Cavell writes in his book on *Walden*, "For the child to grow he requires family and familiarity, but for a grownup to grow he requires strangeness and transformation, i.e., birth."[12] Rousseau himself had already said in his *Emile* that "We are born twice, once to exist and a second time to live."

I think the next thing to say here is that these films do *not* show us what we *should* do. Contrary, I think, my dear sir, to what you seem to believe, film is not and cannot (nor should not) be in the business of portraying moral or political truths as an imperative. Film, rather, "shows what showing the truth is."[13] In this sense, I find that you mislead us when you assume that Mr. Cavell thinks that it is the role of film to teach us lessons. Rather, films can prepare us by making evident a possibility. After all, he writes:

> [I]f these films are studies in perfectionism, then we have a small laboratory for studying moral conversation not as the attempt to persuade someone to a course of action, or as the evaluation of a social institution, but of something I think of sometimes as prior and preparatory to these familiar goals of moral reasoning, sometimes as subsequent and supplementary, namely the responsiveness and examination of one soul by another.[14]

Before exploring what this entails, a certain amount of ground clearing is necessary. Clearly, you exaggerate when you assert that there is a danger when good young American citizens (although I do hope there are as many such as you assume) "dash off to the multiplex" in the hope of "rendering a service to their country and nearly to humankind." Mr. Cavell speaks not of all films (think of all those forgotten operas!), but

[12] Stanley Cavell, *The Senses of Walden* (Cambridge, MA: Harvard University Press, 1979), p. 60.

[13] Jean-Luc Nancy, "La règle du jeu dans *La Règle du jeu*," in Antoine de Baecque and Christian Delage, eds., *De l'histoire au cinéma* (Paris: Complexe, 1998), p. 148. I owe this reference to Keith Reader, *La Règle du jeu* (London: I. B. Tauris, 2010). The rest of the citation says that cinema is a "performance of truth" and does not "show truth as theater does." "Performance" seems wrong to me.

[14] Cavell, *Cavell on Film*, p. 339.

only of those the viewing of which may be thought to be or to become part of an education; Mr. Cavell does not urge that we render a service to our country, but that we call it (and ourselves) to itself, to its promise. It is not like climbing a mountain, but more like marking and pursuing one's path in a woods. And it is not about "one's country," but about America, at least *The Philadelphia Story* is, as are the other "comedies of remarriage." If you do not start from the recognition that America can break your (and Mr. Cavell's) heart – and that it comes and has come close to doing so – you will never grasp the political immediacy of his work. These words were written in 1970:

> It has gone on for a long time, it is maddened now, the love it has had it has squandered too often, its young no longer naturally feel it; its past is in its streets, ungrateful for the fact that a hundred years ago it tore itself apart in order not to be divided; half of it believes the war it is now fighting is taking place twenty-five years ago, when it was still young and it was right that it was opposing tyranny … Yet what needs doing, could he [the American] see his and the world's true need, he could do, no one else is so capable of it or so ready for it. He *could*. It's a free country. But it will take a change of consciousness. So phenomenology becomes politics.[15]

When reading Cavell – on anything and also on film – I come away with the strong sense of the degree of his disappointment and/or distress with his country. But, to be disappointed, one has to have an idea of what the country (or a marriage) could be. The model from Milton is that of a conversation. Thus, Mr. Cavell's disappointment comes from the fact that it's (our) speaking – the words that our citizens use to talk with one another, to talk about themselves, to talk about their country – "keep becoming unintelligible, to it and for it."[16] (Surely you share the sense that recent episodes in American political life exemplify this,

[15] Cavell, *Must We Mean What We Say?*, pp. 345–6. There is more where this comes from. See Anne Mahon, *The Ironist and the Romantic: Reading Richard Rorty and Stanley Cavell* (London: Bloomsbury, 2014), pp. 52–5.

[16] Cavell, "Philosophy as Education," p. 212.

in spades?) It is thus centrally important in *The Philadelphia Story* that again and again the same words are reconceived and their truer meaning (for that context) appears. The morning after the episode with the drinking, the swim, and Tracy's return to her bedroom carried by Mike, George remonstrates with his fiancée. She replies to him in apparent agreement that a man "wants his fiancée to behave. Naturally." Dexter corrects or rephrases this as "wants his fiancée to behave naturally." The removal of the full stop turns Tracy's partial acquiescence to George and his conventional standards into a critique of George and a reminder to Tracy that she is, one might say, facing the wrong way, that she is not behaving according to her nature (a nature about which she has needed to be educated, and not one to which she can be recalled). Or, again during the exchange with George about Tracy's behavior the previous night with Mike, George says to Tracy that her "attitude is a little difficult to understand." Dexter interjects: "Not necessarily." George snaps back: "You keep out of this." Dexter: "You forget. I am out of it." That is, it should be obvious to *anyone* who has eyes and ears (which George manifestly does not) that her attitude is *not* difficult to understand. Or, again, Mike tells the story of depositing Tracy on her bed and returning to George and Dexter, "as you will doubtless remember." To which Dexter says, "Doubtless without a doubt," thereby giving confirmation and reality to the episode, such that it sets up the exchange between Tracy and George that will lead to their breakup.

It is significant that Dexter is generally the character who reformulates words so that they acquire meaning in terms of the plot of the film. The Dexter role is in fact an amalgamation of two roles from the play: Sandy, Tracy's brother (who sets up the relation with Kidd and *Spy* magazine) who does not exist in the film, and Dexter himself. The whole set of events then can be seen as having been hoped for by Dexter; he does not make it happen but he knows or senses that Tracy can be something other than a "goddess." The elimination of Sandy is important for it means the film is about the relation between (potential) husband(s) and wife. Dexter does not transform her – she must do that – but he does make possible the circumstances in which she may be able to transform herself. This is what we *see* and why the film does not instruct us; it is not didactic. It *shows* us a world in which transformation is possible. As Rousseau says, it "persuades without convincing." When Dexter does try to instruct her (as in the "virgin goddess" speech), the effect is to put an end to all possibility of conversation ("Stop using those foul words," says Tracy). He must, I might say, show her (and thus us) her (actual) self.

Such showing is at the root of what distresses you. The core of your distress with Mr. Cavell comes from your distress about the role of the erotic in the political realm. You write: "The mobility [do you mean "motility"?] of eros is incompatible with the political need for institutional stasis" (p. 78). Stasis, I note, has two meanings: it refers in contemporary English to an equilibrium, but for the Greeks it referred to an ongoing struggle between two opposed and competing forces. You mean, I think, equilibrium. (I shall return to this question.) And you pleasantly seek to undercut my anticipated response here with a reference to a book in which I have addressed the question of the erotic in relation to Rousseau. It seems to me that your conclusion rests on the belief that the erotic is the fundament of marriage, something I would argue that Rousseau did not accept, whatever his worries about the relation of the erotic to the political: "Marriage," you say, "is a stable (or unstable) institution of eros." Yet Milton tells us:

> Marriage is not a meer carnal Coition, but a *human Society*: where that cannot reasonably be had, there can be no true Matrimony. (I, 13)

It would seem that for Milton the erotic is not sufficient to make a marriage and certainly not its foundation. What makes a marriage? What impediments keep a marriage from being a marriage? What is to be done about these impediments? Perhaps it is this:

> Let me not to the marriage of true minds
> Admit impediments. Love is not love
> Which alters when it alteration finds.
>
> Shakespeare, Sonnet 116

Shakespeare tells us that a true marriage will triumph over whatever impediments anyone might propose. The morning after the scene where Mike brings Tracy back from the pool in his arms and puts her in her bed, Dinah, who had seen the whole thing, purports to relate the episode in a dream and, with reference to Mike carrying Tracy back in his arms and in her bathrobe, says to Tracy (in ministerial tones), hoping to *prevent* her marriage to George: "If anyone knows any just cause why these two should not be united in holy matrimony …" Dinah functions as a kind of chorus. She knows, as do we in the audience, that George is not a "true mind" for Tracy (at least from when he says that he wants to "put [her] on a pedestal and worship" her) and we sense that Tracy can become such. (Her last words as she goes in to marry Dexter acknowledge her leaving of her father and the hopes he had expressed for her: "I feel … like… a human being" – no longer a would-be goddess, this is her transformation achieved). Thus, there *are* impediments to the marriage of George and Tracy: they are consequent to the fact that they are not "true minds." The effect of Dinah's question is to make possible Tracy's marriage to Mike and/or to Dexter, despite what might appear as impediments. The remarriage to Dexter is now one of two true minds and all the impediments the film has made manifest to us matter naught. But, as we shall see, confronting those impediments is important.

You are the author of a book on, and with the title of, *Pessimism*. I admire it: I have a blurb endorsing it on the back cover. Your intention is to show the political importance of pessimism for what one might see as the chastening of the claims of the political realm. It is clear from your insightful comparison of *The Philadelphia Story* with *The Rules of the Game* that you find the characters in the French film "more poignant and more instructive [in their failures] than the successes of their Main Line [i.e., *The Philadelphia Story*] counterparts." You applaud what you see as the pessimism of the French film. Yet, what is this pessimism? The *Rules of the Game* is not precisely a tragedy. As all commentators note, it is modeled on eighteenth- and nineteenth-century French comedy – and, indeed, the opening tune over the credits is from Mozart's *The Marriage of Figaro*, itself an adaptation from Beaumarchais' play, referring us to comic opera. The film starts as a comedy[17] and moves *toward* a tragedy. Wondrously, during the chaos of the theatrical show and the overlapping attack by Schumacher on Marceau, the Marquis turns to the imperturb-able majordomo (appropriately named "Corneille," the paradigm of the conventions of French theater) and orders him to "Put an end to this comedy." He replies "Which one, Monsieur le marquis?"[18] With explicit irony, the story is *prevented* from becoming a tragedy publically to, that is, those in the film as the Marquis de la Chesnaye[19] addresses the assembly as an audience from the steps of the chateau giving out the pretense that the death of Jurieux was a "deplorable accident" (the gamekeeper is said by la Chesnaye, quite untruthfully, to have thought Jurieux was a poacher and to have shot him *comme c'était son droit*; the General then opines that with this prevarication the Marquis has demonstrated "class"), a pretense that only underlines the tenuousness of the conventions that were barely keeping bourgeois society possible.[20] Note, though, that the Marquis has defended the necessity of violence and in his pretense has taken over the position that Schumacher had earlier espoused ("During the war I shot fellows who had done less than he has," or, as he says to his wife Lisette, "A shot in the dark, in the woods, and no questions asked").[21] Four months after the release of the film the world would explode into flames, but the director of this comedy could foresee disaster without making his film a tragedy. La Chesnaye's words save the situation as it is and they are the wrong words; the conventions are retained, nothing is changed, and

17 Renoir has said that he started off wanting simply to adapt Alfred de Musset's *Les caprices de Marianne*. Traces of Marivaux, Molière and Beaumarchais also appear in the script.

18 *Comédie* in French means any theatrical performance.

19 In the cast list in the film his name is given as "La Cheyniest." The above spelling has become standard, apparently.

20 There is a double identity mix-up which is the stuff of comedy, as is the exchange of clothing and so forth: Octave is planning to run off with Christine; her maid Lisette has given her cloak to Christine; Lisette convinces Octave not to run off with Christine; Octave gives his coat to Jurieux when he urges him to go and run away with Christine; Schumacher thinks that Octave is planning to run off with Lisette (given the cloaks) and shoots Jurieux (thinking him to be Octave), who has in fact come, on Octave's urging, to run off with Christine. It could be Plautus except that people die.

21 Schumacher is Alsatian, hence born as a German, as Alsace was annexed by Germany in 1871 and France only recovered it in 1918. The French pronounce his name SchoomaCHAIRE; the Austrian Christine pronounces it SchuMAKerr.

that means that this comedy calls up the immanent *possibility* of tragedy. There are lessons to be learned from comedies, as there are (other?) lessons to be learned from tragedies. The lesson from this film is what is learned when the film fails (purposively) to be either. *The Philadelphia Story* would be a tragedy if Tracy and Dexter did not come to acknowledge the fact that they are in actuality still married to each other and that what is necessary is for them now to say the right words in the right place. They do and it is a comedy.[22]

So you do not think that film can be "instructive." Certainly, you might seem to be wrong about some films: *Dead Man Walking* tells us that capital punishment is bad; *Gandhi* tells us that civil disobedience can be a good thing. But, you are right in the sense that these films give us none of the sense of complexity that we know is the actual stuff of moral and political decisions and situations. So, what do we learn from films like *The Philadelphia Story* or your excellent counterexample *The Rules of the Game*? What are the lessons and are they different?

Both films raise the question of our relation to rules and conventions. The Renoir film is more properly titled "The Rule of the Game"; the plural is an Anglophone addition. *The "rule of the game" is that there are rules: the question is what our relation to them is or should be.* In *The Philadelphia Story*, I believe the only explicit reference to rules comes, again, at the confrontation after the night at the pool. Mike indicates that he simply put Tracy in her bed and left. Tracy, somewhat miffed, asks why, was she not attractive? Mike responds that she was indeed very attractive but notes that she was, however, "somewhat the worse … for wine" and that "there are rules about that." Tracy acquiesces: "Thank you, Mike. I think men are wonderful." After Dexter's and Tracy's discussion about the events with Mike, Dexter responds to Tracy's assertion that "I don't know anything anymore" with: "That sounds very hopeful."[23] Rule(s) is here the social

[22] See here Stanley Cavell, "Moral Reasoning," in *Cavell on Film*, p. 355.

[23] The exchange is more extended in the play, but amounts to the same. In the play, Dexter says: "occasional misdeeds are often as good for a person as – as the moral virtues," and finds that the event with Mike may signal her "coming of age." Philip Barry, *The Philadelphia Story: A Comedy in Three Acts* (New York: Samuel French, 1969), pp. 108–9. See Liz's comments just after.

conventions *that can only be properly reasserted as our own after having been broken*. Rules are broken all the time in this film: Dexter as the divorced husband should not be at the wedding with George; Tracy's father should be there to give away the bride-to-be and not exiled by Tracy; the uncle is a lech; the father *is* a philanderer; and so on. As Liz says at one point: "We all go haywire at times and if we don't maybe we ought to."

The matter is different and darker in the Renoir film. Those who adhere to "the rule" are the gamekeeper Schumacher, who turns to violence; La Chesnaye, who keeps to social rules and finds fulfillment in mechanical toys[24] (the greatest of which is destroyed by Schumacher's shooting at Marceau), and, as noted, Jurieux, whose insistence on explaining to La Chesnaye that he is going to depart with his wife ("there are rules") leads to his being shot by Schumacher. In fact, despite multiple attempts or desires to, social conventions are *not* ever broken in this film, and the point of the film is to make it clear that *they should have been*. (Octave only does not run away with Christine after Lisette, the maid, insists on social conventions by pointing out that "Madame needs things" and that Octave is too poor to be able to provide them, at which point he sees himself in a mirror and acquiesces.) The preservation (not refounding) of the existing social order has required the sacrifice of Jurieux and the departure of the two characters (Octave and Marceau), who were not part of that order.[25] For the others, social conventions persist. When Julie is collapsing after the shooting of Jurieux, Lisette tells her to hold herself together as she is "an educated person" and Christine warns her that "people are looking at you." The Marquis's marriage is saved, but he has not remarried; as he ushers his wife into the house at the end, they do not embrace; Schumacher and his rifle are restored to the role as keeper of order. Nothing has been made anew. This society rests on violence.

[24] Renoir said that the shot of La Chesnaye presenting his great harmonium took thirty takes and called it the best scene he ever filmed.

[25] It is no accident that for the theatricals Octave chooses to be a bear; Marceau is a poacher, by definition not part of, even if living off, social convention.

It turns out, then, that personal growth and the avoidance of violence, disaster and conventionality is only possible by a breaking of the rules and a revitalization of those rules after their infringement, as if their true worth needed to be made apparent. At stake between us here is precisely what to make of your requirements for "political and institutional stasis." I think that you have a sense of the tenuousness of rules (as the end of *The Rules of the Game* makes clear), but that you think, like Burke or Bagehot, that precisely because of that tenuousness it is important that their fragility not be exposed. Yet the point made in *both* films is that the rules cannot straitjacket behavior: only after they are or could have been broken can they be truly reasserted as one's *own* rule. (If you hear an echo here of Kantian autonomy and his urging that one take one's *eigenes Weg*, you are not mistaken.) Moreover, rules are broken in *The Philadelphia Story, but not* in *The Rules of the Game*. What we learn from the French film is that these rules *should have been* broken. Furthermore, when the polity is in trouble – as are the relations in each of these films – then the rules that govern it must be challenged if they are to be reinvigorated. Civil disobedience breaks existing rules in order that they be reformulated as rules that are truly our own. You tend to speak as if each of these films (or at least the American one) confronted a predetermined and continuing situation rather than one that wanted to be corrected or perfected. (Thus, toward the very beginning of *The Philadelphia Story*, a key to the possibility of change comes when Dinah wants to see Dexter and says so in the middle of a conversation about Tracy's scheduled marriage to George.)

Your second major claim is thus, that film "exposes us in safety to the danger we inhabit personally and politically." You argue, correctly, that such seeing would be a form of pornography, the pleasure in seeing what we should not see from a position of self-privilege. And here is your Rousseauian point: when viewing a film like *The Philadelphia Story* we are, you hold, on a kind of moral holiday. Your underlying argument is that politics requires what Burke had called a "politic well-wrought veil" that keeps in secret that which is essential to its functioning. Thus film, by allowing us to see "secret" functions, is fundamentally non-, or a-, or anti-political, or rather is dangerous to political stasis. Politically, your two critiques come together in your sense that democracy requires secrecy, that it is founded on that which is not to be in public view. You point out that the debates that gave rise to the Constitution were done behind closed doors and in secret and could not have been exposed to the open.[26] "*The Philadelphia Story* rewards, punishes and amplifies our desire to see what goes on within Independence Hall, our unrequitable desire to see the sources of our own independence (p. 26)." As you continue, you point out that, despite all the films that we have seen, "we have yet to see the benefits of this blanketing of our culture with filmed talk in any improved conversations, marriages or political discourses (p. 28)."

This last sentence seems to me to knock at the wrong door. What do you think books, films, that which is composed, can do? One could of course make your same complaint about your books and mine. But perhaps you hold that films cannot be like Greek drama – a civic and moral education to citizens – and that Mr. Cavell's mistake is to assume that they can. Let us explore this, for there are parallels. The American film relies, as did Greek plays, on stichomythia, alternating lines between two characters. Dinah (who is supposedly fifteen, but plays about a year past puberty[27]) serves as a chorus, mostly commenting on the action rather than participating in it (she wants to join the adults with a cocktail early on and is told "certainly not"). Like a chorus, she does nothing, but does see the whole as it develops and asks questions as matters evolve. There are resonances to Greek or any drama.

However, this is a film and not a play. Nevertheless, the similarities (such as they are) raise the question of the place of theater and of its relation to film. *The Rules of the Game* not only has an extended theatrical episode, but on two occasions explicitly sets up other scenes as in a theater: first when Octave recalls Christine's conductor father, and

[26] For a detailed discussion of this and related matters that goes behind and beyond the closed doors, see Pauline Maier, *Ratification: The People Debate the Constitution, 1787–1788* (New York: Simon & Schuster, 2011).

[27] At one point her mother suggests that something is wrong with the fall of her dress in the back, to which Dinah responds that "it is me."

second when La Chesnaye explains the death of Jurieux. Both scenes taking place on the proscenium of the steps of the house, the first addresses everyone (or no one: that is, the film audience) and the second the cast of the film (minus Octave and Marcel). Similar theatricalized scenes occur in the American film: the first part of *The Philadelphia Story*, for instance, comprises an extended acting out by Tracy and Dinah in "welcoming" Mike and Liz as supposed friends of their cousin, and that is followed by Tracy's requirement that her uncle play the part of the absent philanderer father.

Both of these films, then, recall theater to us. Let me then ask what we learn about our political realm in these films? (I will deal later with the importance of theater as opposed to film in this education.) As a play, *The Philadelphia Story* was purposively set by Philip Barry in what was probably the most class-conscious American city at the time, class-conscious to the degree that Grace Kelly (the daughter of a very rich but Irish Catholic Philadelphia family, in 1956 to play the Tracy role in *High Society*, the Cole Porter musical version of this story,[28] and later the bride of Prince Rainier of Monaco) could not be invited to "come out" in the de rigueur elbow-length white gloves at the Philadelphia Assembly Ball, as were the daughters of the older Protestant families.[29] The character of Tracy Lord

[28] The film was directed by Charles Walters and starred Bing Crosby, Grace Kelly, Frank Sinatra and Louis Armstrong.

[29] See Ian Irving, "The Real Philadelphia Story," *The Sunday Telegraph* (April 16, 1995), p.1: "Philadelphia society then exhibited an extreme type of class-consciousness. The flood of wealth that created American family fortunes in the late 19th century settled around a handful of cities and was expressed in different forms of conspicuous consumption and elaborate social behaviour – as chronicled by Edith Wharton in novels such as *The Age of Innocence*. In dynamic New York and Chicago, Vanderbilts and Astors, Fields and McCormicks vied with each other in glitter and the acquisition of European titles through their marriageable daughters, but mere wealth usually provided a sufficient entree to their society."In more traditional Boston and Philadelphia, however, society turned almost feudal, almost English in its attitudes – 'old' money and 'old' families counted for everything. The very term WASP (White Anglo-Saxon Protestant) was coined to describe members of Philadelphia society – its most characteristic institution was the Philadelphia Assemblies Ball. This is the oldest and most exclusive social gathering in the United States. Held every year since 1748, it is strictly reserved for members of the city's Social Register – no amount of money will allow entry; blood is everything. It was here, down the staircase to the great ballroom of the Bellevue-Stratford Hotel, that Hope Montgomery, in ballgown and elbow-length white kid gloves, made her entrance as a debutante in 1922."

was in fact modeled on Helen Hope Montgomery Scott, a friend of Barry's and a rich socialite of much the same age and breeding as Hepburn. (Scott lived until 1995; the fortune of the extended Hepburn family was estimated at half a billion dollars: her mother was heiress to the Corning Glass fortune.) Class comes up several times in the film. Mike refers to it; Liz fantasizes about trading places with Tracy; most notably, when George realizes that he is being thrown over (and not at that point for anyone in particular), he spits out: "You and your whole rotten class. You're on your way out, the whole lot of you and don't think you aren't." Yet, it is clear in the film, as it is in *The Rules of the Game,* that while class is a reality, it does not, or need not, determine the outcome in the end. (La Chesnaye, though Jewish, is defended by *both* the aristocratic General and the cook.) Differences in the role that class plays derive to a great degree from the differences between Renoir's Popular Front sympathies and the very American recognition that, as Mike says as a discovery, some can come from the lower classes and be a "real heel" while others can come from the upper classes and be all right. This is echoed in the irony of the General announcing at the end that the Marquis "has class." Each setting is itself clearly political and class-conscious. At this first level, the films show us a world in which class exists but is not definitive. As such, the message is perhaps important but not very profound, especially given the American and Popular Front sympathies. What difference does it make that this is cinema?

Films are cinema and not theater. Indeed, Mr. Cavell has said that *The Rules of the Game* may be said "to establish the ascension of cinema over theater."[30] This ascension is due to two qualities. First is the ability of film to see from different angles, not only from the audience but from the wings or, as in the *danse macabre* sequence, from behind the players (thus in comment on the fact that the event is staged for an audience as a theatrical performance). It thus takes us behind the rules and the social conventions that they legitimate. In the theater, on

[30] In a talk to the Harvard Film Association in 2010. See also Cavell, *A Pitch for Philosophy*, p. 137.

the other hand, we only watch from our seats in one direction. At the end of the film, where La Chesnaye addresses the participants from a stage (with only the rifle and person of Schumacher in-between), we see him as a theater audience. The scene is thus a theatrical reassertion of theater and social convention and, in doing so, in fact calls its tenuousness into question. However, when this scene occurs, Octave, played by Renoir himself, is absent, as is Marceau. One may suppose that he has resumed his role as cinema director; the last scene is, thus, an assertion of the fact that the players are caught by and in their roles (except for Octave and Marceau) and so of the conclusive primacy of film over theater.[31]

What, then, is the ascendency of cinema over theater? In *The Rules of the Game* it is, I think, this: when society (the polity) and theater become so intertwined that we risk losing the humanity of the social-political world in its theatricalization (when rules threaten to take over), then cinema can show us that this has happened (is happening) and thus give us a critical view on our world, an estrangement from it. Hence the social world depicted in Renoir's film is in fact a world that cannot manage to escape its own rules: Octave's absence (and implied return behind the camera: in the conducting scene he tells Christine that he wanted to be a conductor) lets us see what is wrong with that.[32] Nietzsche's most sour accusation against Wagner was that he had theatricalized opera.

However, do these thoughts reflect on *The Philadelphia Story*? Here what is important is the role the camera plays in this film. Cameras are important all the way through: in particular, they are resisted. We learn early on that Dexter smashed the cameras of all those who took pictures of his first marriage to Tracy; Tracy hates the idea of having cameras come into the house; various comments are made about Liz's photographing and we have a sense that she is doing something inappropriate as she takes pictures of the wedding gifts. At the end, Sidney Kidd, the editor of *Spy*, appears at the wedding with a camera. His camera

[31] This is my reading of Cavell, "More of *The World Viewed*," in *The World Viewed: Reflections on the Ontology of Film* (Cambridge, MA: Harvard University Press, 1979), pp. 221–3.

[32] If I read him correctly, this is what Cavell is saying (ibid., p. 225).

clicks. We then get a frame or two of the wedding party, with Mike almost so far forward as to make it seem that Tracy might be marrying them both. However, the freeze-frame that comes next (we assume) was taken a slight moment *after* the first, as the wedding party is turning to look at Kidd (Tracy's mouth is open in surprise and distress in the second, but not in the first). The photo, however, recalls for us the fact that film is a set of photographs joined in time. These cameras are not smashed, as this marriage is for real.

This leads us to the second element in the ascendency of film over theater. An immediately subsequent photo of the entire wedding party then turns, as if a page in an album, and we see a photo of Dexter and Tracy kissing, by themselves. The film camera moves to focus in on their still-kissing heads, insisting, as it were, that they are now the only two in the frame. Others were necessary to get there, but this marriage is *theirs*. What have we learned from this movement? The effect of Kidd's appearance, of the click of his camera, and the resultant photo/frame is to distance us from the feeling of a participation in the film that we had before. While viewing the film, we were (almost) there. We look, however, *at* the photos. It thus makes us question what our relation to the film is: Tracy's surprise in the photo is our surprise also. The photo of the kiss shows us that marriage (and its conventions) have been re-established, but now as a real marriage. And, as it is now a real marriage, *we are no longer privileged to look at it*. Here, and only here, is there a danger of your pornography. So the film instructs us in what you think we should never have done at all.

Cameras have been resisted all the way through the film, yet the film ends with camera shots. It is as if what happens on film could only happen if the photograph were kept at bay by the development that the temporality inherent in film makes possible. Yet the photograph reappears and closes the film out, except for a reprise of the drawings of the Philadelphia buildings (which in its fixity perhaps underlies the atemporality of the photograph). Kidd's appearance at the wedding in fact confirms George's earlier judgment: "this wedding is of national importance." *But now it is Dexter who says that line*: now the (re)marriage is truly of such importance, for it is a true marriage. Dexter's use of those words again gives them their true, living meaning, that is, the true (re)marriage between Tracy and Dexter is a model of what could happen in the nation. Conventions have been broken and are now reaffirmed, somewhat transfigured, as *our* conventions. (Perhaps one might think of civil disobedience for civil rights.) Or, to pick up the parallels offered by Milton, one might say that the political model proposed in *The Philadelphia Story* is that of a meet and happy conversation. What the photographs do is to renormalize, reinstitutionalize, the conventions of society, but only after they have been broken: only now are they *our* conventions and not ones we have been caught in (as are the characters of the French film). The slightly annoyed looks on the faces of each in the photograph (and, indeed, the freeze-frame) only serve to confirm this.

It is in and by the conversations that our rules are questioned and made our own. And what, over the course of the film, have those conversations been about? They have explored: 1) the relations of different classes; 2) what it might mean to be a "first-class human being"; 3) the question of luxury and inequality; 4) the importance of the availability of leisure; 5) the importance of class and lack thereof; 6) the question of creativity. All these are in the relation of the players to each other and such matters are precisely the substance of the discussions that took place behind doors in Philadelphia during the Constitutional Convention. We view them and learn from them without, however, our being seen by the characters in the film. It is as if we had a cloak of invisibility at the Philadelphia Convention.

What do we see/have we seen? Tracy is upper class, moneyed, and appears to inhabit a magic kingdom. (They are expecting 500 guests for the reception (not a problem!) and, when the mother worries about rain, Dinah says that Tracy will not permit it to rain; Tracy changed her sister's name from Diana to Dinah, wanting, presumably, to retain for herself the only role as virgin goddess.) She grows such that she can pursue her newly perceived vocation, "to be of use to the world." George is self-made from the lower classes, but his expulsion signifies not the triumph of the upper classes but the rejection of a man who cannot be other than externally defined. A "first-class human being" has qualities that are, in principle, available to all, even if most do not choose to pursue or avoid pursuing that path. (So Nietzsche taught us in *Schopenhauer as Educator*, a judgment with which Mr. Cavell agrees.)[33]

What we learn, or rather what we see, in the film is that transformation by conversation requires a set of circumstances, and that is a political as well as a personal lesson. However, the transformation is something that an individual must do once the circumstances have made it possible. The circumstances do not make it happen. Thus, in the exchange between Tracy and Dexter after she emerges from her room quite hungover, he offers her as a remedy "the juice of a few flowers" to "open her eyes." (Do we hallucinate if we hear here an echo of *A Midsummer Night's Dream*? It, too, ends with weddings.) Dexter helps make the circumstances, but he cannot do it alone. If Dinah does claim (in her chorus role) during the marriage ceremony that she "did it all," we know this to be exaggerated and it is in counterpoint to George accusing Dexter of "having something to do [with the breakup]" and Dexter responding with a line, only in the film script: "Some. But you were a great help." Importantly, George is as necessary to Tracy's education as Dexter and the others. What we have here is something like the model of education in Rousseau's *Emile* – where the Tutor does not instruct but places Emile in a sequence of problematic situations, the finding of the solution to which will help him grow – but the model here is not for children but for grown-ups. For children, conversation follows dealing with the situation; for grown-ups it precedes it or is concomitant with it. One might – I begin to go afield here – think of what happens in the film as examples of what Heidegger calls *Fürsorge*, "solicitude." Dexter marks the moment of successful solicitude as the departure of George by pumping his hands up and down the candles on the table and singing the tune of the waltz "Sobre las Olas –The

33 Stanley Cavell, *Pursuits of Happiness: The Hollywood Comedy of Remarriage* (Cambridge, MA: Harvard University Press, 1981), p. 156.

Loveliest Night of the Year" (you will know it from *Sesame Street* as "George Washington Bridge"). Shortly after he breaks into song, the orchestra starts the classic wedding march from *Lohengrin*. Music carries us to the end.

So, this comedy is not, in my reading, pornographic. What it shows us is how transformation (of a couple, of a nation) requires circumstances that make exchange – conversation – possible. Those circumstances can be helped, but they depend on a combination of actors, not always in concert. And they must be taken advantage of. If this were opera, music would make this transfiguration available, would allow us to experience it. This is film: the camera makes the experience of transfiguration available in that it shows us that the actor could become another character.[34] The movement of film in time is for the viewer the equivalent of the effect of music in opera. So I resist M. d'Alembert's judgments about music.

This transfiguration must, therefore, be understood at a level that lies, as it were, under that of the right and the good and the prudent. It corresponds, one might say, to the achievement of a moral and political consciousness adequate to a "first-class" life; it sets it before us as if to say "look! It is possible." In the end, my friend, it seems to me that you miss the fact that (these) films are not about moral behavior or political stasis: they are about what one has to become *in order to be capable of moral behavior and/or political stasis*. The political lesson from *The Philadelphia Story* is to have shown us that we – as individuals and as our nation – can be more than what we have thought to settle for – that we need not live "lives of quiet desperation" – and, or *but*, that it is up to us to take advantage of the circumstances that would make that possible. I began with Plato and I end by recalling a passage from Pindar (*Pythian Odes* II, 72), three-fourths of which formed Nietzsche's favorite encomium: γένοι' οἷος ἐσσὶ μαθών "(having learned, become who you are)". On Saturday night at the cinema, we can learn such from comedy as well as from tragedy.

[34] Whereas in theater the character can be taken by other actors.

4

The tragedy of remarriage in the Golden Age of television

Margaret Kohn

Joshua Dienstag's "Letter to M. Cavell" makes two arguments. It urges us to reconsider the claim that film is the source of insight into moral complexity and a fertile ground for fostering democratic sensibilities. The essay also shows that film can indeed illuminate the human condition, but it does so when it exposes the tension between eros and social structure, not when it suggests that this tension can be easily overcome. It is tempting to say that film can be democratic as long as it has the disruptive effect of atonal music rather than the soporific effect of jazz, but Dienstag does not take this position. Inspired by Rousseau's *Letter to M. d'Alembert on the Theatre* (*Lettre à M. d'Alembert sur les spectacles*), Dienstag does not comfort and flatter his reader by affirming the view that democratic communities are strengthened when the right kind of people appreciate the right kind of movies. There is no satisfying reconciliation of critique and community, which, quite appropriately, makes his essay more like *The Rule(s) of the Game* than *The Philadelphia Story*.

In this response, I will make a qualified case for the opposite view and suggest that films and even television shows can be texts that encourage reflexivity about moral paradox, political obligation and community. I will do this through a reading of a more recent work in the genre of "the tragedy of remarriage": the television show *The Americans*. *The Americans* is a commercially successful spy drama set in Washington, DC in the early 1980s. It incorporates aspects of high and low culture. It combines the elaborate atmospherics of *Mad Men* with elements of the spy genre, but at its core it is a story about marriage and, to a lesser degree, about politics. First, I will briefly review the key theoretical issues addressed in this collection: whether and how we can learn from film. Next, I will clarify how *The Americans* resembles the other remarriage films and can illuminate the issues they raise. Finally, I will explain what insights we can draw from the show and whether these insights could fortify democracy.

I

In addition to the very explicit debt to Rousseau, "The tragedy of remarriage: letter to M. Cavell about cinema (a remake)" also bears the trace of another influence: Adorno. According to Dienstag, *The Philadelphia Story*, a commercially successful Hollywood film, is also a deeply ideological one. Dexter and Tracy's remarriage reaffirms the possibility of reconciling freedom and social order, *eros* and *nomos*. Its popularity was at least partially due to the appeal of this message. It also affirmed the American fantasy of a hierarchical yet egalitarian society. In *The Philadelphia Story*, after a brief period of misunderstanding, members of different social classes treat each other with affection and respect, while still ultimately choosing to remain within their own class. Renoir's *The Rules of the Game* provides neither the hope of psychic nor social reconciliation, and it is not surprising that it was reviled by audiences. The lesson here is that cinema can be critical, but it cannot be both critical *and* popular. This is one of the reasons why Dienstag concludes that it is not suited to the idealized role of instructing democratic sensibilities. Dienstag's essay raises three related questions: Can film inspire critical reflection on ethics and politics? If so, can these films be popular? And, if they are popular and critical, is there still something about the isolating experience of viewing a spectacle that undermines more appropriate forms of sociability?

The Americans unsettles the opposition between popular/ideological and critical/unpopular film. Initially, it might seem to be an odd example to draw on because it is not a film, nor does it obviously fall into the genre of a "comedy of remarriage." It is, however, a "filmlike" television show and one in which remarriage plays an important part. Attending to the theme of remarriage helps illuminate the central themes of the show. Is the difference between film and television a matter of degree or of kind? The distinction between television and film is introduced in Dienstag's essay in the context of a discussion about temporality. Television is associated with the temporality of the present: live television, reality television, and the simulacra of the live studio audience. He concedes, however, that the difference is not absolute. Films are often viewed on television, and television shows can have "filmlike" qualities. I will leave aside for now the important issue of the difference between viewing a show in the movie theater as opposed to viewing it at home. Dienstag does not explain what he means by "filmlike," but the concept makes intuitive sense and I assume that it describes shows that are designed to command sustained attention and ones that reward such sustained attention. *The Americans* is filmlike in the sense that its visual design, sound design, and plotting all remove it from the temporality of the present and draw the audience into a distinctive world, a world that demands and rewards close attention.

The Americans follows Philip and Elizabeth Jennings, two KGB agents who have lived most of their adult lives undercover as a married couple in the United States. They share a bed and have raised two children together (the oldest is a young teenager), but, while they are more than partners, they are not really a romantic couple. Elizabeth has a lover and admits to Philip that "it [marital love] never really happened for me." Midway during the first season, they separate and Philip moves into his own apartment, but, after a mission goes wrong and Elizabeth is shot and almost killed, she briefly wakes up and speaks to Philip in Russian for the first time. She says "come home." This is the remarriage.

How does this remarriage compare with the classic genre? Dienstag's essay juxtaposes two very different kinds of remarriage. Christine's return to her husband is not a renewal of love but a sign of defeat. Love unconstrained by social rules proves impossible and her return to her husband follows from her reluctant acceptance of this fact. Tracy Lord's remarriage to Dexter is precisely the inverse. Tracy recognizes that neither pure convention (George) nor pure rebellion (Mike) is the foundation for a satisfying marriage; it is possible and necessary to overcome this opposition in order to create something that preserves and transcends them both. The remarriage in *The Americans* is based on neither resignation nor reconciliation, but points to a third possibility.

At first, it might seem unlikely that we could draw lessons about marriage or moral perfectionism from *The Americans*, a show in which beautiful super-spies don disguises, fight villains, seduce informants and then return to their normal suburban home to nag their kids about homework and screen time. The premise seems so pulpy that I am sometimes embarrassed to publicly profess my love for the show. *The Americans* differs from the other remarriage films not only because it draws on the spy genre, but also because family plays a central role. Romantic love and parental love are equally important. Elizabeth's dilemma differs in some other key respects from Tracy's and Christine's. Elizabeth is not torn between three different romantic suitors and the options that she considers represent different ways of living. This is due in part to the moral complexity that is explored in the show. The characters in *The Americans* confront what Cavell calls "moral paradox" and they also wrestle with the tension between obligation and desire. These conflicts, which begin as binaries, become increasingly enmeshed in more complicated webs. The conflict between duty and desire is a familiar one, but increasingly we see how duties conflict with other duties and desires conflict with other desires.

In the first episode of the show, a top KGB officer plans to defect to the United States and Philip and Elizabeth are ordered to prevent this by kidnapping him and exfiltrating him back to Russia. Philip, whose easygoing demeanor has made him feel at home in the United States, tentatively suggests that maybe they should defect too. He enjoys the abundance of American life and his enjoyment has weakened his commitment to Soviet ideology. The dilemma he faces is not between duty and desire, but between two desires, his love for Elizabeth, who seems unwavering in her ideological commitments, and his desire to be free from his responsibilities to Mother Russia.

The show eventually introduces at least six different factors that motivate the central characters: romantic desire, familial love, masculinity, honor, duty and political ideology. I use the term "duty" in the Kantian sense of a universal moral law that prohibits certain conduct regardless of the possible beneficial consequences. These concerns become increasingly important in Season Two when Philip has to kill innocent people in order to ensure the success of a mission that aims to expose US support for paramilitary organizations and the use of torture in Central America. They teach their children never to lie while literally living a lie. "Honor" is the term I use to describe the norms that Hegel grouped under *sittlichkeit* (ethical life), including professional identity and social roles. It is a way of describing the tension that characters experience when their professional obligations conflict with other duties or desires. This tension is explored most clearly through the character of FBI agent Stan Beeman, a skilled agent who eventually faces a choice between his professional obligations and his love for Nina, his informant.

In the two films that Dienstag analyzes, the female protagonists are torn between three romantic possibilities which correspond to different sides of themselves and different positions in the social order. Initially, Elizabeth's affair with Gregory would seem an obvious parallel. He is a radical black activist, who shares her political convictions and adventurous spirit. Like the journalist/writer Connor and the musician Octave, Gregory could symbolize a desire that transgresses the social order. Yet this would be a misreading. Nothing in the show suggests that Elizabeth seriously considers leaving her "husband" Philip or that Gregory is the reason they split up. In order to understand the meaning of remarriage, we must know why Elizabeth and Philip split up in the first place. This will tell us how the characters had to change or what they had to accept in order to be able to live together.

According to Cavell, the reason for bringing film and philosophy together is that they enable a fuller understanding of moral perfectionism. He explains perfectionism as follows:

> This is the aim of moral reasoning in perfectionism, not to assess pluses and minuses of advantage, nor to assess whether the act is

> recommendable universally, but yet to see to what those two standard theories wish to accomplish, namely that the one in question make himself intelligible, to others and to himself.[1]

Cavell points out that the challenge of moral life emerges not from of lack of moral knowledge or even the conflict between moral duties, but rather "from a confusion over your desires."[2] In Season One of *The Americans* we see just such a confusion. In an early episode, Elizabeth betrays Philip. The betrayal is not her affair, which had been going on for years, but rather the moment when she denounces Philip to her superior at the KGB. She tells her handler that Philip might defect. Somewhat counterintuitively, I want to argue that this is the turning point in their relationship, the answer to the question why, after fifteen years of marriage, she allows herself to become romantically attached to Philip. This betrayal is an expression of Elizabeth's confusion over her desires. She has always been completely dedicated to the Soviet ideology and to her role in an organization that she believes to be advancing this ideology. Truthfully reporting her doubts about Philip's loyalty to the KGB seems as if it is obviously the right thing to do, but it ends up having the opposite effect. It makes her aware that in fact she feels greater or at least equal loyalty to Philip. This realization motivates her to try to build a stronger marriage with Philip.

Elizabeth discovers that intimacy, however, is also a source of vulnerability. Later in the season, Philip is told to go to New York, where he meets with Irina, a former girlfriend from the USSR, the woman that he had to leave behind in order to accept his professional role and go undercover as an American. He spends the night with Irina but rejects her suggestion that they defect together. Philip's sexual infidelity is not an issue. Both Elizabeth and Philip use sex instrumentally to pursue their assigned tasks, but this infidelity is motivated by desire not duty; moreover, he lies about the brief liaison and, when Elizabeth finds out about the deception, she tells him to move out.

1 Stanley Cavell, *Cities of Words: Pedagogical Letters on a Register of the Moral Life* (Cambridge, MA, and London: Belknap/Harvard University Press, 2004), p. 42.
2 Ibid.

How does this compare with the tripartite structures of *The Philadelphia Story* and *The Rules of the Game*? I want to suggest it is a more subtle variant on the same theme. Elizabeth too is confronted with a choice between three options, the moral certainty of rigid ideology, the sense of control found in autonomy, and the heteronomy of love. When she tells Philip in Russian "come home" she acknowledges her own vulnerability and accepts the possibility of betrayal that comes with loving someone else. In an earlier episode, Nina, a low-level staffer at the Soviet Embassy, told Stan, "You Americans think everything is white and black. For us, everything is grey." In fact, Elizabeth did see things as either black or white, but grey begins to seep in.

The Americans is not a show that teaches moral lessons. It does not tell us to do our Kantian duty or to privilege the family over country, or the cause over self-interest. Instead, it vividly depicts what Cavell calls "the moment of encounter or challenge."[3] Part of the vividness comes from the spy scenario, but its emotional depth and insight comes from the way that it makes these moments resonate with the moral imperfectionism of everyday life. Love is about the possibility of being betrayed and the reality that you can betray someone and still love them. This runs counter not only to the Hallmark card sentimental version of love, but also to the capital "R" Romantic account of love as a source of clarity, identity and purpose. This is quite similar to the message that Cavell wants to draw from *The Philadelphia Story*. He insists that the ceremony that renews the bond between Dexter and Tracy is not portrayed as a resolution to the *eros/nomos* problem, but as an event that marks the protagonists' willingness to try to "be first-class human beings" while recognizing the difficulty of this task and the uncertainty of the result. Perhaps that was not the take-home point for the audience in the theater, but it seems to have been the intent of the director, who ended the film with the intrusive snapshot intended for *Spy* magazine, a sly reminder that everything does not conclude neatly.

[3] Ibid, p. 43.

One of the distinctive features of serialized television is that it is continuous rather than finite. *The Americans* does not end with Elizabeth's request "come home" and in the second season the audience gets to see that this moment, while transformative, does not solve everything. Remarriage is still marriage and marriage is work. Along with some moments of intimacy that are nourishing to both, there are terrible misunderstandings that reveal a gulf between husband and wife. For example, Philip is deeply shaken by some acts of violence that he commits. Elizabeth reminds him that they are at war and he replies in a tired voice, "You don't have to give me the speech. I know we are at war. But you just find it easier than I do." She turns to him and says, "You think I find it easy?" This is a powerful scene, because it reminds us how even the most intimate relationships rest on misrecognition. It also suggests that there can be a kind of emotional division of labor in relationships. When one partner expresses an emotion this may mean that the other is prohibited from doing so, because this reticence is the only way to preserve a balance that must be maintained. If Elizabeth expressed Philip's doubts, then it would no longer be possible to do their jobs and their family would fall apart. The show constantly insinuates that undercover agents are not the only ones who play roles. The rest of us may not wear such cool wigs, but the existence of masks is not exclusive to the world of espionage.

II

The Americans, which has just been renewed for a third season, demonstrates that "cinema" can be commercially successful and still provide a place for moral reflection. By bringing together thought and emotion and situating moral puzzles in a register that is both fantastic and yet familiar, it could plausibly fit into the category of "Emersonian perfectionism."[4] We are asked to think about what it means to be a good

[4] Ibid.

person and we are constantly reminded to question our certainty that we know the answer to that question. The very premise of the show, which asks the audience to identify with KGB agents who kill innocent people, implies that it is not easy to distinguish the good guys from the bad.

The second part of this response considers some objections to the ideas presented in the first part. The first objection follows directly from the preceding claim. If the show fosters emotional identification with "the bad guys" doesn't this prove that Rousseau's concern is legitimate? The problem with poetry/drama (and by extension film and television) is that it incites intense emotions that hinder judgment rather than enhance it. According to Rousseau, Molière encourages his audience to laugh at the honest man and to identify with the knave. Rousseau's second point is that it is a mistake to pay exclusive attention to the content of spectacle and overlook the structure of reception. What was true of the theater is even more true of cinema and television. Even the most exciting and morally provocative television ensconces us in our dark basements and isolates us from fellow citizens, thereby weakening real solidarity. The next part of this response will respond to these two objections.

Does *The Americans* hinder our judgment by romanticizing the KGB and encouraging the audience to identify with brutal killers? Does it suggest a moral equivalence between the United States and the Soviet Union? In answering these questions there are a few things to consider. First, if it were a show aimed at a Russian audience, these might be more serious concerns. The show does point to a certain moral equivalence, and, while the USSR of Brezhnev was not the USSR of Stalin, the show may indeed fail to highlight the full extent of repression and material deprivation in Russia (but it certainly does acknowledge these facts). This story, viewed in Russia, might possibly contribute to a nationalist mythology by reinforcing an ideological picture of KGB agents as morally conflicted and well-meaning patriots trying to make the world a better place. In the United States, however, it does not have that ideological effect and the moral equivalence serves to cast doubt on a different ideological picture, that of the United States as a beacon of integrity and justice.

Another response to this line of criticism is that the show forces the audience to acknowledge and consider moral ambiguity and conflict rather than to simply identify with the protagonists. It does this in two ways. First, it does not sanitize its characters by ensuring that they never do anything that really violates conventional morality. In the first season, Elizabeth executes a source because the center is worried that he could betray the KGB; she kills someone who is on the same side, someone who risked his own career and life to help the cause. Throughout the show people who are not involved in geopolitics are killed or exposed to grave danger when it is necessary to attain political objectives. Elizabeth explicitly endorses the consequentialist logic of the ends justifying the means. By encouraging us to identify with Philip and Elizabeth while fully exposing their brutality, we are forced into the same dilemma the characters are confronting, the tension between affect and judgment.

The show is also structured around a parallel between the KGB and the FBI. A central character is Stan Beeman, an FBI agent and neighbor of the Jennings. He is a serious and dedicated professional who has sacrificed his family for his job; he no longer feels at home after spending several years undercover with a white supremacist organization. He is neither cruel nor corrupt, yet he murders a low-level Russian intelligence officer in retribution for his partner's death and begins an affair with one of his sources. *The Americans* is not merely a show that makes villains into heroes. Instead, it does something much more unusual. It humanizes the characters on both sides of the binary between good guys and bad guys, cops and robbers. While the characters are sometimes moralistic, insofar as they express moral certainty and rigidity, the structure of the show itself does just the opposite, it provides a context for reflecting on moralism.[5]

[5] Wendy Brown, *States of Injury: Power and Freedom in Late Modernity* (Princeton, NJ: Princeton University Press, 1995).

Even if my sympathetic account of the content is persuasive, this means little if the very position of the spectator is fundamentally harmful. There is a strong and a weak version of this argument. The weak version is that a spectacle is fine as entertainment, but problematic when political theorists place this form of enjoyment at the center of their understanding of politics. To put it crudely, the objection goes something like this. Meetings, leafleting and deliberating about policy are difficult or boring. Instead of trying to change wordly things in association with others, we want to believe that a subtle reading of our highbrow shows is an important contribution to democratic politics. The stronger version of the argument, introduced by Rousseau and tentatively endorsed by Dienstag, is that going to the movies is like sojourning in the land of the lotus-eaters: "we are apt to let it take the place of those more truly democratic experiences, until the day arrives when we have lost our ability to tell the difference or, worse, when we prefer the dream, which we think we control, to the waking life, which we know we do not."

This is related to the argument made by Joseph Heath and Andrew Potter in their book *The Rebel Sell*.[6] *The Rebel Sell* mercilessly mocks the pretentions of academics and hipsters who cling to the conceit that their lifestyle choices and aesthetic preferences constitute meaningful political action. They remind us that buying an ironic T-shirt does not weaken the dominant discourse and that raising backyard chickens is not a decisive blow against capitalism. The regime of the sensible is not reconfigured by our art installations or facial hair. Heath and Potter's point is not just that these lifestyle choices are consumerist in their own niche way, but rather that they are a classic form of mystification. Critical consumerism takes dissent and channels it away from practical and effective political activity toward narcissistic expressions of personality. Not only do the aesthetics of the self come to replace political mobilization, but they also make it difficult to recognize that this

6 Joseph Heath and Andrew Potter, *The Rebel Sell: Why the Culture Can't Be Jammed* (Toronto, ON: Harper Perennial, 2005).

substitution has taken place. For Heath and Potter, the political goals of the left – fulfilling basic material needs, dismantling social hierarchies, and making space for individual freedom – are advanced through community organization and political participation.

The Rebel Sell is not focused primarily on cinema, but cinema could be an example of this broader tendency. Dienstag makes a similar point at the end of his essay. Following Rousseau, he argues that we should spend more time engaging in political activity and less time hypnotized by representations of the actions of others. There is empirical evidence for the claim that these activities are indeed mutually exclusive. In *Bowling Alone*, Robert Putnam suggests that up to 40 percent of the decline in associational activity may be due to the increased time spent watching television.[7] Theorists who are more sympathetic to the view that cultural criticism is a key dimension of political activity argue that aesthetics can foster a democratic ethos. But, as Ella Myers points out in her book *Wordly Ethics*,[8] the connection between democratic ethos and political action is seldom spelled out. Even if we sympathize with others, this does not mean that we are willing to act on their behalf or that we are capable of acting in ways that foster equality rather than *noblesse oblige* or of creating political associations.

Before assessing this line of criticism, we need to disentangle different parts of the argument. To do so, I turn back to Rousseau in order to understand his objection to the theater and how his argument might illuminate the contemporary debate. For Rousseau, the theater is a paradigmatic example of a certain type of collective experience, one that functions as a substitute for authentic public life. It simulates something that reassembles public life by bringing strangers into contact with one another, but, according to Rousseau, this commonality is based on an illusion. An emotional feeling of togetherness hides the lack of any real interaction that could overcome the isolation of modern, urban life.

7 Robert D. Putnam, *Bowling Alone: The Collapse and Revival of American Community* (New York: Simon & Schuster, 2000).

8 Ella Myers, *Worldly Ethics: Democratic Politics and Care for the World* (Durham, NC, and London: Duke University Press, 2013).

Rousseau also points out that the commercial nature of the theater exacerbates inequalities and encourages invidious comparisons. He contrasts commercial theater with public festivals that bring people together as equals and citizens.[9]

At first, Rousseau's *Letter to M. d'Alembert* appears to be a polemic against the theater, very much indebted to Plato's argument in *The Republic*. Like Plato, Rousseau worries that the theater appeals to the emotions rather than reason, and glorifies morally dubious modes of conduct. Rather than elevating, instructing, or challenging the spectator, the theater must appeal to the tastes of masses in order to maintain its commercial viability. Rousseau also stresses the negative consequences of the theater for Geneva, a city not yet corrupted by the habits of city life. Introducing the theater to Geneva would seduce citizens and draw them from more wholesome pursuits, thereby setting in motion a dynamic of consumerism and competition that would undermine the solidaristic basis of the republic. It is crucial to remember that he emphasized that theater functions differently in different places. It might actually prevent the corrupt Parisians from engaging in even more decadent activities, but it would lead to Geneva's decline.

Rousseau makes four distinct arguments:

- Theater is a bad influence in places where people would otherwise engage in more worthwhile activities.
- It is a form of public life based on hierarchy, comparison, and vanity rather than solidarity and equality.
- The commercial nature of the theater makes it ill-suited to challenge conventional taste.
- The narrative/dramatic form appeals to emotion and may enervate reason.

In response to the first, I think it is clear that we are Parisians and not Genevans. There is no going back to the real or imagined time when we

[9] Jean Starobinski, *Jean-Jacques Rousseau: Transparency and Obstruction* trans. Arthur Goldhammer (Chicago, IL: University of Chicago Press, 1988).

spent our evenings in serious conversation, political action and musical performance. Were it not for the pleasure of spectatorship in the golden age of television, I probably would not be pursuing particularly decadent pleasures, but I might well be surfing the Internet in a state of semi-distraction.

Rousseau's second criticism, too, was aimed at a particular time and place. The social experience of the eighteenth century theater was highly stratified and the physical arrangement of space enabled a very public performance of status. The opposite is true of the modern cinema, which may not be democratic in the sense of encouraging public spiritedness or deliberation, but is egalitarian in pricing and access. Viewing television, of course, is even less an expression of vanity and status. Some people may view their shows on a gigantic high-tech television, but the television is located in a private space and, therefore, it is not primarily a form of conspicuous consumption.

The third and fourth points have already been addressed above. Commercial entertainments do have to find a way to balance mass appeal with aesthetic innovation and critical perspectives. Sometimes this entails a hint of doubt after the happy ending, as in *The Philadelphia Story*. In "Golden Age" television shows such as *The Sopranos*, *Breaking Bad*, and *The Wire*, this involves taking popular genres – the Mafia, cops and robbers – and rewriting them with protagonists who are not stock characters, and introducing visual and sound effects that open up new perspectives and scenarios that cast doubt on dominant ideology. They are able to do so in part because technological changes have made it easier to make money on shows that do not attract a mass audience.

Cable television has made it possible to produce shows that appeal to a smaller but committed audience, bypassing the mass audience necessary to attract national advertisers. Streaming makes it even easier to match individual tastes with specific content. In the eighteenth century, if a play did not appeal to a wide cross-section of the local population, the actors would perform to an empty theater and ticket sales would not cover their salaries. The age of mechanical reproduction allows for more specialization, but cinemas still need a large number of people to come to the same place at the same time. This requires costly infrastructure, which in turn requires marketing budgets to attract audiences. Internet-based television makes it possible to attract a geographically dispersed audience and to do so in a more gradual fashion. Rather than inundating people with costly advertising, it is possible to wait until reviews, word of mouth and commentary draw interested viewers who can catch up on older episodes by downloading them. These technological conditions make it possible, in a way that perhaps was not in Rousseau's day, to create spectacles that do challenge conventional wisdom and critique dominant ideology.

Dienstag does not write about television, but his comments imply that he thinks that it exacerbates the problems associated with cinema. Since television is viewed in private, it is even more isolating and individualizing than cinema. It has none of the aura of a spectacle, but all of the disadvantages: representation, commodification and passivity. I am not so sure. Spectatorship is not necessarily passive. Often a text – a film, television show, play, or novel – poses a puzzle rather than preaching a sermon. It invites the viewer to take part in a process of decoding and interpretation. Rousseau worried that the theater might turn us all into actors, people who are comfortable with dissimulation and masks. I am hopeful that the Golden Age of Television may turn us all into critics, taking the skills that we use to decipher television shows and use them to interpret our own lives. I have learned about marriage through viewing *The Americans*. Television shows can also serve as a kind of social glue. The experience of viewing may be isolating, but the task of interpretation can be collective. Popular niche television shows provide something to talk about other than real-estate prices, work and schools. Outside of a book club or university seminar, it is unusual to read a book together with other people at the same time, but movies and television shows are still events that create the possibility of a shared experience of interpretation.

The logics of spectatorship and quest are not necessarily opposed, but nor are they necessarily interrelated. Like Machiavelli donning his ancient robes, we sometimes read texts (including cinematic ones) and try to enact the insights that we draw from them. Other times, however, cinema is a form of escape, a reproduction of ideology, or an exercise in nostalgia. Notwithstanding the specific objections presented in this response, I think that Dienstag's motivating concern is valid. He is right to worry that the quest of political action – the struggle to improve the world – is more challenging and more important than watching a movie or an innovative and insightful show on television. It is not enough to see things through a slightly different lens. We must also create a different world.

5

"That dangerous contention": a cinematic response to pessimism

Davide Panagia

> Games are places where intention does not count, human activities in which intention need not generally be taken into account; because in games *what happens* is described solely in terms set by the game itself, because the consequences one is responsible for are limited a priori by the rules of the game.
>
> S. Cavell, "A Matter of Meaning It"[1]

To begin, I feel I must be forthcoming by means of an apology: Prof. Dienstag has given us too much to think about, and too much to respond to, and I cannot be true to the markings I have made in his text and respond to all the things I wish and hope to respond to in the remarks that follow. Indeed, what Dienstag has offered is a lifetime of topics for conversation about the marriage of film and democracy, and I look forward to furthering all the possible strands and moments of conversation, though not in this response piece.

Here I wish, instead, to begin with a dangerous contention I hold to be true: film is in direct competition with God for the creation of worlds. No other art could claim as much, though all other media have tried. Every other art form relies on the presence of a viewer/spectator to enact worlds via the enlivening motility of the imagination. Poetry, novels, painting, sculpture – even theater and dance! – all these require an audience. Film does not. For film has absolved the spectator from

[1] Stanley Cavell, *Must We Mean What We Say?: A Book of Essays* (Cambridge: Cambridge University Press, 2002), p. 236.

the burden of imagining movement through its own technical automaticity – a simple gear borrowed from a sewing machine and a perforated strip of celluloid; this was all that was needed in order to overcome the power of the human imagination. Film does not require humans to create moving images, it does so on its own by projecting them onto a screen. In this way – and like no other art form – it is in direct competition with God, who is said to have created life and movement.

No doubt such a contention is absurd, blasphemous to some. But I hope the reader will accept it as a provocation that Dienstag's "Letter to M. Cavell" invites; that is, the demonic coupling of film with democracy is the dangerous contention of which Dienstag accuses Cavell. But, we might respond, echoing that other great reader of Rousseau, "the contention contends."[2] And what does it contend? It contends that there is a non-human presence that competes with humanity in the organization of worlds. Call that non-human presence film, or God. In this shadow, Dienstag's countercontention is that the ameliorative spirit of perfectionism found in Cavell's comedies of remarriage, and especially in *The Philadelphia Story*, is a dangerous supplement that degrades viewers to a state of animalian existence incapable of presenting and admitting vistas to one another. In the movie theater, Dienstag affirms, "We relax into the comfort of a prehuman isolation only to enjoy the spectacle of human travails" (p. 71). And no happiness or freedom, never mind democracy, can come of this. *That* is the dangerous contention: there is no politics, democratic or otherwise, when we humans give ourselves up to an experience of aesthetic presentness that, as Diderot describes in his Salon writings, is so intense and absorptive that it denies the presence of others.[3] For, as Dienstag affirms, "We go to films with preexisting friends precisely to compensate for enduring the loneliness of experience. For, however marvelous an experience, it is a lonely one, not one that can be truly shared" (p. 72).

2 Jacques Derrida, *Of Grammatology* (Baltimore, MD: The Johns Hopkins University Press, 2013), p. 154.

3 Michael Fried, *Absorption and Theatricality: Painting and Beholder in the Age of Diderot* (Berkeley, CA: University of California Press, 1980) pp. 7–70.

"Truly shared" is a curious – uncharacteristically optimistic – expression that I find to be at the heart of my disagreements with Dienstag's position. I should note – quite ironically – that my disagreements are rooted in a friendship with Dienstag born of (amongst other things) the sharing of films and a love of cinema, and of the conversations that films invite. This is despite the fact that, in the history of our friendship, Dienstag and I have never gone to a theater to see a movie together. This aside, I do not know what can be "truly shared" or, for that matter, proximately shared. But, elaborating on this is not my concern in this reply, as I am not an epistemologist. Rather, my concern regards the conceptual ties between sharing, education, and influence in Cavell's work on film, and how my understanding of this mediation differs (radically) from Dienstag's. In this regard, I read the title of Cavell's *Pursuits of Happiness* to be less descriptive than autobiographical. In that book, we discover an author recounting, sharing and partaking in the pursuit of happiness (of going to the movies).

Much of my disagreement with Dienstag, then, rests on my inability to recognize his account of Cavell's motivation in writing about film. I simply do not read Cavell's words in the same way as Dienstag does, and he and I do not share a sense of film's activity. In part this is because I do not read Cavell as making prescriptive arguments about film's relation to democracy, nor to the ameliorative potential of film for democracy. Instead, I sense great hesitancy in all of what Cavell writes about film – a hesitancy born of the "imponderable evidence"[4] he champions. Cavell's mood is not regularian but adverbial:[5] there is no subliming of an ought here, but a sense of frustration that, however hard he might try to point us to a source of conviction in a claim about film, such indexing inevitably fails. It is in light of what I take to be Cavell's antinomianism that I read his book *Pursuits of Happiness*, not as instruction

4 Ludwig Wittgenstein, *Philosophical Investigations* (3rd edition, Englewood Cliffs, NJ: Prentice Hall, 1973), p. 228e.

5 Richard E. Flathman, *Reflections of a Would-Be Anarchist: Ideals and Institutions of Liberalism* (Minneapolis, MN: University of Minnesota Press, 1998) p. 74.

for the place of film in democracy but as a set of reflections on the kinds of tuitions our intuitions might afford.[6]

From a formal perspective, the book models a course syllabus, or an attempt at a syllabus, plagued by an anxiety in addressing the pairing of philosophy and film in a university curriculum. Let us recall, briefly, the era in which Cavell's studies on film were written. Though published in 1981, *Pursuits of Happiness* was composed throughout the 1970s and followed *The World Viewed* as the only other book that took film seriously as a philosophical topic, written by an American author tenured in a philosophy department at a prominent American university. By any standard, *that* is an achievement given what we know of the orientation of American philosophy departments in the post-war period.[7] More to the point, Cavell is writing about what he considers "works," and about his sense of what constitutes the nature of a work. Moreover, he does not take this ontological question lightly, as we can all agree; for an answer to the question of what constitutes a work provides a very important first step to answering the question of whether a film can contribute to a philosophy curriculum. That is, for Cavell, the ontological question of the nature of a work must first be answered before any account of the value of a specific work can be given. Hence, the anxiety, and the inevitable disappointment, in discovering that he (Cavell) cannot provide adequate epistemic evidence for the existence of a filmic work. There is, then, a curious instance of habeas corpus to his project: if Cavell cannot provide evidence for the existence of a work (what he refers to as "the question of film's legitimacy"),[8] can there be any value attached to cinema and/or the philosophical study of cinema? The short answer is ambiguous: yes and no. Indeed, I would argue that a first lesson that we learn from reading Cavell on film is the antinomian

6 Ralph Waldo Emerson and Mary Oliver, "Self Reliance," in *The Essential Writings of Ralph Waldo Emerson*, edited by Brooks Atkinson (New York: Modern Library, 2000), pp. 132–53.

7 John McCumber, *Time in the Ditch: American Philosophy and the McCarthy Era* (Evanston, IL: Northwestern University Press, 2001), *passim*.

8 Stanley Cavell, *Pursuits of Happiness: The Hollywood Comedy of Remarriage* (Cambridge, MA: Harvard University Press, 1981), p. 270.

position (first elaborated by Immanuel Kant in the third *Critique*) that there can be no rules for expressing or indexing or proving the existence of value. Thus, the best that we can do, to use Cavell's famous term, is *acknowledge* it; and by acknowledging value, we are acknowledging the sensation of an experience. So, when acknowledging something like the work of cinema, Cavell can only access his experiences with the hope or ambition or anxiety "that others have a similar kind of experience, that they will recognize themselves in his words."[9] The alternative, as Cavell puts it starkly, "is having nothing (political) to say."[10]

Therefore, the political question of *Pursuits of Happiness* seems to me less about the semblances or usefulness of film for democracy (because aesthetic objects aren't instrumental) than the question of democratic participation: what is entitled to partake (i.e., share) in a curriculum? And, more devastatingly, can one's experience of value partake (i.e., be shared) in that curricular project? Such questions imagine a conjoining of participation (*qua* sharing) and acknowledgment in the forging of what Cavell refers to as a university's "commitment to the idea of curriculum."[11] By "curriculum," I take Cavell to mean both the idea of a plan of study (hence my formal reading of *Pursuits of Happiness* as a syllabus) and the sense of a shared way (or path) of learning. Keeping Cavell's anxieties regarding the validity of subjective experiences of value in mind, then, the questions he asks are what are the elements that can be shared in a way of learning, and are one's intimacies in viewing legitimate participants in those sharings? The study of film is nothing other than the pursuit of experience as a source and resource for the learning of and about value; to wit, aesthetics. Can the curriculum in and of democracy bear such pursuits? Can it avoid them?

However, the problem of curriculum – of a path of learning – does not end here. For when Cavell was writing his works on and of film, he

[9] Daniel Morgan, "Stanley Cavell: The Contingencies of Film and Its Theory," in Murray Pomerance and R. Barton Palmer, eds., *Thinking in the Dark: Cinema, Theory, Practice* (New Brunswick, NJ: Rutgers University Press, 2015).

[10] Stanley Cavell, *The Claim of Reason: Wittgenstein, Skepticism, Morality, and Tragedy* (New York: Oxford University Press, 1999) p. 28.

[11] Cavell, *Pursuits of Happiness*, p. 269.

did not have access to our visual media (i.e., he was not writing at a time when he could access vistas via a VHS or DVD player, or a tablet). Cavell pursued his curriculum not only with intuition, but with memories, the *least* reliable sources of evidentiary support out there and certainly not something that could count as a robust testimony for the pursuit of "film's legitimacy."[12] In a courtroom, this would be akin to responding to the charge of habeas corpus by saying, "I remember to have seen a body." But Cavell's aesthetic philosophy reminds us that, when issues regarding the nature of value arise, we are not in a courtroom and the epistemology of legitimacy has little sway. So what does have sway?

"A reading of a film," Cavell states, "sets up a continuous appeal to the experience of the film, or rather to an active memory of the experience (or an active anticipation of acquiring the experience)."[13] It is at the point at which memories count as the fragmented traces upon which to construct a claim about film's legitimacy that Cavell encounters Dienstag's mood of pessimism which affirms that "Nothing is permanent, and we suffer most from the lack of permanence in the people and things that we most care about. Indeed, the more we care, the more we suffer."[14] For, if we might entertain (with some difficulty) the possibility that Cavell is endorsing the ameliorative function of film for democracy, the fact that his readings of films are grounded in the impermanence of memories – and memories are, essentially, dying thoughts – suggests a strain of suffering throughout Cavell's pursuits of happiness: his happiness is dying because his memories – those things we care deeply about – are fading. Films – and our experiences of films – point to nothing other than the lack of permanence in our lives. I wish to call that lack of permanence *discontinuity*.

[12] Cavell, *Pursuits of Happiness*, p. 270. At this point, I ponder, as an aside, whether "an anticipation of acquiring the experience" is not what Cavell means by "pursuits of happiness"? And to ponder this means, once again, to acknowledge that Dienstag and I do not partake in a shared reading, despite reading the same words and viewing the same films. There is here a veritable dissensus, not a disagreement.

[13] Cavell, *Pursuits of Happiness*, p. 11.

[14] Joshua Foa Dienstag, *Pessimism: Philosophy, Ethic, Spirit* (Princeton, NJ: Princeton University Press, 2009), p. 23.

I thus read the mood that Dienstag names *pessimism* to be at the heart of Cavell's pursuits of happiness. The things most impermanent – the memories of views and experiences of value – are the quicksand upon which Cavell chooses to ground his pursuits of a life of learning, a life of curatorship dedicated to the impossible sharings that relate things like film and philosophy, or Kant and Capra. These are, to anyone's eyes, perverse couplings or risky marriages, to be sure. The claim(s) Cavell makes about film(s) are not representational where x and y films are said to offer better understandings or a more capacious or effective semblance of democratic life. Cavell cannot make those claims, given his own anxiety about claim-making, and his acceptance of the fact that aesthetic experience is neither verifiable nor prescriptive.[15] That is to say, Cavell's claim(s) of and about film(s) do not assign an experience of value to objects in the way that I read Dienstag recommend they do.

Cavell's claim(s) of and about film(s) are, rather, presentational – not surprisingly, of the *look and see* variety – as when Wittgenstein says this: "I wanted to put that picture before him, and his *acceptance* of the picture consists in his now being inclined to regard a given case differently: that is, to compare it with *this* rather than *that* set of pictures. I have changed his *way of looking at things*."[16] Being "inclined to regard differently" is not a seeing differently, nor a thinking differently, nor an agreement or a consent on the validity of the statement of value. It is an acceptance of the projection of value in the form of a linguistic utterance which recalls a moment of experience. What Wittgenstein and Cavell are accessing, in short, are sentimental reflections on the nature of taste.

Of course, by taste here I mean neither "preference" nor "liking." I mean, rather, that ambiguous set of practices and capacities that enable pairings and couplings to come into occasion – let us call such pairings and couplings "assemblages" (Deleuze), or "queer connexions" (Wittgenstein), or "partitions" (Rancière). Recall how Cavell begins

[15] Stanley Cavell, "Aesthetic Problems in Modern Philosophy," in *Must We Mean What We Say?, passim.*

[16] Wittgenstein, *Philosophical Investigations*, para. 144.

Pursuits of Happiness by declaring that the object of study of his book is genre, and that his first – explicit – debt is to Northrop Frye's "The Argument of Comedy." Of course, the matter of genre as a practice of literary inquiry is not far from the issue of curriculum as an object of ontological inquiry, and it does not surprise me at all that the bookends of *Pursuits of Happiness* are the topics of genre ("Introduction") and curriculum ("Appendix"). These bespeak, in some sense, the same activity that parallels the activity of filmmaking: that is, these are activities that give priority to the human capacity for selection and arrangement, call it the human instinct to cut and paste. They are activities, in short, that understand the practices of and about taste to be activities fundamentally committed to the forging of relations and structures of participation (and hence sharing) that previously did not exist – like, for instance, the participation of *The Philadelphia Story* with a treatment of *La Règle du jeu* in a discussion of the democratic value of cinema. What dispositions do such forms of sharing admit? What is taste's scene of instruction? Whatever answers might arise from these questions, one thing is for certain: the issue of sharing is a matter of taste.

Pursuits of Happiness is a book that enacts its own argument about taste by putting a picture before us and exacting a movement of comparison with *this* rather than *that* set of archival pictures (Shakespeare, marriage, Freud, Bazin, etc.). But, more than this, it is an exercise in remarking upon pictures and fictitious narratives, as if Cavell had taken this passage from Wittgenstein as his professional epigraph: "Don't take it as a matter of course, but as a remarkable fact, that pictures and fictitious narratives give us pleasure, occupy our minds."[17] The (erotic) pleasure of a mental occupancy, or what the history of taste otherwise calls "absorption," is at the heart of Cavell's reflections on film. His are reflections on how to take as remarkable the fact that memories of streaming images persist in our consciousness, and what we make of the "queer connexion(s)"[18] that ensue.

[17] Wittgenstein, *Philosophical Investigations*, p. 142e, para. 524.
[18] Wittgenstein, *Philosophical Investigations*, p. 19e, para. 38.

The issue of aesthetic absorption bespeaks a further element of Cavell's writings on film-learning that Dienstag's "Letter" sidesteps; namely, the matter of ekphrasis. I have already noted the technical environment within which *The World Viewed* and *Pursuits of Happiness* were written. This was a time when one could not readily access the films themselves, and if one did have such means at one's disposal, the kind of stop-action viewing available to film scholars today was not possible then. Thus, much of Cavell's hesitancy in claiming is related to the acknowledgment that a) affirmations of taste are not prescribable; b) that the film/philosophy pairing might be deemed in bad taste; and c) that faded memories are a poor source of evidentiary support for something as important as an ontology of film; but d) that the faded memories of viewings compete for mental occupancy with the faded memories of other lived experiences, making the memories of films as real as the memories of other peoples or events.[19] Hence Cavell affirms the following in the "Foreword to the Enlarged Edition" of *The World Viewed*:

> I wrote primarily out of the memory of films, though between the time of the parent book and the time of its offspring I had begun the practice of taking notes during and after screenings, thus altering my preparation for future writing about film, thus altering what *could* be written by me about it; I was always aware that my descriptions of passages were liable to contain errors, of content and of sequence. I have not attempted to correct such errors in this reprinting, wanting neither to disguise the liabilities of the spirit in which the work was composed nor to disguise the need for a study of what may be remembered in any art and for a study of how using an analyzing machine

[19] And here I am making the blasphemous (Humean) point that, to the extent that mental life relies on memories of experiences, no appeal to a robust realism can be made as regards the difference between memories or images or impressions of peoples and memories or images or impressions of things (like films or pictures or paintings). "Real" people and "real" events are, to our mental occupancy, indistinct from the films we view on the screen. To buttress such blasphemy, I point the reader to Daniel Kahneman's theory of the experiencing and remembering selves as outlined in his *Thinking, Fast and Slow* (reprint edition, New York: Farrar, Straus and Giroux, 2013).

> may modify one's experience of a film. The absence of both such studies helps to keep unassessed the fact that in speaking of a moment or sequence from a film we, as we might put it, cannot *quote* the thing we are speaking of.[20]

To write not *from* memory, but "out of the memory of films" – this is Cavell's ekphrastic ambition; as if memory is not a storage device but a spring to thought. Writing about film is thus not the pursuit of an accurate semblance *in* films, this because vistas cannot be cited and memories are impermanent. Herein lies Cavell's flirting with pessimism, despite his own pursuits of happiness.

How does any of this make Cavell's writings on film an ekphrastic exercise? Simply put, he is writing of things that *do not* exist in the world precisely because his (and our) views and experiences and memories of vistas *do not* exist in the world. The allure or prestige of aesthetic criticism is to make the audience/reader believe that the object in question actually exists even though there can be no corollary to it. This is the ekphrastic ambition of film-writing and thinking that is akin to Homer's description of Achilles' shield, or Keats's Grecian Urn. The ekphrastic in all these instances regards "the illusory representation of the unrepresentable, even when that representation is allowed to masquerade as a natural sign, as if it could be an adequate substitute for its object."[21] Thus, I would say, Cavell's recommendations of films read less like the commending of a tuition than as an attempt to create a system of signs that can adequately address the flux that arises from the experience of remarkableness. "A study of what may be remembered in any art"[22] is the study of aesthetic criticism, and what is remembered is not the object itself, but the subjectivity of encountering a felt impression. There is no doubt that *The Philadelphia Story* exists: it has a material (celluloid) existence. But there is no such object-thing as Cavell's

[20] Stanley Cavell, *The World Viewed: Reflections on the Ontology of Film* (Cambridge, MA: Harvard University Press, 1979), p. ix.

[21] Murray Krieger, *Ekphrasis: The Illusion of the Natural Sign* (Baltimore, MD: The Johns Hopkins University Press, 1992), p. xv.

[22] Cavell, *The World Viewed*, p. ix.

(or mine, or your) vista of it; and, when we speak of *The Philadelphia Story*, or *La Règle du jeu*, or *Blade Runner* or *The Man Who Shot Liberty Valence*, we are never speaking of the film, whatever that may mean, but are always speaking of our vistas of them – and *that* means that we are speaking, or writing, ekphrastically, about a non-existent object, a virtual *res*. Hence the impossibility of a commendation (how can one commend something that doesn't exist?), yet the invitation to look and see for yourself.

This sense of the ekphrastic is Cavell's scene of instruction that I understand as a curatorial disposition that invites us to take up a view, to bear or support a view, like a strewn blanket might bear light if it were a makeshift screen holding "a projection, as light as light."[23] With this in mind, let us take a look at that dangerous contention once again, the scene of instruction (one of many, no doubt) that sets off Dienstag's penning of his letter:

> But the idea of what happened in Philadelphia during the making of our Declaration of Independence and our Constitution is not the whole daydream. It projects further a conversation between film's preoccupations and some three or four texts or moments in the working out of those covenants in their subsequent two centuries.[24]

What a couplet! It's almost Shakespearean! The idea that what happened in Philadelphia is a daydream in exactly the same way that what happens on film is a daydream, and they are daydreams because they are events that cannot correspond to anything in the world, unless memories and recountings (call them histories, if you must) are things in the world. But they are not. History is not something that exists in the world, it is a *poesis* of recounting temporal happenings, and such ekphrases can manifest themselves numerically, or orally, or archivally, or textually. And all of these things may represent truths about the world in exactly the same way that film does, by projecting views and vistas and imaginings.

[23] Cavell, *The World Viewed*, p. 24.
[24] Cavell, *Pursuits of Happiness*, p. 154.

So what are film's preoccupations? They are varied and variable, no doubt, but, at least between the cover pages of Cavell's *Pursuits of Happiness*, there is a sense that a central preoccupation that film is not so much the stories it tells, but how to tell those stories by creating associations and relations (e.g., kinships or marriages) between things that do not actually belong together: this shot with that camera angle, this film with that other film, this set of concerns (e.g., cinema) with those others (e.g., democracy) – to wit, this genre or that curriculum. In short, the preoccupation of film *is* a preoccupation for democracy: namely, it is the preoccupation of partaking in and assigning lots to things. For, if there is one thing that film does very well – exceedingly well, indeed – it is to assign lines of sight and auralities. Film parses the world in order to make worlds. This is at once its technical and aesthetic achievement, and why it is in competition with God.

It seems, then, that a central preoccupation of Cavell's own scene of instruction is not so much to exact representations for prescription or adoption, but to beg the question as to what transubstantiating force of mediation enables distinct and unrelated objects to exist in proximity (spatial and temporal) to one another. The aesthetic version of this question is "how is value shared?" And this *is* a political question that for Cavell arises out of the fact of film's automaticity and the further fact that film is "cut" (automatically) twenty-four times per second (in the case of conventional celluloid) and then cut, once again, between shots and scenes. It is also a political question because, if nothing else (and as Dienstag's Masonic picture of American founding projects), democratic politics involves selecting cuts and apportioning parts so that disaggregated units are seen to hold together. Such a holding together is not simply impermanent, it is ekphrastic – an illusion akin to the idea of a natural sign.

My response to Dienstag's letter is nearly exhausted, though inevitably incomplete. Nevertheless, allow me, then, two further qualms. The first is this: what are we to make of Dienstag's implicit contention that a proper democratic learning involves an active citizenry of reading and writing subjects? We know of Dienstag's penchant for narrative and prose: he is a great reader of novels and his work in political theory places great emphasis on narrative in political life. Notably, Dienstag never – and I mean *never* – actually claims the privilege of reading to viewing for education in his "Letter to M. Cavell." And yet, there is something of a *punctum* – a wounding pinprick – that glares at me when I encounter his view of spectatorship, and in particular his sociology of the isolationism of filmic spectatorship. No doubt he is right that going to the movies is a "lonely" experience where "We relax into the comfort of a prehuman isolation only to enjoy the spectacle of human travails" (p. 71). But, how much more lonely is this activity from that of reading? Is reading not equally something we tend to pursue in isolation, with our heads "buried" in our books, as we are accustomed to saying? Our ordinary language likens reading to a grave, for heaven's sake! How's that for isolation?

As Dienstag's work shows, there is nothing more solitary (and perhaps more antipolitical) than death. But though Dienstag has much to say about film's capacity to distract us from one another, he has little to say of reading's similar capacities; curiously, scriptural activities somehow remain immune from charges of demonology in political education. And yet, what benefit to democracy does reading or writing bring? Neither is (for us, today) a social activity. To paraphrase Dienstag's own words, "I have never yet made a friend *in* a book, and I expect I never will" (p. 72). For, however marvelous the experiences of reading and writing may be, they are not ones that can be "truly shared." What does it say for democracy that reading and writing are not shareable activities? What does it say about a democratic education that they are not? To share someone's perspective, you must first acknowledge its difference from your own; literature affords no space for this experience. Or, at the very least, and if I may continue to be coy, it offers the same "no-place" that film does. (I could, at this point, make a direct riposte by way of quoting one of I. A. Richards' most memorable lines: "A book is a machine to think with."[25])

[25] Ivor Armstrong Richards, *Principles of Literary Criticism* (2nd edition, London: Routledge, 2003), p. 1.

I might be exhausting the reader's patience, but it is worth noting how the issue of sharing as a social activity in Dienstag's analysis of cinema partakes in similar concerns as the issues of curriculum, editing, and genre in Cavell's writing about film. The crux of the concern is this: the nature of influence and collaboration in and for democracy is undetermined, and to assume that influence and collaboration require a correspondence model of transmission that relies on a telegraphic account of sharing is, I believe, limiting. As others have shown, such an account of social influence is rooted in a late nineteenth- and early twentieth-century commitment to theories of unconscious imitation. The idea is as straightforward as it is familiar: consciousness implies attention and intention, unconsciousness implies coercion and manipulation by another authority, whether that authority is the power of a mental illness (hysteria), or a trickster (the hypnotist), or a spectacle (cinema).[26]

My point here is this: the debates over the uses and abuses of cinema for politics rest on an understanding and appreciation of the power of the image, of its architecture, and the forms of influence the image can excite. Indeed, it is excitement itself, and it is the concomitant sense of the uncontrollable (as in the early twentieth-century film-going archetypes of the hysteric and the somnambulist) that is at stake. For the uncontrollable is akin to the unspecifiable, or the unpredictable; to that sense of anxiety that Cavell admits to when having to rely on the sensations of an experience, or the vagueness of a memory, to index value. The uncontrollable is also what is at stake in our appreciations of mediatic theories of influence in and for democracy. In democracies, we tend to want to defend the absolute value of freedom, but not defend the absolute value of the uncontrollable for fear that the uncontrollable can generate undemocratic impulses, like cinematic demagoguery. I take this point to be at the heart of Dienstag's concerns regarding the sociality of sharing, and cinema's failure in generating "those more truly democratic experiences" (pp. 72–73).

[26] Rae Beth Gordon, *Why the French Love Jerry Lewis: From Cabaret to Early Cinema* (Redwood, CA: Stanford University Press, 2002), *passim.*

I fear that I have now embraced Dienstag's horrible subject of cinema: the one incapable of distinguishing between dream and reality, or, worse perhaps, of preferring the dream of a world of moving images, or (*summum malum*!) of the sinner who believes the world is nothing other than a stream of moving images. This is the vista of the democratic somnambulist who is maligned because she is passive and incapable of seeing other perspectives. This is what she shares with animals. But is this spectatorship? What do we make of the element of play in movie theaters that makes a collective writhe and squirm with pleasure, pain, or horror while viewing?[27] Must the education of the city occur without play?

Here, then, is my second and final qualm over Dienstag's position: there is absolutely no room for play (*Spiel-Raum*) in his discussion of film and in his representation of a democratic education. "If we are to experience a democracy of moments," Dienstag affirms, "we can never learn to do so from an art that exists to subvert them" (p. 76). Such an assertion can only be true if we excise any sense of play from art, learning and democracy. It is perhaps the case that Dienstag might associate the element of play in art with the kind of ameliorative aspirations that he sees in comedies, thereby adding to the "myth of optimism that happiness and freedom walk hand in hand" (p. 73). But, if this is true, it is simply a category mistake. For there is no 1:1 correlation between play-comedy-happiness-freedom-democracy-optimism. This is not a fixed series.

It is telling that, in his treatment of *La Règle du jeu*, Dienstag spends much time on the issue of rule and ruling, and little time on game playing. And it is further telling that Dienstag's account of the doll scene in *La Règle du jeu* interprets the automaticity of the doll as an absence of willpower. In short, the relation is analogical, and the analogy speaks of an absence of freedom, hence the dangerous tendency

[27] In his *The Theory of Moral Sentiments* (Indianapolis, IN: Liberty Fund, 2009), Adam Smith says this of his idea of fellow-feeling (or sympathy, or sharing): "The mob, when they are gazing at a dancer on the slack rope, naturally writhe and twist and balance their own bodies, as they see him do, as they feel that they must do if in his situation" (I.i.1.3).

"of the mechanistic life toward violence and death" (p. 45). But dolls and games and automata are complicated things. From one perspective (e.g., Dienstag's optimistic vista regarding the existence of something like human will and freedom), dolls and automata inevitably represent a limit to human will, and automaticity is akin to an absence of individual freedom. But this is only one side of the dice. For Renoir, as for Cavell, automata offer an occasion to explicitly explore the nature of human sentiments; Cavell does this in his example of the "striptease of misery"[28] in *The Claim of Reason*, and Renoir (as Dienstag rightly notes) does so in such scenes. But, more than Cartesian carriers of the problem of human freedom vis-à-vis mechanization, dolls and other automata also represent (for the early twentieth-century viewer like Renoir) the quintessential site of cinematic play as a force of freedom. For, what the automata show is exactly the opposite of an absence of freedom but, rather, a freedom from the habituation of ritual that narrows the scope of freedom's play. Doll and automata for the early twentieth-century viewer were things that enabled a kind of play that liberated one's sense of servitude to (class and spiritual) ritual.

Consider, in this regard, Walter Benjamin's famous essay, "The Work of Art in the Age of its Technological Reproducibility." Rather than reading the compromised third version of that essay (found in the *Illuminations* collection), however, let's follow Miriam Hansen's advice and read the second version – the final version written by Benjamin before Theodor Adorno's distortive hands took over.[29] I cannot do justice to Hansen's treatment of play theory in cinema, and especially in Benjamin's theory of technological reproducibility. But, there are two things I do want to note, which I believe (at the very least) complicate Dienstag's image of the passive spectator. The first is what Benjamin has to say about play and cinema, and the second is the emphasis Benjamin places on innervation (a synonym for the unpredictable), that culminates in his esteem for Chaplin.

[28] Cavell, *The Claim of Reason*, pp. 403–16.

[29] On Adorno's distortion of Benjamin, see Miriam Hansen's discussion in *Cinema and Experience: Siegfried Kracauer, Walter Benjamin, and Theodor W. Adorno*, edited by Edward Dimendberg (Berkeley, CA: University of California Press, 2011),pp. 195–9.

Much rests, in Benjamin's essay, on his treatment of mimesis as the interplay of semblance and play. But it is cinema, which Benjamin at several points calls "games of light" (*Lichtspiele*), that holds the greatest promise for game-play, and for extending the scope of play so as to dissolve and dissociate the power of semblance, or what he refers to as the "decay of the aura." Here, Benjamin's task is to distance himself from the age of "auratic perception" that he associates with Hegel's beautiful semblance – indeed, with bourgeois capitalism. Throughout the second version of *The Work of Art* essay, Benjamin insists on exploring forms of emancipation from auratic perception that "technological reproducibility emancipates the work of art from its parasitic subservience to ritual."[30] Further, in footnote 23 of this second version of *The Work of Art* (a footnote ultimately cut from the *Illuminations* edition), Benjamin says this: "what is lost in the withering of semblance and the decay of the aura in works of art is matched by a huge gain in the scope of play [*Spiel-Raum*]. This space for play is widest in film. In film, the element of semblance has been entirely displaced by the element of play."[31] Why might this be the case? Simply put, because "it manages to assure us of a vast and unsuspected field of action [*Spielraum*]."[32] In short, Benjamin finds the political importance of film in the conjunction of play and action because no other art, technology or medium provides occasions for the innervation of semblance via repetitive play in the way that cinema does.

Recall that Benjamin's interest in play is tied to his interest in childlike imitation and the learning that comes through the child's "creative innervation."[33] Benjamin believes children are unique (but not innocent) in their capacity to generate new images for the *an-archive* of humanity: "To each truly new configuration of nature," Benjamin writes

[30] Walter Benjamin, *The Work of Art in the Age of Its Technological Reproducibility, and Other Writings on Media* (Cambridge, MA: Belknap/Harvard University Press, 2008), p. 24.

[31] Benjamin, *The Work of Art*, p. 49.

[32] Walter Benjamin, *Walter Benjamin: Selected Writings, Volume 4: 1938–1940*, edited by Howard Eiland and Michael William Jennings (Cambridge, MA: Belknap/Harvard University Press, 2003), p. 117.

[33] Hansen, *Cinema and Experience*, p. 36.

in *The Arcades Project* (*Das Passagen-Werk*), "and, at bottom, technology is just such a configuration – there corresponds new 'images.' Every childhood discovers these new images in order to incorporate them into the image stock of humanity."[34] That "database aesthetics"[35] is disconnected and discontinuous, innervated, a broken heap of pictorial traces, something that each generation, and each epoch, carries with it. Repetitive technical reproducibility guarantees the constant cutting and circulating of such a pictorial bricolage. Indeed, we could say that the element of play identified by Benjamin in cinema, which far from an ameliorative happiness (as it offers no guarantees for joy or redemption) interplays the tragic with the comic (i.e., fragmentation and play), is encapsulated in the two great archetypes of modernity that he projects: the bricoleur and the flaneur. What we quickly discover via *The Work of Art* essay is that, for Benjamin, the flaneur is the bricoleur in motion – or cinema.

For this reason, Chaplin – the quintessential bricoleur in motion – takes on "historical significance" for Benjamin, for "he was the first to inhabit new fields of action opened up by film."[36] Whether this is an accurate account of Chaplin or not is, of course, beside the point. The point is that what cinema offers politics is a transfiguration of motor-perceptual energies, a heretofore unavailable technical transformation of the human sensorium itself.

In a posthumously published 1935 fragment entitled "The Formula in Which the Dialectical Structure of Film Finds Expression," Benjamin writes this:

> The formula in which the dialectical structure of film – film considered in its technological dimension – finds expression runs as follows. Discontinuous images replace one another in a continuous sequence. A theory of film would need to take account of both these facts. First of all, with regard to continuity, it cannot be overlooked that the assembly

[34] Walter Benjamin, *The Arcades Project* (Cambridge, MA: Belknap/Harvard University Press, 2002), p. 390.

[35] Hansen, *Cinema and Experience*, p. 202.

[36] Benjamin, *The Work of Art*, p. 38.

> line, which plays such a fundamental role in the process of production, is in a sense represented by the filmstrip in the process of consumption. Both came into being at roughly the same time. The social significance of the one cannot be fully understood without that of the other. At all events, our understanding of this is in its infancy. That is not quite the case with the other element, discontinuity. Concerning its significance we have at least one very important pointer. It is the fact that Chaplin's films have met with the greatest success of all up to now. The reason is quite evident. Chaplin's way of moving [*gestus*] is not really that of an actor. He could not have made an impact on the stage. His unique significance lies in the fact that, in his work, the human being is integrated into the film by way of his gestures – that is, his bodily and mental posture. The innovation of Chaplin's gestures is that he dissects the expressive movements of human beings into a series of minute innervations. Each single movement he makes is composed of a succession of staccato bits of movement. Whether it is his walk, the way he handles his cane, or the way he raises his hat – always the same jerky sequence of tiny movements applies the law of the cinematic image sequence to human motorial functions. Now, what is it about this behavior that is distinctively comic?[37]

The movement-innervation-gesture-discontinuity sequence as embodied in Chaplin's innervated *gestus* is the site of cinema's politics of play, a politics that, though not exclusively democratic, isolates the discontinuity of human movement in the face of the recursive, auratic pressures of ritual semblance. Interestingly, Benjamin holds out no hope for an actual (real) distinction between human and automaton. In the fragmented world of his modernity, it is impossible to do so, and unwelcome as well. The cult of the human – and the aura of human freedom – is dissolved by the innovation of Chaplin's gestures, in his bodily and mental postures that parallel (indeed, imitate) the innervated sequences of cinematic movement. What Chaplin shows us, by embodying the motorial law of the cinematic image sequence, is an

[37] Benjamin, *Selected Writings*, p. 93.

embodied automatism, or a human *something* "unlike anything else we know."[38]

The godlike feature of cinema, and its aesthetic and political value, is its capacity to give us something unlike anything else we know. And *that*, to be sure, is a dangerous contention.

[38] Cavell, *The World Viewed*, p. 26.

6

Letter to Mr. Dienstag

Thomas Dumm

Dear Joshua,

There is little I can offer here in response to your letter to Stanley Cavell on film and what you are calling the tragedy of remarriage. (Since I am recently remarried, and find our marriage meet and happy, I have to say that I am not inclined to sympathize with your perspective on *The Philadelphia Story*.) This is not to say that I have not thought about the issues you have raised concerning film and politics, or that I do not have an ongoing concern about the relationship of what we call culture to political thought. As you know, I have written fairly often on specific films as exemplary moments in the unfolding of the American political drama, as I have with a variety of cultural artifacts, novels, poems, songs, memoirs, paintings, performances and other narratives in our united states of life. As you also know, I have been deeply influenced by Cavell's understanding of film, and his understanding of skepticism and its relationship to moral perfectionism.

I guess that this background is one reason I have been asked to be a respondent to your letter to Professor Cavell and your argument against a specific film, indeed a genre of film, that he admires, and more generally the idea of film itself as a potentially positive force in democratic life. But here is my first problem. For me, the culture we create is something we also metaphorically swim in, the enormous intelligence whose lap we lie within, to twist awkwardly the words of Emerson. It may be of some value to think about distinctions between theater and film as media of communication, for instance, but that is not my most serious interest. In other words, it is as impossible for me to imagine not watching and then trying to assess the meaning of films such as *The Philadelphia Story* as it is for me not to do the work of interpreting the meaning of *The Federalist Papers* or the secret debates concerning the collective writing of the American Constitution, or the strange call for a civil religion of Constitution-worship advanced by Abraham Lincoln in his speech to the Young Men's Lyceum in Springfield in 1838. (By the way, I do not think the secrecy of the proceedings of the Constitutional Convention in Philadelphia were much more than a consequence of the Thermidor-like quality, the self-knowing reactionary move of anti-democratic powers interested in restraining, not ordering democracy, during that period. The retrospective sainting of these guys has always irritated me. Not for nothing do I claim the status of being a student of Theodore Lowi.)

In short, I find myself disengaged from most of the substance of your letter, wondering what is at stake here, for you, for me, for all of us really. Are you actually suggesting that it would be better not to watch movies than to watch them? Is the argument you make an attempt to show that Cavell does not understand the dangerous relationships of culture and politics, or that his politics are somehow Whiggish, unduly hopeful in a world where pessimism is the only legitimate response?

The former claim leads us to questions about what constitutes a democratic culture. I will speak more directly to that set of issues shortly. The latter claim concerning Cavell's political naivety, if that is indeed what you are claiming, seems to me to be simply mistaken. Cavell has, from his very first publications, been concerned with the abilities and disabilities of philosophy to address the problems of culture itself, in its most oppressive as well as most liberating phases. His work on Wittgenstein as a philosopher of culture has influenced a wide range of contemporary political thinkers, from Hanna Pitkin to Simon Critchley. His work on skepticism has been crucial to the work of many more: I think of someone fairly far afield from his core concerns here, Veena Das, and her studies on violence and everyday life. His lengthy, if *sub rosa*, debate with Jacques Derrida over decades concerning the priorities of writing, speech and the question of voice have even yet not received the attention they need and deserve (though Aletta Norval, among others, has begun to make amends for that slight). His critique of Rawls presents a full-fledged alternative understanding of what the conversation of justice could be. And some people go so far as to suggest that he actually established film as a proper object of philosophical examination (though on this count, they would be mistaken; he only started to make American philosophers begin to take film seriously as an object of philosophical reflection.) So for me, a letter *to* Cavell suggesting that he is somehow naive or ignorant or disingenuous is simply a non-starter. (It is remarkable as well to me that you are arguing so extensively on a turf of Cavell's own making: after all, both the terms "remarriage comedy" and "moral perfectionism" are inventions – exclusively, in the case of his identifying the genre of remarriage, and largely in the case of specifying the meaning of moral perfectionism – of his own coinage. And "the melodrama of the unknown woman" – again, his coinage – is a cousin, at least, to your description of the tragedy of remarriage.)

There is another thing going on here in your letter to Cavell that requires at least brief attention. You seem to see Rousseau's letter to be friendship-ending, a public contestation that will result, or at least risk the result, of an estrangement, an end. There is an irony here, in that the remarriage comedies are for Cavell explorations of how the estrangement of a husband and wife can be overcome when they find themselves again learning from each other. This learning occurs in fits and starts, setbacks and advances, does not always result in a meet and happy ending, but it is part of the ongoing activity of being human. Marriage is a form of friendship, I dare say, and while it may seem a reach to you, it seems to me to be a simple refutation of your thesis concerning the incompatibility of becoming friends and going to movies that one of our most popular forms of dating and gathering with friends is to meet them at the movies. Of course, no one talks to each other during a film, if the film is engaging at all, but one attends in the presence of others who are experiencing that movie in one's company. That commonality leads to conversation and is how we come to share another's perspective, recognizing and acknowledging the differences from and commonalities with our own. (Here I am paraphrasing your own words.)

"Cinema," you say, "affords no space for this experience" (p. 72). What experience are you talking about? I am reminded of the intransigence of the son in Don DeLillo's novel, *White Noise*, who drives his father around the bend by insisting that, because the present is constantly slipping into the past, we can never know whether it is raining at the moment we *say* it is raining, because by the time we *say* it, the rain may have stopped.

I know, I know – I am proceeding encased in my *own* set of privileges and assumptions. I am not even trying to make an argument in defense of Cavell against your charges. But here I am interested only in explaining why I do not want to engage in such a defense in this response. It is not where my energies or interests lie. (I also have had the opportunity to read Tracy Strong's contribution to this volume, which I believe does take on your specific charges in fine detail and does a better job than I might have done had I the energy and inclination to do so.)

However, I do want to ask some questions, assuming you will be responding to your interlocutors at the end of this volume, assuming that whatever collegial friendship we have enjoyed is not at an end, but instead in mid-flight. These questions have to do with *why* you were so concerned to write this letter. That is, what is your motivation as an actor here? I once thought my main question would be, "What does Joshua Dienstag want of Stanley Cavell?," but I do not think that is really the most pertinent question to ask you. Instead, when I think of the question you are asking (the demand you are making), it is not simply addressed to him, but to all of us, and that question is, "What do we want of democracy?" or, "When finding democracy wanting, what are we to do?" Somewhere within this concern is your motivation, but I am unclear as to whether you are a democrat or a critic of democracy. I realize that the two are not necessarily exclusive, but here I want to emphasize that the criticism of democracy you seem to be launching requires as a solution a stifling of democratic activity.

Some of what you are explicitly concerned about in your letter is the strange intermingling of secrecy and publicity, especially the balance and imbalance of the two, in the up-building, perpetuation and decay of our democratic institutions. Despite my protest over your example of the Constitutional Convention, I like that theme a lot, as it seems to me to be precisely one of the pertinent motifs Cavell explores in his various readings of *The Philadelphia Story* and other remarriage comedies, as well as in his parallel studies of the other genre he identifies: the melodramas of the unknown woman. (I think here especially of Cavell's reading of the concluding wedding scene in *Stella Dallas*, in which Stella, played so painfully well by Barbara Stanwyck that I dread watching that film every time I assign it to my students, observes from the city street the wedding of her daughter, a strange comingling of public display and privately felt validation or pain or ecstasy, depending on how one reads the expression on Stella's face as, chewing her handkerchief, she walks away from the wedding scene into the city and her future alone self.) But, for me, it is the intermingling and intersecting of private and public, of secrecy and publicity, indeed of the official and the informal, not simply as represented on the screen but as people experience it in the constant movement between mini-publics and mini-privates, so to speak, that constitutes so much of the experience of popular culture. The sharp separation of public and private and the accompanying denigration of social life is one of the reasons I have never accepted, in the end, the political theory advanced by Hannah Arendt, at least as I, an unwashed democrat, have understood it.

What I have always thought unifies Cavell's concern in his studies of films, as well as in his studies of opera, Shakespeare, music and even his study of his own life as a philosopher, is not an authoritative (authoritarian?) desire to be a pedant plying civic lessons, but the desire of a democrat to show the multiple and complex crossings of private and public so necessary to following a life worthy of existence. He has pursued what Tracy Strong and I have both (separately and perhaps not quite compatibly) named a "politics of the ordinary."

I think you understand this democratic desire quite well. Why do I think this? It is not your implicit embrace of Rousseau that does it for me. I have never trusted Rousseau as a democrat, especially because his romantic vision is so blind to the damage he does to others in pursuit of it. Instead, I think your more measured American romanticism is tied to a democratic vision that, should you ever choose to pursue it more thoroughly, and, dare I say it, with more self-awareness, would make me feel much easier about the extent to which you are friendly to democratic life. You are as worried as anyone I know about the direction that our poor world is taking, and hence I want you to worry less about how we are to be instructed and more about whether we are to be instructed at all, rather than simply being ordered around. An inclination to worry is something I think we share in common with those theorists we consider to be our fellow travelers. Indeed, I would go so far as to suggest that political theory begins out of worry.

I suspect you are interested in pursuing democratic culture in ways that are at odds with your explicit worry about film, theater and all the bread and circus elements that inevitably follow from them. Trying to draw you out on this theme, I want to linger over a parable you relate to us early on in your essay.

Your parable is that of a stranger, a traveler who finds himself in a village. It begins with a young bicyclist lost in rural New Hampshire, apparently traveling alone one summer in the halcyon days before cable television, VCRs and, of course, without the existence of GPS to help him find his way. The hidden-in-a-valley village he stumbles upon could have been a creepy, Stephen King sort of isolated, gothic place, where the smiles disguise malevolent intent. But it is not that sort of village at all. I think the term one might use is Shangri-La:

> It took me some time to realize what was unusual about the place. There was no movie theater – it would have been on the one main commercial street and there was none there. Nothing so strange about that, of course; it was a small village and no doubt there was some theater or other not far away. But most convenience stores in that area and at that

> time would have had a television going … When I commented on this to whomever had sold me a soda, they told me that the position of the town in the valley meant that no television signals could be received without elaborate antenna equipment. A rich person could afford such equipment perhaps, but there was no one that rich in this little town. So they did without. This was in the days long before video recorders and cable and satellite television, mind you, which only came much later. There were simply no images to be seen there. (p. 26)

I have tried to figure out how you could be both old enough to be cycling through New Hampshire and young enough so that there were no VCRs (which took off as a device in the late 1970s), no coaxial cable (which first began in 1948 and was widespread by the early 1970s in the United States), but never mind. We are dealing with Shangri-La here. How old were you anyway? You appear to have been born sometime in the mid 1960s – I looked at your CV online out of curiosity – which would mean that you were barely in your teens while cycling through New England on your own. Pretty amazing!

You note that the citizens of this town were not perfect, and you say you resist romanticizing them, though you easily could do so. Is romanticizing something different from sentimentalizing?

> I will not contend that the people of this town were simple and virtuous. I will not romanticize, as it would be easy to do, New England in the 1970s or at any other time. Film and television are hardly the only media that could connect them to the outside world and, if they lacked these, they had all the others. But, they did seem a tad friendlier than those of the other towns I passed through that summer, a little more inclined to chat, to be sociable toward a traveling stranger who had come into their midst. (p. 27)

A "tad friendlier," a "little more inclined to chat," to be "sociable toward a traveling stranger in their midst." "I will not romanticize," you write in precisely the same passage that you engage in romanticizing. (I love this passage, it shows me that, despite yourself, you want to mix it up in the demos, not instruct it from a distance. This is the sort of romanticism I can abide.)

Memory is a funny thing. Recently, when trying to recall the weekend of the (first) Kennedy assassination for a writing project I am immersed in, I got the date and time of day of the shooting of Lee Harvey Oswald totally wrong, and in a consequential way for the supposed lesson I was drawing from my memories of the days between Kennedy's death and his funeral. My point is simple: our subjective states color enormously what we remember, how and when. So, I want to ask you bluntly, maybe whimsically, are you sure you were in New Hampshire and not in North Carolina, home to Andy Griffith and the denizens of the imaginary town of Mayberry? (Mayberry was based on Griffith's hometown of Mount Airy, North Carolina, and named after the town of Mayberry in Virginia.) Wikipedia tells us, "The town only had one long-distance telephone line, as referenced in the episode 'Man in a Hurry,' that two old ladies shared each Sunday preventing others from using the telephone." This sounds like the sleepy place you are thinking of, and, as in other sitcoms of the era, nobody on these programs would do something as mundane as retire to their home in the evening to watch television. Perhaps you watched that show as a kid and, even as you went to New Hampshire, your experience was deeply colored by the sentiments expressed in this popular television show of the time (perhaps in syndicated rerun by the time you took your bicycle trip). I wonder – and I also wonder whether it is something akin to this blurring of memory that makes you worry about the televisual arts – about the extent that you seem to want to keep us away from our television sets, and to shut down the movie theaters to boot. But do you, really?

Your parable continues, at this point sounding themes closer to Meredith Wilson's *The Music Man* than to *The Andy Griffith Show*. I apologize for quoting at length, but this paragraph worried me enormously when I first read it, in part because it reveals a view of technology and its relationship to culture that seems to me to be extraordinarily flat-footed in its sense of causality, and strangely limited in its sense of what might constitute the range of meaningful engagement of citizens with one another, their conversation.

> Now let us imagine that this isolated town were to be suddenly graced by the presence of a theater. Do we foresee that the character or the governance of the town would be thereby improved? Let us go further and imagine a cinema purged of its worst elements – careless violence, unfunny comedy and lifeless romance. It would therefore have to remain dark most of the time, but still we can imagine from time to time a film of quality would appear and, duly approved by the canons of good taste whom we would appoint, merit a screening. The prices would have to be fairly high, of course; without the subsidy of the normal dreck to subtend it, the few good films that played would have to support the whole cost of the institution. So, whatever good the films did would have to be weighed against what they subtracted from the budget of those who attend them. But, let us imagine what may not be true, that the cost is not prohibitive. What then? Would we expect the town meetings to be ennobled? The managers more responsible? The citizens more engaged? Would not the contrary be more likely? Would not the representation of a good conversation undermine the capacity to engage in one, as recorded music has undermined the ability to make music? Would a subtle depiction of intimacy really improve our capacity to engage in it? Or would it, on the contrary, deprive us of both the free time and the components of willingness to do so? (p. 27)

Why does this passage make me think of *The Music Man*? Because the perspective you present at this moment in your parable is one of (slightly) frightened rectitude, the view of the village elder, a view so well parodied in that musical. I think here especially of Robert Preston's performance in the film version of "Ya Got Trouble," in which the presence of a new pocket billiards hall allows the salesman Harold Hill to sound the warning of cultural decline to the citizens of River City.

Of course, "Professor" Hill's cure – why, oh why is the professorate so often so disparaged in our united states? (I think I know) – is probably exactly the opposite of the one that Socrates would endorse, the establishment of a boy's marching band. But, we must also remember something crucial: *The Music Man* is a musical that has been an exceedingly successful entertainment, one that gently and kindly pokes fun at the town that Meredith Wilson grew up in, Mason City, Iowa. It has inspired an extraordinary number of amateur productions throughout the United States, which would seem to counter the idea that listening to recorded music discourages the performance of live music. (As someone who listened to records as a teenager specifically in order to learn to play guitar and to play piano by ear, as everybody I knew who hoped to be a rock-and-roll star did, or just to be able to make ourselves slightly more impressive to those we were finding attractive and wanted to impress, I found your claim of audience passivity especially puzzling. And, as someone of a certain older age than you, my guess is that, for you, the 1984 Kevin Bacon film *Footloose* might provide a similar narrative to that of *The Music Man*.)

Your enactment of this tale of your experience in New Hampshire seems to me to be a frustrated *cri de coeur*, an expression of your true desire to have some fun, but told in such a way as to repress the evocative powers of the popular culture from which your memory of it must have sprung. But must you really embrace a position that entails rendering a judgment of film that is disconnected from most of our experiences of it, for better or worse, so as to make us not take some of your more serious claims, well, seriously?

I feel like I must tell you something that you already know. There are no pure pasts. There are no unsullied New England towns (trust me on that last point!). When I am in small villages in New England (I am writing this missive from Newfane, Vermont, a town of a little over 1,000 souls spread over a goodly number of square miles), I am reminded of my first experience living in a village a quarter of a century ago in Chimayo, New Mexico. While helping my landlord put up drywall one day, after I waxed on about the beauty of the desert, the friendliness of the people, and so on, I asked him how he liked his village. His response was, "You know, we find it really boring living here."

Let me repeat, I deeply suspect you know these things. But, for some reason, you seem to persist in pretending otherwise. This pretense troubles me, because it suggests that you are burdened by some fear that lies beyond the ken of your critique of film. I think this in part is because the quality of humor contained in your essay hesitates at that threshold where we might discern whether or not you are ascending into satire. It confuses me. I want to know better what you are most deeply worried about. If it truly is your worry that film corrupts democracy, I want to reassure you that of all the phenomena that may corrupt democracy, film is the least of our worries. If it is instead democracy itself that is the danger we must worry about, then I think we have a deeper disagreement, which I hope we might be able in some other venue, someday, further explore.

I am hopeful it is the former worry and not the latter. Maybe there is a third path through, maybe we simply have different ideas about what sort of ethos democracy requires in order to persist. While literacy, substantial equality, access to public goods, respect and comity are all important for democracy to thrive, there is something else that is not so often discussed that I think is essential to democracy. (Call this my American romanticism.) I think that democracy requires not simply a tolerance for degrees of ignorance, impertinence and boundary crossing, but their active, if selective, celebration and pursuit. What seems absent in your letter to Cavell is that happy mischief – could we call it anarchy à la, say, The Ramones? – which would enable us to be assured that you would not, if given the opportunity, assume the position of one of the censors in our ongoing *Kulturkampf*, become John Lithgow to Kevin Bacon, the Mayor of River City to Harold Hill, Vladimir Putin to Pussy Riot. I want, and I think we need, instead for you to liberate that child on the bicycle, the kid who could appreciate the soft bed without accepting the stultifying moral code of an isolated village (not for nothing did Marx call it the idiocy of rural life). We need the confidence of the boy who is sure of his supper, someone who would join us in mustering the common courage to say, "Fuck you!" to the powers that be, the ones who are always dependably there to worry so much about the health of our souls as to forget that our health vitally depends upon our pertinent impertinence.

Yours in the struggle,
Tom

Part III

Reply

7

A reply to my critics

Joshua Foa Dienstag

Dear Friends! Dearer Opponents! I find myself strangely cheered by your criticisms. At any rate, I find them easier to read than my own letter, written some time ago, the words of which now return to haunt me with their crudeness. I am in your debt.

If I speak in another's guise, I will at least not seek to emulate his hostility to the opinions of others nor his paranoia about their motives. On the contrary, I think our exchange will reveal that the spirit of friendship can survive disagreement and, in fact, even be strengthened by it.

But again I remind you that we can only disagree and be nourished by our dissensus *after* the film has ended and not while it still plays. I remain undaunted in the thought that this small community of five or six, like the larger one of which we are but a part, will be strengthened by an equal, reciprocal and boisterous conversation and not by a quiet collective viewing, however pleasing the latter might be.

I have not, in this response, spent much time on the particulars of the two films I discuss at length in my "Letter to M. Cavell." While I want to acknowledge the many fine points and interesting interpretations of the films that the respondents make, I do not have the space to debate particulars and I believe our audience would, in any case, find it tiresome to do so any further. So, I have focused on what I take to be the larger points.

One theme I have found in several of these objections is the following: that I have spoken wrongly for Cavell; that I have made him mean what he did not mean; that I have made him mean something particular when he meant something abstract; that I have made him command when he meant only to indicate or to suggest or to exemplify. To this charge, I might plead a qualified "guilty," but the qualification is an important one.

As several of the commentators remind me, Cavell is the author of *Must We Mean What We Say?*, a book which indicates the difficulty of answering that question, and also a book which insists that meaning is not something fully under the command of an author. At the very least, I think it is wrong for my respondents to rely on what they believe Cavell *meant*; more important is what his work *means* to us now, how his claims (and those of others like him) about cinema and about our culture resonate today and what effect they will have going forward. In particular, I think it is of no avail to say that Cavell has no desire to command or instruct if his words are taken for instructions or commandments. One could say the same of many philosophers or sages, that their followers are more zealous than they ever were. We must judge also by effects and not merely by intentions.

I will, therefore, repeat my opening sentiment: I have no wish to wrong Cavell. If there is an agreement that fosters the disagreements aired in these pages, it is that we have all read and learned from him. I have tried only to speak for myself *to* him and to others, like the respondents, who share similar thoughts about what is best for our democracy and our culture. If I have misheard him, I apologize, but that is ultimately something for the reader to judge. And, in judging, I would ask the reader to consider more the substance of the argument between us; that is, the *matter* of our conversation and not the words or voices we used or intended in speaking of it.

Let me (very) briefly rehearse my position, the better to answer my detractors. I have argued against an optimistic account of the relation between film and democracy. I have claimed that the pleasures of cinema come at the expense of democracy, not in its service. I oppose the comfortable assumption that artistic achievement in this genre and democratic freedom naturally support one another.

Can we learn to be better citizens and better people by observing a representation of human life that is meant to instruct or inspire us? I maintain – to the contrary, like Rousseau – that this misunderstands the relationship between original and copy, even more so in the medium of film than in the medium of theater. Although the immediate focus of the essay is M. Cavell, the larger target is the general Enlightenment position, revived today in more than one quarter (e.g., William Connolly, Richard Rorty, Robert Pippin, Jacques Rancière) that popular film can serve to instruct us in democracy. Indeed, perhaps here is the place to re-emphasize that I criticize Cavell not because I think he is the worst of these figures, but because he is the best of them and puts forth the most powerful and subtle case for his position, in addition to all the other ways in which his philosophy improves us.

Still, I contest his position both on specific and general points. I contest, first, his interpretation of *The Philadelphia Story*, a film that he has said exemplifies the connection between Emersonian perfectionism and the "remarriage comedies" of the 1930s and 1940s. Rather than demonstrating moral improvement, the film reveals the dangers and pleasures involved in the representation of the instability of erotic relations. It warns, I argue, against thinking that we can learn to democratize by watching a representation of democracy, however artful.

In the second section, I turn from *The Philadelphia Story* to its dark twin *The Rules of the Game* (*La Règle du jeu*), a film made at roughly the same time with roughly the same plot but with a much more pessimistic account of the relationship between eros and politics. In this film, instead of the miraculous resolution of eros and law, we see the vicious conflicts between these two more starkly depicted; in the end, the erotic desires of the characters are brutally policed by social regulations that appear beyond the control of any individual. Unlike *The Philadelphia Story*, *The Rules of the Game* was not a commercial success and only decades after its initial release became a darling of film critics. The reason, I argue, is not hard to understand: its pessimistic depiction of democracy indicts its audience and their desire for instruction and moral uplift from aesthetic works. This tragedy of remarriage,

I maintain, would be a better instructor of a democratic community, if such a community were prepared to listen. That it is not is one of the obstacles that aesthetic optimists fail to acknowledge.

In the final section, to get to the root of our differences, I take up more directly the aesthetic, phenomenological and ontological issues that the first two sections have raised. I first consider Cavell's contention that time is a "barrier" between film and audience and argue, to the contrary, that time is in fact the medium that forms the aesthetic connection between humans and film, something we can understand better by contrasting cinema with television.

Next, I argue that we must understand film as an interruption of the sociability and mutual recognition that we enjoy, potentially at least, with other humans in democratic relations. Our ability to see pictures as pictures in the first place (as animals cannot) has its root in our recognition of the plurality of other views that actually exist. Film takes advantage of this human ability for picture-seeing, but also takes it out of its ordinary and original social context and returns it to a kind of animal captivation. Rather than expanding our vision, I maintain, cinema in fact narrows it and deprives us (quite pleasantly, it must be admitted) of the relationality and independence we ought to enjoy as free, autonomous beings.

Whatever the content of particular films, the medium itself does not empower its audience but, on the contrary, disables us. Rather than teaching us how to democratize, it substitutes an experience that feels instructional but is actually enervating. While I do not repeat Rousseau's claim that the theater simply substitutes illusion for reality, I do echo his concern that the spectacular experience can *feel* empowering when it is actually politically crippling. We must take the hard lesson that our pleasures and our freedom are in some contest with one another, that we may have to sacrifice some of the former to secure the latter.

I take it as some confirmation of my siting of Cavell with the other figures I mentioned that Clare Woodford, in her essay, puts him together with Jacques Rancière and forges a defense of film's democratic potential from this alliance. While this defense is attractive, I am not certain that it is in fact Cavell's defense, nor that, in fact, what it asks of us is really possible.

But first I must object to hearing my own position described as a "cynical" one. Never that! Perhaps it will surprise some readers that, having called myself a pessimist, I take offense at being labeled a cynic. Are not the two words more or less synonymous? I think not. Though they often go together in public consciousness today, I have taken some pains in the past to differentiate them and now I fear I must do so again.

Originally, of course, the Cynics were so called for their "doglike" behavior – they were indifferent to human conventions and mocked traditional morality. In modern times, however, cynicism has come to mean a more generalized indifference and even an active suspicion of the motives of others. To be a cynic now is akin to thinking the worst of others and that, I take it, is what Woodford means to accuse me of when she claims that I express "disappointment in the human condition" (p. 90). I hope that I do no such thing.

On the contrary, while it is true that I avoid optimism and suggest that others avoid it as well, I take that to mean that I, in fact, am more accepting of the people who exist today, with all their flaws, and ask others to refrain from fantasizing about them or projecting onto them [n. b.] qualities that they do not possess. Is it wrong of me to ask that we take humans as they are? Rousseau was not embarrassed to do so and neither am I. As to what humans might be, my account creates no limitations but asks only that we not proceed by the imitation of the imaginary beings we see on film *as if they were human*.

On the topic of imitation, Woodford defends Cavell by an ingenious argument that creates two kinds of exemplarity. There is, she argues, exemplarity of the ordinary kind, where a model is held up for one to imitate; and then a second kind, which I will call "meta-exemplarity," where an exemplar is offered not that one should imitate its traits or behaviors but only its meta-characteristic of being unique or individual. I attack the first, Woodford claims, but Cavell only defends the second.

It is true that Cavell, following Emerson and Nietzsche, speaks of this kind of meta-exemplarity. But I do not think that he speaks of it exclusively. Indeed, I do not know how we could really think about it exclusively, certainly not in relation to film. It is true enough, in a logical sense, that we can distinguish between the imitation of a particular trait and the more general, if vague, sense in which an example of individuality provokes an admiration that is not confined to the traits of the individual on display. However, if a general encouragement of individuality was all that was being urged, why would Cavell repeatedly make it so hard for us to distinguish this point from the other by suggesting films with such avatars of imitability? What man does *not* start to imitate Cary Grant's suave graciousness, in all its fastidious detail, after watching his comedies of remarriage? I cannot say whether Katharine Hepburn inspires an equivalent reaction, but it would be no surprise to me were it so. Surely Cavell is aware of this? Surely, too, he is aware of how such imitation of mannerisms, costumes, dialogue and poses is the *most ordinary* result of a film's popularity?

If the meta-exemplarity occurs at all, surely it must occur *through* and *after* the ordinary kind? We might (might!), on reflection, see that there is more to C. K. Dexter Haven than charm and wit and a well-tailored wardrobe, but I doubt whether we could ever be brought to such reflection if we had not been charmed by the wit and wardrobe in the first place. In any case, Cavell does not simply make the Emersonian case that we should each be ourselves, but offers us *particular models* that he goes out of his way to describe at great length. Why review so many films in such detail if the point is to abstract away from all of them? Indeed, I would make the same claim about Emerson. Do we really think that he wrote *Representative Men* in order to inspire us only generally "to be more active … citizens" (p. 92)? Does it not make more sense to think that we are supposed to both learn particular lessons from particular figures, *as well as* have the meta-inspiration to be our own best selves? So I am not sure that the two kinds of exemplarity can be so neatly separated in practice, nor that Cavell intended to do so.

While I think Woodford is right to find a resonance between Cavell and Rancière, this does not, naturally, incline me toward the view of either. I have my doubts as to whether Cavell would really go as far with

Rancière in emancipating the spectator as Woodford believes. But, let me set this aside and acknowledge a larger point on which I believe we can agree: surely a democratic conversation to aspire to is one in which each participant trusts his own judgment or, at least, does not defer automatically to the judgment of any other. To be able to make one's own judgments, and to be able to live by them, ought to be understood as the core capacities of a free citizenry. However, in order to distinguish judgments from whims, they must meet with contrary views and have some cause to respect them so that they earn their status in a real contest of faculties.

At a certain point, therefore, I wonder if the model of emancipated judgment begins to collapse in on itself. Woodford makes the point, quite correctly, that Rancière has no reason to favor a particular genre, like the comedies of remarriage, as a focus of judgment: "all films and all types of performance can play their role in our journeys of self-reflection" (p. 97). Indeed. But why stop there? Why think that judgment of art is any different from judgment of nature or politics or technology? When trust in our own judgment becomes our only principle, there is no one and no one thing that we need to pay attention to. And, if we choose our own objects of reflection, we are very close to choosing our own conclusions.

Alexis de Tocqueville saw this characteristic already developing in the Americans of the 1830s and he deplored its logical consequence: when we trust only ourselves, we cut ourselves off from others – not just from their domination or possible wisdom, but in every way. Each person seeks "the light of truth nowhere but in their own understandings. Every one then attempts to be his own sufficient guide."[1] Rancière thinks of contact with others' judgment as domination, never as education. But if everyone's judgment is perfectly independent, no one is forced to confront the opinion of any other. For that to work would require more than Jacotot's "equal intelligence," it would require what is impossible: that everyone's judgment be equally true.

[1] Alexis de Tocqueville, *Democracy in America* (New York: Appleton, 1904), vol. 2, ch. 22, p. 489.

If there is an important difference between Cavell and Rancière to point to here, I would say that, in focusing on the value of *conversation*, Cavell makes the claim (as Rancière does not) that we cannot pursue our own emancipation in intellectual isolation from others. On this much, at least, he and I concur. (I will return to the topic of conversation later.) Cavell's aversion to conformity is never a rejection of education and conversation. If all we have to learn from others is that we too can judge for ourselves then, once we have learned this lesson, there would be no need to ever converse again.

It is clear that Woodford rejects such an isolated life and insists that we live in conversation with other exemplars. But my question is: what are we meant to learn from such partners? Must we be reminded over and over to be ourselves (does it take that much reminding?) and yet never imitate them in any particular way? Again, the firm distinction between two kinds of exemplarity seems to fall apart in practice. So we must ask again: if the democratic citizen is prone to be influenced both by other people, as well as by art and the natural world, will our theory say nothing about which of these might be healthier and which more dangerous? That we are emancipated cannot mean that we are invulnerable.

My concern has been that in watching film we have a kind of hidden experience of domination that degrades our character as democratic citizens who might otherwise be engaged in reciprocal relations with our peers. Woodford reports that her own mind in fact wanders during her visits to the cinema. I am very glad to hear it. Would that it happened more often and to more people! But I can only speculate that the films in question must have been very bad to fail to hold her attention when they had so many means at hand to do so. If we all found cinema routinely unabsorbing we would all surely cease to attend, and then my concerns would be answered in a different way.

I am no enemy of solitude and I share with Woodford the sense that real solitude can contribute greatly to our being. Is it not a strange fact of modern life, however, that anyone would seek solitude in a cinema, a crowded room full of sound and light? I will not insist, like Emerson's sometime friend Thoreau, that we abjure society and live in the woods to find ourselves. But, if asked to choose between the two models, I would say that at least Thoreau knew what he was about and chose the shorter path to his goal, if not the only one.

Finally, I am glad that we can agree that finding the balance between moment and law is the difficult task on which we are endeavored. Even if we disagree on the means, the task itself is of such overriding importance that the more we reflect upon it, the better off we will be. Only we must really reflect upon solutions and not let them be reflected or projected onto us.

"Saturday Night," though he declines Cavell's voice, probably speaks more purely in Cavell's generous spirit than any other in this volume. Like Woodford, Tracy Strong believes that I misconstrue how Cavell thinks film educates us, though his version of the proper account is at some distance from Woodford's. Film does not "teach us lessons," he says, "Rather film can prepare us by making evident a possibility" (p. 114). Again, I wonder whether this distinction can remain as firm as Strong would wish it – how long can we admire something as a possibility before seeking to imitate it? – but let me return to this later.

First, I want to make more explicit something that I hope my readers already appreciate: I know that Cavell is not d'Alembert. In putting one in the place of another, I do not mean to imply that their theories overlap in every detail. While d'Alembert was a sophisticated man, his aesthetics would be hard to defend today. He did indeed seem to possess a cruder account of the good of theater than Cavell's far more complex defense of film (and the other arts, such as music). I do not believe I accused Cavell of being d'Alembert.

Rather, I put one in place of another because of their parallel employment of the arts in relation to politics. D'Alembert, like Cavell, suggested that we take the *best* examples of a medium and isolate their effects on a potential audience. I, like Rousseau, insist that we cannot really hope to expose a population to some examples of a medium that improve it while allowing other examples (the great majority) to degrade it – we must evaluate the medium as a whole. And we must evaluate the effect of the structure of its experience and not simply the content of its best instances.

D'Alembert suggested that the Parisian theater could be purified for Geneva by maintaining strong laws against the poor behavior of actors. Cavell (and Strong) tell us that we are to respond, or to be taught responsiveness, by *good* films. Such films are supposed to be those, as Strong reminds us, that can withstand criticism. But how are we to find them? Are Cavellian censors to be established who will keep the worst films from us? More importantly, how did *Cavell* find these films? Like the nineteenth-century music critic, he must have endured many hundred poor operas to find the few worth listening to a second time. What effect did these bad films he had to endure have on his character? Perhaps none at all in his case, his genius being so remarkable to begin with. But for the rest of us? Whoever gives us a theory of good film and its effects must give us an account of the effects of bad film, or else give up the title of social critic for that of curator of fine arts. Either a censor chooses the good films for us and we are the slave of that person's taste or we endure a genre *in toto* and *in populo* (for the films that we see will be tuned to the taste of the public, not that of the philosopher).

We often laugh at self-appointed moral censors who judge films bad without ever having seen them. Does not Cavell encourage a similar conceit? That we could know which are the good films *before* we see them?

I admit that Milton's model of a "meet and happy conversation" as a basis for politics is a charming one, though I doubt that the experience of watching fine conversations on film will make us more likely to conduct them. But is there not something quaint in this description? Is that not part of its charm? Although I know that this is not Strong's intent, nor even Cavell's, does this model not smack too much of the liberal theory of perfect discourse? All talk and no action?

Yes, Rousseau thinks human relations, including marriage and politics, are fundamentally erotic, but that certainly does not mean that "mere carnal coition" is the whole of eros. What it means is that passion cannot be extirpated from politics – the wish to do so is inhuman, or anti-human. What binds us together in large and small societies is a passionate attachment to one another that cannot simply be talked into existence. Perhaps Milton's Puritan denial, or avoidance, of this point is one factor in his own dismal marital relations. Thus Rousseau disdained any role for the Church in politics but substituted a civil religion – it was not possible, he thought, to have a successful state without a passionate attachment to it on the part of its citizens and some institution to channel that attachment.[2] Though I did not dwell on this point, it could also be said that one point of superiority of *The Rules of the Game* (and Greek tragedy) over *The Philadelphia Story* is the clarity with which it depicts the power, as often destructive as productive, of sexual attraction. Eros is hardly wordless – many volumes of poetry attest otherwise – but the Miltonic model of marriage, to its detriment, avoids a frank discussion of passion's power. However marvelous Milton may be on other points, this is a weakness in his political theory.

In this vein, I am glad that Strong points to Cavell's passionate engagement with the politics of his time. I fear his style hides that attachment too much from his contemporary readers. And, indeed, I do share their disappointment in the debasement of our political discourse. The question is what to do about it. Strong's suggestion comes in response to my reading of *The Rules of the Game* – we should take the lesson, he claims, that the rules "should have been broken" and that rules "can only be properly reasserted as our own after having been broken" (p. 121).

To this interesting and subtle argument I can only reply in part. First, I am concerned that this depicts the rules by which we live as too much a matter of private conscience rather than of public culture. The rules of property, for example, would be pretty meaningless if we each were free to break and remake them. Living together by rules is difficult because we are *not* free to remake them at will, even when we may have discovered a better one. That is part of the inevitable cost of housing eros within a stable institution. *The Philadelphia Story*, I fear, makes light of

2 As Tom Dumm notes, this suggestion was repeated by Abraham Lincoln, no less.

this cost, as if marriage itself makes no claim on its members but can be whatever they would like it to be. While we are surely not condemned to repeat the institutions of our parents and ancestors, we can see from our current politics how much effort is involved (and how much *public* effort) in remaking the institution of marriage that we have (and in an innocuous way that harms no one!).

Renoir's characters know better that the rules by which they live cannot be remade at the drop of a hat. They hesitate to break the rules because they know the costs and are *not free to change them*. The fate of Christine and the death of André are strong evidence of this. I say again that our rules are not as inflexible or immutable as those of chess or poker (and even these, of course, have changed over time). We serve neither God nor nature in obeying them, but this is all the more evidence that long-standing institutions are hard to change, since they sustain themselves without divine or natural support. It is also evidence that, as Hegel understood, they are *already* ours even before any breaking and remaking that we might undertake.

Second, despite the difficulty of such projects of self-overcoming, there is a danger of romanticizing them so that, as with Rancière, they become the *whole* of politics, as if we could live a revolutionary life at every moment. The dream of the 1960s dies hard, but it is time to lay it to rest. Living with institutions, I would say, is the real challenge and a project that Rousseau, for all his transgressive tendencies, was committed to, however difficult it was for him. Though Strong is committed to reasserting rules after breaking them, his philosophy does not really tell us how to do so or how to live with them after it has happened. Continuing a relationship is just a less cinematically compelling subject than making or breaking one, and it is hard to imagine that it will be the subject of many "Saturday Night Fevers."

Third, as with the later related claim that the films in question are not about moral behavior but about "what one has to become in order to be capable of moral behavior" (p. 130), I wonder if the argument abstracts away too much from what is clearly depicted, in favor of a conclusion that one already needs to be a moral paragon to reach. In any case, my main argument is not that film cannot show us something admirable (clearly it can), but that, even in such a case, the substance cannot defeat the effects of the form. That is, even as a film is *giving* us something, I worry that it is simultaneously *taking* something from us that we do not notice until it is too late.

As with Woodford's claims on behalf of exemplarity, I wonder whether the distinction that Strong strives to make on Cavell's behalf can really operate in practice. Even if I grant that the best films show us what Strong claims they show, it is not clear whether the effect of watching is to make us more or less likely to become "what one has to become." If watching Astaire dance does not make us dancers, how much less likely is it that watching moral paragons will make us such? Or, if we simply need assurance that such behavior is possible and yet cannot find it in the world around us, then the film has sailed past optimism and into fantasy.

Setting this aside, my more particular claims about the substance of these films is that the need to please the audience, in cases like *The Philadelphia Story*, leads them to refrain from addressing the tensions that they touch upon in the most honest way. This brings me to Margaret Kohn's remarks and the challenge that she offers via her analysis of *The Americans*, a series well suited to our topic since its very title ironically refers to a pair of imposters (actors?) faking a marriage in a country that is/is not their own and in need of moral repair.

I must admit that I am not very familiar with this series, beyond seeing the well-executed posters that dominated that Los Angeles skyline for a few months while it was being launched. But that is not unusual, because it seems that not many of my fellow Americans are watching *The Americans*. According to what data I could find, the show is seen by three million people at most every week (yes, including those who record it and watch it later). In a nation of over 300 million, that is not all that impressive. I believe it does not even crack the list of the top 100 shows on the air today.

So, I am tempted to say that, whatever the content of this show, it will not "[unsettle] the opposition between popular/ideological and critical/

unpopular," (p. 132) as Kohn maintains, and leave it at that. Like *The Rules of the Game*, it seems to have met with critical acclaim but little love from the public, Kohn's own enthusiasm notwithstanding. Its continued existence seems to reflect something else Kohn mentions much later in her essay: that the changing economics of the television industry has made it feasible to eke out profits on shows with small audiences.[3]

However, that would be a cavalier response to Kohn's very serious effort to alter and expand our understanding of what a remarriage drama might do. I am first of all attracted to the notion that some of the structures of television might be to the advantage of those interested in depicting marriage more realistically. "One of the distinctive features of serialized television is that it is continuous rather than finite," she writes, adding that this allows the show to demonstrate that "Remarriage is still marriage and marriage is work." This is a consideration that the comedy of remarriage in film hardly depicts. The film always ends at the moment of remarriage. However, as a serial television show, *The Americans* continues well beyond that point. That this is an argument in its favor, I cannot deny.[4]

This does mean that part of the force of Kohn's argument relies on a distinction between the two genres, which she initially rejects in claiming (using my admittedly vague category) that the show is "filmlike." But, like her, I do not think it makes sense to rely too much on genre distinctions here until we have analyzed the substance a little further. Knowing so little about the show, I can only proceed so far, but I have some questions. I wonder, first of all, if the title is even more ironic than it seems. Is this couple, perhaps, intended to be the "real" Americans in the show? That is, is their actorly identity as a married couple, perhaps repaired over the course of the show, a hint that our own political union is less than sincere? The 1980s setting and critique of American foreign

[3] It is important to note that the general fragmentation of the television audience has *not* been matched by a similar phenomenon in the audience for film. A truly popular film in the United States can still reach tens of millions of people in a few days. It has been decades since that was true of any television show. For those tempted to dismiss film as a declining element of our popular culture, it is important to note this fact.

[4] Although this is also the structure that permits soap operas and sitcoms.

policy that seems to be involved in the show surely points in that direction. I wonder, therefore, whether there is a deeper level of insincerity or cynicism (!) about the whole enterprise that might make it less than it seems in terms of a model of remarriage. Can it be a "remarriage" if it was not a real marriage in the first place? I realize, of course, that the whole Cavellian theme of remarriage is predicated on a degree of failure and falseness to the first marriage, but *The Americans*, from what I understand, takes this to an extreme.

A spy drama that is also a family drama seems to maximize the possibility for secret-keeping among its characters, but, therefore correspondingly, I would say, for the quasi-pornographic enjoyment of its viewers. Kohn wants to argue that we learn from the moral ambiguity of the characters or their situations. I would be inclined to guess that whatever popularity the show has results less from this element than from the endless opportunities it affords to peek into a scene that is usually unseen (espionage, a marriage, affairs, etc.). Again, I insist that we must ask not what intelligence might have written the script, but what emotion keeps the viewers seated? Kohn is leery of her own attachment to the series – is this perhaps the reason? Does it offer an endless number of veils to be torn away, one after another, like a roller-coaster of peeping?

My view is not just that, as film viewers, we are lotus-eaters; it is worse than that. My concern is that we actually dull our capacities for engaging with others by enjoying ourselves with the simulacra of personality that we encounter on screen. Kohn offers some reasons why this might not be so. I acknowledge, of course, that we may discuss television shows and bond over them. But, I ask again (and by now the reader is no doubt a little tired of this), if this is the Golden Age of Television (and who am I to doubt it?), then where is the "Golden Age of Politics" or "Friendship" or "Conversation" that is supposed to result? Why should we be afraid to draw a conclusion from the simple correlation that our politics seems to have gotten worse while our television has gotten "better"? Whatever good may come from the reflections Kohn describes, why should we believe that it is not outweighed by the known drawbacks?

Kohn says we are clearly all Parisians now and "there is no going back to the real or imagined time when we spent our evenings in serious conversation, political action and musical performance" (p. 144). That we cannot reverse time is beyond dispute; nor would I want to. But that is not our only choice. In reality, we do not face one big decision of whether or not to "have" film or television. Rather, we face a thousand smaller decisions. Shall I watch a film on my phone as I eat dinner? Shall I let my children watch a show or make them read a book? Shall we subsidize the film industry and penalize printing? Shall I take my beloved to the movies or take a walk in the Hollywood hills? Shall I write a letter or take a selfie? We need not answer all these questions in the same way, but we must have some principles to live by in answering any of them. Are we satisfied to let our lives, our culture and our politics be dominated by screens or do we choose to resist that domination? Why do the prophets of total revolution quail at the idea that we might attempt to limit our consumption of screened images? This is not a domination we can overcome perfectly or completely, but to collapse without a fight will hardly be thought a brave decision by our descendants, who will have their own aesthetic, technological and political challenges.

I am glad, for more than one reason, to see Davide Panagia ascribe godlike powers to film. I would not have put it that way, but in some sense I agree with him, and it is this agreement about film's power that forms the basis of a political disagreement of no small importance. For he would have us bow down to this new god while I would have us resist, to the last, anything that makes our human world less human. Democracy needs gods like it needs a hole in the head. As Rousseau well understood, any uncivil religion locates a moral authority beyond the people and therefore undermines their political authority. The people's choices are then always second best. Democracy must make its own standards of judgment – is that not the true Emersonian legacy?

I am glad, in the second place, because Panagia gives me grounds for answering one of his other objections to my argument, one that I have heard before from other quarters, and found difficult to counter. "Is reading not equally something," he asks, that isolates us and therefore defiles our social capacities (p. 159)?

When this question has been put to me, I have tended to concede the point, to admit that my critique of cinema must apply to some of the other arts as well and to wonder whether I could find grounds for saying that it applied less completely. But now Panagia has supplied the ammunition I have been seeking by insisting that cinema has a special world-creating capacity that the other arts have sought but never fully possessed. I want to agree with him, because that agreement would excuse me from the task of differentiating film from other media and supply perfectly what my argument otherwise lacks, a simple way to differentiate films from novels and paintings and the like. All these arts "absorb" their viewers to a degree, but film absorbs us in a special way because it can completely immerse us in another world like no other media, though perhaps it will be superseded in this by future artistic technologies.

"One says this, and then one hesitates." Shall I really admit the existence of a god within our world and then deny her proper respect? Perhaps I can find a better response in another register.

I am very struck by Panagia's invocation of Benjamin and the concept of "play" as an alternative vocabulary with which to defend the democratic potential of the medium of film. A quick reply to this contention would be to say that Benjamin was simply wrong to look to the films of Charlie Chaplin as an encapsulation of the medium's aesthetic potential, though this was a very common move in cinema criticism before the World War II. While Benjamin may (perhaps) have been correct that Chaplin's antics would have worked less well on stage (although Chaplin began his career in vaudeville), still I'm not sure that we can say that his films fully demonstrate the kind of world-creating absorption of which we know the medium to be capable.

But this kind of response is clearly insufficient. I reply to Panagia's invocation with one of my own: Hans-Georg Gadamer. It is not often remembered today that Gadamer's *Truth and Method* also has at its core a theory of absorbing play as an essential model for human activity and even art. But, for Gadamer, this account points us in the direction of language and dialogue – that is, reciprocal exchange – as the core practice for human beings, something quite at odds with Panagia's contention that we can find play in the experience of watching a film.

Gadamer's account draws from history, etymology and anthropology to argue that our many uses of the term "play" center on the "to-and-fro movement that is not tied to any goal that would bring it to an end … rather, [play] renews itself in constant repetition."[5] Play, and absorption in play, are exemplified in this account by the way in which we become part of a shared activity with other people, where we participate in an exchange that involves each of us, at some point, taking action. The game provides a structure for our interaction, but while we engage we do not think much of that structure, but only of our actions in the game.

In this sense, a game is like a conversation, in that we do not think of the rules of grammar and syntax while we converse but only about what we, and the other people involved, are saying. We think of the substance of our exchange and of the other people with whom we are conversing. Whether we win or lose a game (or an argument), the activity is a reciprocal one between equals, an equality that is recognized by our very participation in the activity. Many games (like catch) as well as (non-forensic) conversations do not have winners or losers at all, but still have the essential game structure of reciprocal equality.

Just for this reason, Gadamer writes, games "are in danger of losing their real play character precisely by becoming shows."[6] Though a contest might be exhibited for others, it gets the character of play from having equal participants. This might even include art, for Gadamer, so long as the audience is a necessary participant in what is created. But, as Panagia reminds us, film does not need its audience (as novels and even theater plays do) to create its worlds. If we value play as a model of equal, open-ended participation and engagement in a joint process that is equally contest and cooperation, we must guard against

5 Hans-Georg Gadamer, *Truth and Method* (New York: Continuum Press, 1994), p. 103.
6 Ibid., p. 109.

its deterioration into something that mimics this form but is in fact one-sided. Perhaps it is correct that novels and theater are already too imbalanced in this regard, but with film we have reached some kind of apogee.

When Benjamin spoke of films as containing room to play, he was perhaps thinking of the creative freedom that they afford a certain category of artists (and, again, in the context of Charlie Chaplin and Buster Keaton, this seems understandable). But, if he meant that the exchange between a film and its audience was one of play, I would have to conclude that he was deeply mistaken. There is no equality in such a relationship, indeed there is a hardly anything that you would want to call an exchange. The throwing is all on one side and the catching all on the other. Again, we may have a wonderful conversation *about* a film after it is over, but to say that we have a conversation *with* a film is to display a sadly depleted idea of what it means to have a conversation or to play a game.

Here too is a better response to Panagia's claim that my concern for the cinematic citizen might be extended to the reader of novels. Gadamer points to language as the essential medium of democratic equality; it is through language that we engage each other as equals, hear one another out, and agree or disagree while retaining a relationship of parity. Even an encounter with an ancient text whose author is unknown can result in a conversation.

Gadamer does think of art as something with which we can have a conversation. Although he discusses many art forms in his book, he has little to say about film, and for good reason. First, as Panagia maintains, film is autonomous from its audience, independent from their imagination and judgment, in a way that other arts are not. Films contain language, to be sure, but if there is anything that generations of film theorists have agreed upon, it is that film is primarily a visual medium. But, unlike dance or theater, the presence of the audience is not necessary to distinguish rehearsal from performance. Its ontological properties, whatever they are, will not be easily equated with those of text. For all these reasons, it is hard to understand an interaction with film as a dialogue.

I confess that Gadamer's aesthetics is inadequate to film – he has no good vocabulary for expressing film's artistry, as does that of M. Cavell. But it has never been my claim that film is not beautiful, or powerful, or fine. It may be all these things, but it is not a medium, like language, which installs equal reciprocal exchange at the ground floor of its being. It is because I want no gods to violate the equal reciprocity necessary for democracy that I want no films to violate it either.

The play theory of language, it seems to me, gives expression to a crucial element of Rousseau's theory of human equality. We are not equal by virtue of God's fiat, nor by some biological fact about our physical constitution. Neither are we unequal by such measures. Rather, we are equal politically by virtue of our mutual constitution of one another as humans, by means of a reciprocal exchange, something that happens through language. There are many different practices that can draw upon and extend this process, but not all human activities do so. Some retard it. Whether cinema is an art or a god it is not a partner to this process, but an opponent to it, a powerful one.

So, things can be truly shared in language – as a game is shared – disagreement as easily as agreement. I do not believe it is optimistic to say so. Optimism would mean believing that language had some natural power over the opponents of this sharing when it seems more likely that the reverse is the case. We must protect this element of our culture and politics and not assume that it is so fundamental that it does not need protecting. Well-wrought constitutions may afford us some of these protections, but they are certainly not idiot-proof – we can break them with our idiocy, even a culturally induced idiocy. (Taking "idiot" in its original meaning of someone so private – so disengaged from conversation with others – that he or she has no interest or aptitude for public affairs.)

I have no objection, I should say, in film forming some part of our democratic curriculum. Like all powerful and dangerous objects, it should be studied and that study may well be part of our political education. But, just as ballistics is a necessary but unhappy science, so I think should we regard the study of film as an important field without hoping that our need for it will expand indefinitely. Naturally, some will fall in love with this field, as happens with all the forensic sciences. That makes them no less morbid pursuits.

Tom Dumm: Felicitations on your meet and happy nuptials! I hope you will enjoy many years of marital concord! I am sorry, though, that your happiness put you in the wrong mood to hear my unhappiness, which is not with real relationships and places, such as those that currently occupy you, but with their representations. Surely you would not suggest to those who lack partners and homes that they be satisfied to see *The Philadelphia Story* any more than one would suggest to the hungry that they enjoy *My Dinner with Andre*? No, where we disagree can only be with regard to what role these representations can play in our democratic culture.

Is Cavell naive? I do not think so. Insensitive to danger? Probably not. Whiggish? Well, there we may disagree. I do not know if pessimism is the "only legitimate response" to our world but, as you know, in my opinion it is one of the best. And, from that perspective, yes, Cavell's perfectionism does look a bit Whiggish despite his many disclaimers. Cavell's optimism is not Kant's or Hegel's; it is Emerson's. But, it is real enough. There is, after all, a reason that Emerson is on every American high-school curriculum and it is not his complex and sensitive treatment of democratic culture. There is a bit of *faith* at the core of his account of the growth and development of the soul and some of that faith I think has found its way into Cavell's perfectionism. I have long thought that this reliance on the future as a cure for the present was the basis for Nietzsche's lament: "In Emerson we have lost a philosopher." I would not say that of Cavell, but I do think there are moments when his hopes get the better of his judgment.

I am glad you perceive that, in the end, my questions are ultimately not for Cavell but for democracy and cinema, and especially, I would add, for our modern representative democracy. You do not trust Rousseau as a democrat? I reply that, on formal terms at least, Rousseau is the *most democratic* figure in the traditional canon of political theory. It is he, and only he, who insists not only that equality is a fundamental principle and that slavery can never be justified, but also that *every law* must have the direct authorization of the majority of *actual individuals* for it to be legitimate. Not even the Levellers go so far. Neither Mill nor Kant, Emerson nor Cavell say anything like it. While democracy as a concept has become increasingly popular in the last two centuries, the burden of most democratic theory today is still to separate political power from its direct exercise by majorities, and then to justify that separation.

So who, really, is the unwashed democrat here? The unvarnished one? Shall we praise democracy as we find it (when we find it), or as we hope it will be, a democracy to come (as Derrida puts it)? No doubt political theory should elaborate ideals and give voice to them, but we cannot become the captives of our own fantasies. We cannot mistake the democracy for which we wish for what majority rule today would mean. I am more inclined to think that those who hesitate to embrace Rousseau's enthusiasms are the ones who are truly wobbly on democracy. It is marvelous to believe that democracy has a future of increasing perfectibility, but is it an act of faith or reason to do so? If you sense some hesitation on my part, it is not because I lack imagination but because I read the polls.

I find much to agree with in your defense of (and Cavell's insistence on) "the multiple and complex crossings of private and public so necessary to following a life worthy of existence" (p. 171). I do not think our disagreements lie here. But I do share Arendt's concern, not that public and private know their separate places, but that the public as we know it may simply disappear. Surely your rightful concern for the politics of the ordinary does not blind you to the many forces that eat away at the ability of our citizens to care for and speak to those outside their daily circle of activity. We are encouraged by many economic and social forces to turn inward, not to our souls but to our families, our jobs, our hobbies, until we have little contact with those with whom we are supposed to be democratizing. Will film counter this tendency? I am concerned that it gives us a *feeling* of participating in something greater while *in fact* it substitutes for that participation and makes it less likely.

How can I answer your blunt questions about a memory when, as you rightly say, memory is inclined to play us false? It was 1979; I was 14; I swear I had never even been to North Carolina! Beyond that, what can I really know for certain? Like a character in *Rashomon*, I speak truthfully but only out of my own recollection. I am really too young for *The Andy Griffith Show*. If I were tempted by nostalgia, its color would be more like *Bewitched, Gilligan's Island* and *Happy Days* (all sadly unwatchable now). For inspiring musicals of liberation from custom and censorship, I would take *The Commitments* over *Footloose* any day (and *Guys and Dolls* over *The Music Man*). But I am not nostalgic and I really think that you have largely misunderstood me here.

Who is really the censor in this debate? Who is the one issuing judgments of quality and edification? I am not the one making the distinctions between those films that are "good film" and those that are … – what word would you have me use? Bad? Evil? Less than good? Some such distinction is what Cavell's aesthetics require, though he chooses largely to ignore those films that do not appear in his canon. I do not really judge individual films at all here, but the institution in which we receive them.

Nor have I – not once – argued that our citizens will lose some kind of native virtue by their exposure to cinema. My argument is, in the main, ontological. I claim that we lose the experience of equal reciprocity in the cinema and find it replaced with a pleasurable experience of power. The loss is political and not moral. Whatever we do afterward, in the movie we give up the presence of other humans and replace it, as Cavell says, with a "human something" that does not make demands on us as a real conversation partner would. It is the fragility of the reciprocal exchange that should concern us. The morality of the humans who carry it out is of less concern to me. I have no nostalgia for village life; if anything, it is life in cities that increases our exchange with others, though not in the cinema.

I have already given above, in response to Margaret Kohn, some of the reasons why I think that the ubiquity of film today is no answer to my concerns. While we may not be in a position today to close the cinemas, we still face many questions about whether to resist, or enhance, the cinematic qualities of our political life. There are recent books (like Jeffrey Green's *The Eyes of the People*) that suggest democratic citizens in a modern state should resign themselves to the role of spectators. I do not expect you would agree with that at all, but I think a stronger defense against such a position is constructed when we acknowledge a general danger of passivity in the cinematic situation, rather than celebrating cinematic edification and implausibly claiming it as a source of activism.

So many of the laws governing our practices of citizenship (in areas like voting, federalism, campaign finance, corporate "speech," assembly, etc.) reflect, at least in part, our sense of what it means to have representatives in a democracy and how we can and should relate to them. All of these, I would say, can be more or less cinematic in many particulars. Perhaps, in a large country, we "must" have representatives in the same way that, as a modern country, we "must" have cinema. But that does not mean that we have no choices about *how* we have them, to what extent, and what rank we give them. All this, to me, is what is at stake in this debate. I am surprised that you think otherwise.

Is it really from Cavell that your taste for anarchy and The Ramones springs? Somehow, I doubt it. Did you know I once saw the The Ramones play live? *That* was a democratic experience: very loud, crowded, slightly violent, corny, boozy, invigorating, and a better date than any movie. But their recordings never meant as much to me – there's a difference, after all, between seeing someone perform in front of you and hearing a human something through a machine. Still, your comments and those of Tracy Strong, too, make me realize that there is something about music and film *together* that I have not yet come to grips with. I hope to do so in the future. In any case, at future concerts, I will look for you in the mosh pit. I think it more likely that you would be there than M. Cavell.

If pessimism is truly at the heart of Cavell's pursuits, as Panagia contends, then the fault is mine for not perceiving it more clearly. But, in the end, I do not write for the Cavells, who are past hearing, but for the rest of us. Perhaps Tom Dumm is right that cinema is not the greatest challenge that our democracy faces. I would suggest that it is a challenge that contains many others, most of all what it means for us to live together in the presence of other humans and to do so freely. For, whether we close the cinemas or leave them open, we shall not come to know our fellow citizens in darkened rooms, lit from behind, where we all face in the same direction, never seeing one another, as if chained from birth.

Bibliography

d'Alembert, J., *Discours préliminaire de "l'Encyclopédie."* Online at: http://fr.wikisource.org/Discours_pr%.

—, *Lettre de d'Alembert à M. J.-J. Rousseau sur l'article "Genève," from l'Encyclopédie*, vol. 7. Online at: http://fr.wikisource.org/wiki/Lettre_de_d%E2%80%99Alembert_%C3%A0_M._J.-J._Rousseau_sur_l%E2%80%99article_Gen%C3%A8ve (accessed January 19, 2016).

Barry, P., *The Philadelphia Story: A Comedy in Three Acts* (New York: Coward-McCann, Inc., 1939; New York: Samuel French, 1969).

Baudrillard, J., *Simulacra and Simulation* (Ann Arbor, MI: University of Michigan Press, 1995).

Baudry, J.-L., "The Apparatus: Metapsychological Approaches to the Impression of Reality in Cinema," in Leo Braudy and Marshall Cohen, eds., *Film Theory and Criticism* (6th edition, Oxford: Oxford University Press, 2004), pp. 206–23.

Benjamin, W., *The Arcades Project* (Cambridge, MA: Belknap/Harvard University Press, 2002).

Benjamin, W., *Walter Benjamin: Selected Writings, Volume 4: 1938–1940*, edited by Howard Eiland and Michael William Jennings (Cambridge, MA: Belknap/Harvard University Press, 2003).

Benjamin, W., *The Work of Art in the Age of Its Technological Reproducibility, and Other Writings on Media* (Cambridge, MA: Belknap/Harvard University Press, 2008).

Boal, A., *Theatre of the Oppressed* (London: Pluto Press, 2000).

Brown, W., *States of Injury* (Princeton, NJ: Princeton University Press, 1995).

Carson, A., *Eros: The Bittersweet* (Princeton, NJ: Princeton University Press, 1986).

Cavell, S., *The Senses of Walden* (Cambridge, MA: Harvard University Press, 1979).

—, *The World Viewed: Reflections on the Ontology of Film* (Cambridge, MA: Harvard University Press, 1979).

—, *Pursuits of Happiness: The Hollywood Comedy of Remarriage* (Cambridge, MA: Harvard University Press, 1981).

—, *Conditions Handsome and Unhandsome: The Constitution of Emersonian Perfectionism* (Chicago, IL, and London: University of Chicago Press, 1990).

—, *A Pitch for Philosophy* (Cambridge, MA: Harvard University Press, 1994).

—, *The Claim of Reason: Wittgenstein, Skepticism, Morality, and Tragedy* (New York: Oxford University Press, 1999).

—, "Aesthetic Problems in Modern Philosophy," in Cavell, *Must We Mean What We Say?*

—, "A Matter of Meaning It," in Cavell, *Must We Mean What We Say?*

—, *Must We Mean What We Say?: A Book of Essays* (Cambridge: Cambridge University Press, 2002).

—, *Cities of Words: Pedagogical Letters on a Register of the Moral Life* (Cambridge, MA, and London: Belknap/Harvard University Press, 2004).

—, *Cavell on Film*, edited by W. Rothman (Albany, NY: State University of New York Press, 2005).

—, "The Good of Film," in Cavell, *Cavell on Film*, pp. 333–48.

—, "The Fact of Television," in Cavell, *Cavell on Film*, pp. 59–86.

—, "Philosophy as the Education of Grownups," in N. Saito and P. Standish, eds., *Stanley Cavell and the Education of Grownups* (New York: Fordham University Press, 2012), pp. 19–32.

Conant, J., "Stanley Cavell's Wittgenstein," *The Harvard Review of Philosophy*, 13:1 (2005): pp. 51–65.

Dean, J., *Publicity's Secret* (Ithaca, NY: Cornell University Press, 2002).

Debord, G., *Society of the Spectacle* (New York: Zone, 1995).

Derrida, J., *Of Grammatology* (Baltimore, MD: The Johns Hopkins University Press, 2013).

Dienstag, J. F., *Pessimism: Philosophy, Ethic, Spirit* (Princeton, NJ: Princeton University Press, 2009).

Dizikes, J., *Opera in America: A Cultural History* (New Haven, CT: Yale University Press, 1995).

Doane, M. A., *The Emergence of Cinematic Time* (Cambridge, MA: Harvard University Press, 2002).

Emerson, R. W., *The Essential Writings of Ralph Waldo Emerson*, edited by B. Atkinson (New York: Modern Library, 2000).

—, "The American Scholar," in Emerson, *Selected Writings.*

—, "Experience," in Emerson, *Selected Writings.*

—, "Nature," in Emerson, *Selected Writings.*

—, "Seal-reliance," Emerson, in *Selected Writings.*

—, *Selected Writings of Ralph Waldo Emerson* (New York: Signet Classics, 2003).

Emerson, R. W., and Oliver, M., "Self Reliance," in Emerson, *The Essential Writings*, pp. 132–53.

Flathman, R. E., *Reflections of a Would-Be Anarchist: Ideals and Institutions of Liberalism* (Minneapolis, MN: University of Minnesota Press, 1998).

Freud, S., *The Interpretation of Dreams* (New York: Avon Books, 1965).

—, "Some Additional Notes on Dream Interpretation as Whole," in *Complete Works*, vol. 19 (London: Hogarth Press, 1966–73), pp. 123–8.

Fried, M., *Absorption and Theatricality: Painting and Beholder in the Age of Diderot* (Berkeley, CA: University of California Press, 1980).

Gadamer, H.-G., *Truth and Method* (New York: Continuum Press, 1994).

Gordon, R. B., *Why the French Love Jerry Lewis: From Cabaret to Early Cinema* (Redwood, CA: Stanford University Press, 2002).

Hanford, J. H., "The Chronology of Milton's Private Studies," *PMLA,* 36 (1921): pp. 268–74.

Hansen, M., *Cinema and Experience: Siegfried Kracauer, Walter Benjamin, and Theodor W. Adorno,* edited by E. Dimendberg (Berkeley, CA: University of California Press, 2011).

Heath, J., and Potter, A., *The Rebel Sell : Why the Culture Can't Be Jammed* (Toronto, ON: HarperPerennial, 2005).

Heidegger, M., "The Age of the World Picture," in *The Question Concerning Technology* (New York: Harper & Row, 1977), pp. 115–54.

Irving, I., "The Real Philadelphia Story," *The Sunday Telegraph* (April 16, 1995), p. 1.

Kahneman, D., *Thinking, Fast and Slow* (reprint edition, New York: Farrar, Straus and Giroux, 2013).

Krieger, M., *Ekphrasis: The Illusion of the Natural Sign* (Baltimore, MD: The Johns Hopkins University Press, 1992).

Leaf, J., "America's Opera Boom," *The American* (July 20, 2007). Online at: www.aei.org/publication/americas-opera-boom (accessed January 20, 2016).

McCumber, J., *Time in the Ditch: American Philosophy and the McCarthy Era* (Evanston, IL: Northwestern University Press, 2001).

Mahon, A., *The Ironist and the Romantic: Reading Richard Rorty and Stanley Cavell* (London: Bloomsbury, 2014).

Maier, P., *Ratification: The People Debate the Constitution, 1787–1788* (New York: Simon & Schuster, 2011).

Maslan, S., *Revolutionary Acts: Theatre, Democracy, and the French Revolution* (Baltimore, MD: The Johns Hopkins University Press, 2005).

Milton, J., *The Doctrine and Discipline of Divorce: Restor'd to the Good of Both Sexes, From the Bondage of Canon Law* (1643, 1644). Online at: www.dartmouth.edu/~milton/reading_room/ddd/book_1/index.shtml (accessed January 19, 2016).

Morgan, D., "Stanley Cavell: The Contingencies of Film and Its Theory," in Pomerance and Palmer, *Thinking in the Dark.*

Morris, D., "Privacy, Privation, Perversity: Toward New Representations of the Personal," *Signs,* 25:2 (2000): pp. 323–51.

Mulhall, S., *Stanley Cavell: Philosophy's Recounting of the Ordinary* (Oxford: Oxford University Press, 1994).

Myers, E., *Worldly Ethics: Democratic Politics and Care for the World* (London: Duke University Press, 2013).

Nancy, J.-L., "La règle du jeu dans *La Règle du jeu,*" in A. de Baecque and C. Delage, eds., *De l'histoire au cinéma* (Paris: Complexe, 1998), pp. 145–64.

Nietzsche, F., *Daybreak* (Cambridge: Cambridge University Press, 1982).

—, *Human, All-too-Human* (Cambridge: Cambridge University Press, 1986).

Pomerance, M., and Palmer, R. B., eds., *Thinking in the Dark: Cinema, Theory, Practice* (New Brunswick, NJ: Rutgers University Press, 2015).

Putnam, R. D., *Bowling Alone: The Collapse and Revival of American Community* (New York: Simon & Schuster, 2000).

Rancière, J. *The Ignorant School Master: Five Lessons in Intellectual Emancipation,* translated by K. Ross (Stanford, CA: Stanford University Press, 1981).

—, *Disagreement,* translated by J. Rose (Minneapolis, MN: University of Minnesota Press, 1999).

—, *The Future of the Image* (London: Verso, 2007).

—, "The Emancipated Spectator," in *The Emancipated Spectator,* translated by G. Elliott (London and New York: Verso, 2009), pp. 1–24.

Reader, K., *La Règle du jeu* (London: I. B. Tauris, 2010).

Renoir, J., *My Life and My Films* (New York: Atheneum Press, 1974).

—, *La Règle du jeu: Scénario original,* edited by Curchod et Faulkner (Paris: Édition Nathan, 1999).

Richards, I. A., *Principles of Literary Criticism* (2nd edition, London: Routledge, 2003).

Rousseau, J.-J., *Politics and the Arts: Letter to M. d'Alembert on the Theatre* [*Lettre à M. d'Alembert sur les spectacles*], translated by A. Bloom (Ithaca, NY: Cornell University Press, 1968).

Smith, A., *The Theory of Moral Sentiments* (Indianapolis, IN: Liberty Fund, 2009).

Stevens, J., *States Without Nations* (New York: Columbia University Press, 2009).

Starobinski, J., *Jean-Jacques Rousseau: Transparency and Obstruction* (Chicago, IL: University of Chicago Press, 1988).

Strong, T. B., *Jean-Jacques Rousseau: The Politics of the Ordinary* (Thousand Oaks, CA: SAGE Publications, 1994).

—, "Music, the Passions and Political Freedom in Rousseau," in S. Hoffmann and C. McDonald, eds., *Rousseau and Freedom* (Cambridge: Cambridge University Press, 2010), pp. 92–110.

—, "Rousseau: Music, Language and Politics," in K. Chapin and A. Clark, eds., *Speaking of Music* (New York: Fordham University Press, 2013), pp. 86–100.

de Tocqueville, A., *Democracy in America,* vol. 2 (New York: Appleton, 1904).

Wingrove, E. R., *Rousseau's Republican Romance* (Princeton, NJ: Princeton University Press, 2000).

Wittgenstein, L., *Philosophical Investigations* (3rd edition, Englewood Cliffs, NJ: Prentice Hall, 1973).

—, *Zettel* (2nd edition, Oxford: Basil Blackwell, 1981).

Woodford, C., "From Nora to the BNP: Implications of Cavell's Critique of Rawls," *British Journal of Politics and International Relations*, 15:4 (2013): pp. 586–609.

—, *Dis-orienting Democracy: Aesthetics, Knowledge and the Subject After Rancière* (London: Routledge, 2016).

Index

absorption, aesthetic 154–5
Adorno, Theodor 132
adversity 48, 90
aesthetics of the self 141–2
d'Alembert, Jean 3, 94, 110–11, 189–90
America, disappointment in 115
Americans, The (television show)
- confusion of desires 136
- emotional division of labor 138
- the family 134
- filmlike television 133
- knowledge of good and evil 138–9
- misrecognition 138
- moments of encounter/challenge 137
- moral ambiguity 140
- moral conflicts 134–5
- moral equivalence, US – USSR 139–40
- moralism 140
- popular/ideological – critical/unpopular nexus 132–3
- ratings 193
- remarriage 133–4, 194–5
- synopsis 131–2, 133
- tripartite structure 137

Andy Griffith Show, The 174, 203
animals 47, 68, 69–70, 71
Arendt, Hannah 171, 202
art
- film as 67
- good vs. bad 94n14
- relationship with spectator 94–5, 99, 102, 147–8, 196–7, 199; *see also* film – audience relationship

ascendency of cinema over theater 125–6
attention 59–60, 103–4, 133, 160, 188
audiences *see* film – audience relationship; spectatorship
automata 42–3, 161–2, 165–6
avarice 8
aversive thinking *see* thinking for oneself

Barry, Philip 124
Baudry, Jean-Louis 61, 68
Benjamin, Walter 162–5, 197, 199
Bondu Saved from Drowning film 32
Burke, Edmund 122

Carson, Anne 51
Cavell, Stanley
- America, disappointment in 115
- ascendency of cinema over theater 125
- aspirations, giving up 85
- automata 162
- "Aversive Thinking" 92–3
- *Cavell on Film* 5–6, 20, 55, 85, 88, 100, 108–9, 111, 114
- *Cities of Words* 10, 101, 136, 137
- *Claim of Reason, The* 151, 162
- comedies of remarriage 5–6, 9, 87
- *Conditions Handsome and Unhandsome* 90, 92, 93, 99, 101, 102, 103, 105
- conversation 188
- democracy 102
- ekphrasis 155–6, 157
- Emerson 101
- exemplarity 87–8, 92–3, 93–4, 99, 104, 185–6
- experience 152, 153
- film's roles 111–13, 114
- film vs. television 55

games 147
"good" films 190
happiness 88, 90, 108–9, 149, 152
hesitancy 149
human frailty 90
interpretation of film 99–100
learning 169
meaning 182
memory 152, 153, 154, 155–6
moment of encounter/ challenge 137
music 111
Must We Mean What We Say? 112, 115, 147, 153, 182
perfectionism 5–6, 10, 20, 87, 90, 102, 103, 105, 113–14, 135–6, 201
" Philosophy as the Education of Grownups " 113, 115
A Pitch for Philosophy 112
political knowledge 168–9, 201
politics of the ordinary 171
preoccupation of film 158
Pursuits of Happiness 9, 87, 99, 129, 149–51, 152, 154, 157, 158
Rules of the Game, The (film) 125
Senses of Walden, The 114
taste 153–4
time 53, 184
value of film 150–1
World Viewed, The 53, 103, 155–6, 157, 166
ceremony 24
Chaplin, Charlie 164, 165–6, 197
cinema *see* film; film – audience relationship; film – democracy relationship
class, social 11, 32, 49–50, 124–5, 132
collaboration 160
comedies of remarriage 5–6, 9, 77, 87–8, 115, 194; *see also* *Philadelphia Story, The* (film); *Rules of the Game, The* (film)
Constitutional Convention 10–11, 15–17, 18, 128, 157, 168
continuity 164–5
contracts 8–9
control, lack of
over audience 94–5
over eros 25, 43, 89
over film experience 70–1, 141
conversation
living in, with others 101–2, 169–70
marriage as 113, 190
moral 114
reciprocal equality 199
transformation by 128–30
value 188
word reformulations 115–16
criticism 111–12, 156
Cukor, George *see Philadelphia Story, The* (film)
curricula 151–2
cynicism 85, 90, 185

danger, safe exposure to 26, 122–3
Dean, Jodi 16n13
democracy
art's impact 94n14
foundation 8–9
happiness 88
hopes for 202
pleasure and freedom 74
preoccupation of 158
publicity and secrecy 16, 73–4, 123
as quest 87
reality vs. hopes 202
see also film – democracy relationship
democracy of moments 31, 39, 45–6, 54, 71, 73, 76, 81, 106
democratic vision 81
Derrida, Jacques 148, 168–9
Dienstag's replies 181–4, 204–5
to Dumm 201–4
to Kohn 193–6
to Panagia 196–201
to Strong 189–93
to Woodford 184–9

discontinuity 152–3, 165
divorce 24–5, 112–13
documentary films 58–9
dreams 60–4, 66–7, 70, 74, 75, 81, 85, 100–1, 103–4, 157

education
  by conversation 101–2, 128–9, 188
  by doing 81
  by film 94, 111, 113–15, 120, 189; *see also* exemplarity; imitation
  of grown-ups 113–14
  inequality of power 95–6
ekphrasis 155–7
emancipation 85, 96–100, 163, 187–8
Emerson, Ralph Waldo
  dreams 100–1, 103
  exemplarity 92–3, 186
  faith 201
  solitude 104
  thinking for oneself 99, 100–2
  willingness to change 5
emotions 60–1, 61–2, 65, 138, 139, 143
equality, human 96, 97–8, 100, 198–9, 200, 201–2
eros
  binding/destroying 49
  eros – stability balance 86–7, 106–7, 117
  marriage as institution 7–8
  regulated and tamed 42, 44, 52
  three-point circuit 51
  ubiquitousness 190–1
  volatility 21, 31, 77, 105, 183
exemplarity
  distinguishing between models 93, 100, 108–9, 185
  imitation model 87–8, 93–4
  inspiration model 92–3, 99, 104, 185–6
  relationship 98, 102, 188

film
  as art 67–8
  ascension over theater 125–6
  commercial success/failure 73
  documentaries 58–9
  godlike powers 147–8, 196, 197
  perfect tense 55, 57
  as photography 54
  preoccupation of 158
  presence 63, 64, 65
  repetition 57
  roles 25
  study of 151, 200–1
  technology 67–9, 71, 162–5
film – audience relationship
  attention 59, 103–4, 188
  domination 70–1, 196, 199–200
  dreamtime 60–4, 66–7, 103–4
  emotions 60–1, 61–2, 65, 139, 143
  engagement 195
  exemplarity *see* exemplarity
  interpretation 99
  loneliness 72
  memory 66, 152, 154, 155–6, 155n19
  play 161–4, 197–9
  pleasure 74
  popularity, continued 194n3
  possibilities, showing 112, 114, 116–17, 137, 189
  reciprocity, lack of 199, 203
  recognizing ourselves 63–4
  safe exposure to danger 25–6, 122–3
  self-reflection 97
  time 53–4, 58, 62, 64–5, 67, 184
  vision 70
  voyeurism 18, 88, 91
film – democracy relationship
  active/passive citizenship 54–5, 93, 95–6, 98, 141–2, 145, 146, 151, 204
  challenge to sociality 205

democratic experience 72–3
democratic role 102–3
education 94, 111, 113–15, 120, 189; *see also* exemplarity; imitation
friendship 72, 77, 78, 105, 169–70
human equality 96, 97–8, 100, 198–9, 200, 201–2
live television events 58
participation 151, 154, 198–9, 202
public/private life 24–5, 28–9, 91, 171
quests 79–81, 87
social engagement 72, 78, 91–2, 101–2, 169–70, 199
solitude 104
thinking for oneself 92–3, 96, 97–8, 99, 101–2, 103, 104, 187
value 108, 150–1, 158, 166
filmic experience 67, 72–3
film studies 151, 200–1
frailty 75, 90, 91
freedom 8, 73, 74, 162, 163, 184
Freud, Sigmund 62, 63
friendship 37–8, 46, 72, 77, 78, 105, 169–70
Frye, Northrop 154

Gadamer, Hans-Georg 197–200
games 35–6, 147, 161–2, 198
Geneva 3, 76, 143
genre 154
Godard, Agnès 55

happiness 6, 73, 88, 90, 105, 107, 108–9
Heath, Joseph 141–2
Heidegger, Martin 68
Holiday film 32
Homer 63–4

imitation 87–8, 93–4, 94–5, 100, 160, 185–6
impermanence 152
inequalities 95–6, 128, 143
influence 94, 160, 188
inspiration 92–3, 97, 99, 100, 104, 106, 108, 185–6
interpretation 86, 96, 98, 99–100, 145
intimacy 17, 19, 20, 24, 136
isolation 7, 60, 72, 142, 148, 159, 188; *see also* solitude

Jacotot, Joseph 96

Kahneman, Daniel 155n19
knowledge 95–6

Lacan, Jacques 63
language 37, 115–16, 127–8, 199, 200
liveness 55–6, 57, 58, 59
loneliness 72
Luce, Henry 13

marriage 8, 9, 16, 89, 113, 117–18, 127–8, 169; *see also* remarriage
Marriage of Figaro, The (Beaumarchais) 52–3
meaning 29–30, 65, 182
memory 66, 79, 152, 154, 155–6, 155n19, 174, 203
Milton, John 112–13, 117, 190, 191
misunderstanding 37–9, 138
momentariness 20
moments 29–30, 35–6, 137; *see also* democracy of moments
moon landing 58, 79, 81
moral ambiguity 140, 195
moral behavior 130, 192
moral intelligence 20–1
Morris, Debra 28n18
music 43–4, 111, 130, 175–6, 204
Music Man, The (musical/film) 174–6
Myers, Ella 142

New Hampshire cycling trip 26–7, 171–4, 176, 203
Nietzsche, Friedrich 62, 63–4, 92, 126, 129, 130, 201
non-publicity 28–9

operas 112, 126, 130
optimism 73, 161, 185, 200

participation 142, 151, 154, 198–9, 202
perfectionism
  dreams 103
  emancipation 98–9
  eros – stability balance 107
  growing up 113–14
  happiness 90
  interpretation 99
  moral 5–6, 86–7, 98–9, 102, 107, 135–6, 169
  never above reproach 105
  personal – political interaction 112–13
pessimism 50, 118–19, 153, 183, 201
Philadelphia Story, The (film)
  ascendency of cinema over theater 126–8
  class relations 11, 32, 125, 132
  commercial success 34–5
  compared to play 11–15
  compared to *The Rules of the Game* 30–5
  contingency of outcome 21–2
  conversations 128–30
  democratic pornography 18, 19–20
  Eros, dance of 21–2
  exemplarity 10, 93
  false happiness 73
  freedom and social order 132
  heroine 34n22, 48
  human frailty 75, 90
  human inconsistency 23–4, 24–5
  intimacy and union 24
  miniature solution 77
  momentariness 20, 30
  moral intelligence 20–1, 21–2
  moral struggle 137
  order restored 47
  perfectionism 10
  photography 12–15, 17, 18–19, 126–8
  plot 11n8
  politics 12
  power 13–14
  public pledges 25
  re-enactment of Constitutional Convention 10–11, 26
  release dates 32n20
  remarriage 133–4
  representation of democracy 183
  rules 120, 121, 122, 128
  solicitude 129–30
  as theater 123, 124
  thinking for oneself 92
  Tracy as "Red" 22n16
  Tracy as "yare" 22–3
  transformation, possibility of 116–17, 130
  True Love boat 18–19, 23
  true marriage 118, 120, 127–8
  voyeurism 91
  wedding ceremony 23–4, 89, 90, 97, 126–8
  word reformulations 116
Philadelphia Story, The (play) 10
  class, social 11, 124–5
  compared to film 11–15
  plot 11n8
  True Love boat 18–19
photographic invasion 12–15, 17
photographic reproduction 57–8
Pindar 130
Plato 5, 94n14, 110, 143
play 161–4, 197–9, 200
pleasure 74
politics of the ordinary 171–2, 202
popular/ideological – critical/ unpopular nexus 132–3, 193–4

pornography 17–18, 20, 25–6, 45, 74, 76, 122, 127
possibilities, showing 112, 114, 116–17, 137, 189
Potter, Andrew 141–2
privacy 15, 28–9, 91, 171, 202
Proust, Marcel 65, 66
publicity 16n13, 19, 20, 73–4, 88, 171
Putnam, Robert 142

quests 79–81, 87, 145–6

Ramones 204
Rancière, Jacques 85, 86, 94–8, 99, 100, 184–5, 186–8
Rawls, John 105
reading 158–9, 196–7, 199
remarriage
  in *The Americans* 133, 194–5
  perfectionism 5–6, 90
  in *The Philadelphia Story* 22, 23–4, 89, 127–8, 132, 133–4
  in *The Rules of the Game* 52, 133
  taming of eros 42, 77
Renoir, Jean *see Rules of the Game, The* (film)
repetition 56–7
republic of laws 31, 45–6, 54, 73, 106
Ricahrds, Ivor Armstrong 159
Rousseau, Jean-Jacques
  democracy 172, 201–2
  education 129
  Emile 114, 129
  human equality 200
  human relations 190, 191
  Lettre a M. d'Alembert sur les spectacles (Rousseau) 3, 74, 143–4
  religion 196
  theater, arguments against 139, 142–4
  transformation 114, 117
rulers 35
rules
  breaking and reasserting 120–2, 128, 191–2
  of games 35–6
  and love 41–2, 44, 52–3
  meanings 35
  misunderstanding 37–8
  no escape 39–41, 48
  powerlessness to change 36–7, 192
  rule of law and the law of rules 45–6
Rules of the Game, The (film)
  ascendency of cinema over theater 126
  automata 42–4, 161–2
  ban 49–50
  calliope as metaphor of film 44–5
  class, social 32, 49–50
  comedy and tragedy 118–20
  commercial failure 35, 107n60
  compared to *The Philadelphia Story* 30–5
  editing history 31n19
  eros
    energy 51–2
    as game 37–9
    regulated and tamed 42, 44, 52
    stability, balanced with 49, 106–7
    volatility 105
  friendship 46, 72
  games 35–6
  hallways scene 51–2
  heroine 34n22, 47–8, 106
  hunt scene 46–7, 51, 52
  misunderstanding "the game" 37–9
  moment and narrative 37
  pessimism 50
  power 45, 191
  release dates 32n20
  remarriage 52, 133
  representation of democracy 183–4
  rules 35–6, 38–41, 42, 44, 45–6, 47–8, 120, 121, 122, 192
  as theater 123–4, 126
  violence 46–7, 121

Schopenhauer, Arthur 28
secrecy 15–17, 18, 74, 122–3, 171
Shakespeare, William 117–18
sharing 19, 66–7, 72, 149, 161, 161n27, 198–9, 200
Smith, Adam 161n27
solicitude 129–30
solitude 104, 188–9; *see also* isolation
spectatorship
  active/passive 95, 98, 145, 204
  emancipation 96, 97–8
  interpretation 86, 94–5
  isolation 159
  and quest 145–6
  see also film – audience relationship
Stella Dallas film 171
stichomythia 123

taste 143, 153–4, 155
technology 45, 55, 67–9, 71, 144–5, 162–5, 174–5
television
  active spectatorship 145
  aesthetic innovation 144
  attention/non-attention 59, 60
  education 145
  isolation 142, 145
  liveness 55–7, 58, 79
  social glue 145
  specialization 144–5, 194
  technology 55, 144–5
  temporality 133
  see also Americans, The (television show)
temporality 67, 127, 133
theater 123–6, 142–4
thinking for oneself 92–3, 96, 97–8, 99, 101–2, 103, 104, 187
Thoreau, Henry David 189
time 53–4, 62, 64–5, 67, 69, 184
Time/Life International 13
Tocqueville, Alexis de 187
transformation 113–14, 116–17, 128–30

uncontrollable, the 160
union 20, 24
universal teaching 96, 98–9, 100
Until the End of the World film 62, 66

value 108, 150–1, 158, 166
viewing the Earth whole 80
violence 46–7, 77, 107, 121
vision 70, 81, 184
Voltaire 3
voyeurism 18, 88, 91

Wagner, Richard 126
Wenders, Wim 62, 66
Wilson, Meredith 174
Wingrove, Elizabeth Rose 8n1
Wittgenstein, Ludwig 36, 46, 153, 154
worry 172, 176–7
writing 158–9